A Life of Her Own

A Life of Her Own

A Countrywoman
in Twentieth-Century France

by Émilie Carles,
as told to Robert Destanque

translated and with an introduction
and afterword by Avriel H. Goldberger

Rutgers University Press
New Brunswick, New Jersey

Second printing, July 1991

Originally published in French by Jean-Claude Simoën, 1977
Translation published by arrangement with Editions Robert Laffont.
Translation copyright © 1991 by Avriel H. Goldberger
This edition copyright © 1991 by Rutgers, The State University
All rights reserved
Manufactured in the United States of America

Library of Congress Cataloging-in-Publication Data

Carles, Émilie, 1900–
    [Soupe aux herbes sauvages. English]
    A life of her own: a countrywoman in twentieth-century France / by Émilie
Carles, as told to Robert Destanque ; translated by Avriel H. Goldberger.
        p. cm.
    Translation of: Une soupe aux herbes sauvages.
    ISBN 0-8135-1641-2
    1. Carles, Émilie, 1900–   . 2. Briançon Region (France–Biography.
3. Teachers — France — Briançon Region — Biography. 4. Farmers — France —
Briançon Region — Biography. 5. Pacifists — France — Briançon Region —
Biography. 6. France — History — 20th century. I. Destanque, Robert. II. Title.
DC801.B853C2713   1991
944'.97 — dc20
[B]   90-41861
                                                                                CIP

*For Ellen Margaret
my daughter and dear friend*

Contents

Illustrations follow page 152

Acknowledgments

I would like to thank all those who have generously given me assistance as I prepared this book, in particular Claude Laugier Parisot and Edith W. Finch. Over many months, Mme Parisot scoured the libraries of Paris, and phoned possible sources to track down obscure or dialectal terms and references; indeed she proved to be a veritable Commissaire Maigret of the intellectual domain. Mrs. Finch once more read a manuscript of mine with extraordinary care, making my project her own, pushing me to the rethinking and refinement of detail that are part of the translator's pleasure and travail.

I did the initial work on the text as a fellow at the N.E.H. Translation Institute at the University of California, Santa Cruz; my colleagues there, particularly Anne Harleman, Lina Brock, and Joanna Banquier, codirector of the Institute, provided useful discussion and comments.

For the released time granted me at Hofstra Univesity in each of three semesters for the project, I thank the Dean of Hofstra College, Robert C. Vogt, and the University's late Provost, Sanford Hammer.

Certain regional terms, mostly buried in the lost past of the Briançonnais region, proved an intractable stumbling block even for Mme Parisot. At last it occurred to me to write the Head Librarian of the Municipal Library of Briançon. Within two weeks I had my answer. Mme Catherine Fromm in her enthusiasm for Émilie Carles, whom she knew, and for this book, had obtained the elusive information.

The following have helped with technical terms: Régine de Guillebon, Michel Pourrier, William Mittelman, Liliane Lazar, and Josh Oppenheim. It is rightly said that the good copyeditor is gold; my luck has indeed been golden in having Irene Fizer work with me in this capacity. Ann Sweeney, Assistant Manager of Production and Design at Rutgers Press, and Steven Curti are to be thanked for coming up with the English title of this book, and Ms. Sweeney also for shepherding it through production.

Once again, I have found it a special pleasure to work with Leslie Mitchner, Executive Editor of Rutgers University Press.

And finally, I say bravo to my personal cheering section for joyous encouragement and objective reading of Mme Carles's text and my own: Ellen M. G. Oppenheim, my daughter, and Arnold Goldberger, my husband.

Introduction

In 1977 Jean-Claude Simoën's small firm published Émilie Carles's autobiography, *Une Soupe aux herbes sauvages* (A Wild Herb Soup), with the hope that it would sell a respectable number of copies. After all, the seventy-seven-year-old author from the mountains of southeastern France was known through television and news media for having just led a vigorous movement to save her pristine valley from the environmental destruction planned by a faceless bureaucracy in Paris. However, the book did not just sell nicely: it was an instant bestseller throughout France at all levels of society, and was quickly translated into a number of languages including German and Italian but, inexplicably, not English.

Why did a story by a woman whose region and way of life had to be remote to most of her readers immediately seize their imaginations? That was my own question to friends in the summer of 1978. I was in Nice to direct Hofstra's Summer Program. My daughter, who recently had spent a semester at the University of Besançon, joined me there as companion-assistant. Practically everyone we met told us emphatically that we had to read Carles's book, so we bought it and then spent our free time wresting it from one another. Once we finished, we wrestled with the question of why it was so compelling.

Speaking impersonally, I might begin by saying that Carles wrote an autobiography that reads like a novel. She propels us from one chapter to the next, creating — or re-creating — a world with her storytelling that readers can enter fully even without a prior knowledge of French history or of the peasant society in which she lived. Only a phenomenon, a one-of-a-kind person like Carles, who stayed put in the environment she loved even as she broke with it radically in education, talents, intellect, and goals, could make her bygone and present France a palpably accessible reality for contemporary readers, whether or not they are French.

But while all of this is true, it does not make clear the very personal impact of the book upon my daughter and me, and potentially for the American public. What we discovered in our endless discussions that sunlit summer was how much of the impact of the autobiography came from Carles compelling us to "reread" our own lives, dilemmas, and hopes, how much we each identified with her and were strengthened by her. We found that the book had the same power of attraction for my husband, who joined us several weeks later. For the fact is that Carles has given us an archetypal exemplary tale — like "Cinderella," "The Ugly Duckling," or "Horatio Alger" — with all its anguish, beauty, and hope.

For each of us, after all, there is a story which begins: "Once upon a time . . ." And so I was reminded of a little girl in Philadelphia, her nose always in a book, like Carles refusing early on to do what her world expected. I thought back with some wonder to the child who had so passionately refused the "feminine mystique" years before she could put a name to it, who had longed to break free of the ironclad cycle of the female life she witnessed, the child who dreamed of "becoming," and knew, however obscurely, that education was the key.

Although Carles never specifically speaks to gender issues, clearly they are implicit throughout the book in her struggle against ignorance and stereotypes, against built-in evils in her peasant society, and the problems she faced in her own family life. Carles's memoir is not only a history of twentieth-century France through her educated peasant eyes, but also a story about women: for example, the ignorance of their own bodies and sexuality that effectively killed her sister Catherine. Carles describes the ironfisted patriarchy that precluded women from making the simplest personal choices, forcing them to endure loveless marriages, endless childbearing, and spousal rape, and that granted custody rights automatically to the father — even when that father was like Carles's brother-in-law Jacques Mercier who had tried to burn his family to death.

Carles fought that patriarchy all her life. She had the wit and the will to brave public derision when she acted in unconventional ways: developing friendships with men as well as women; bringing her infant niece to the village where she taught when the mother could not care for her — oblivious at first to what people would think; marrying the man she loved against the strongest and meanest objections. When she recalls playing the "ant" to Jean

Carles's "grasshopper," we realize the pressures on her, as the woman, to hold the family together in the face of her husband's impulsive generosity. She worked four jobs at once: teaching school; keeping house and cleaning the hotel she opened with Jean; rearing six children, her own two and her four wards. Jean persuaded her to become the legal guardian of her nieces and nephews.

She never complains. On the contrary, her example shows us what determined individuals can accomplish when faced with anonymous bureaucracies that threaten what we hold most precious: the environment, peace, our civil rights. She demonstrates to us that it is often possible to get what we want if we fight hard enough, and she reminds us that the struggle is lifelong, that stasis is death. Thus, her tragic and triumphant life stands as a model to us all.

How did this unusual book come to be written in the first place? From what the author tells us, as well as from Robert Destanque's introduction in the original French edition, we learn that Carles had intended for many decades to write the story of her life, filling schoolchild notebooks as she went along, and then stacking them on top of her upright piano. Finally she began to organize her material into chapters, working at a square table in the living room of the tiny chalet built for her last years. She wrote in a large, stoutly bound notebook with a green and white marbled cover, reminiscent of old-fashioned account books or hotel registers. Eventually an illness — it was to be her last — threatened the project, and she "talked" her autobiography to M. Destanque over a period of three months in the spring of 1977. The manuscript was completed in November and published in January 1978.

Yet as we read what was compiled from those notebooks and dictation, we may occasionally wonder if anyone could recall so clearly events and dialogues spanning more than seventy years, if things really happened as neatly as she describes. But is not all autobiography fiction to the extent that it necessarily selects and arranges lived reality, bringing a personal viewpoint to bear, even if it makes every effort to avoid distortion and invention? Thus, for example, one might easily have the impression that the village of Val-des-Prés had only one mayor from 1900 to 1978: throughout the book, the mayor has only the name of his function, wears the same official face, and acts in the same arrogantly shameless official way. Clearly, Carles is making a statement on the influence of power and position: in her eyes, as she shows with many different examples from all political levels, mayors, deputies, presidents, and the like are all irredeemably corrupt.

Émilie Carles was born at the turn of the century in the harsh, primitive land that was France's Appalachia of the time. Hers was the generation scarred from youth by the First World War, and indelibly marked by the social and technological upheavals that followed. Like many of the great writers of her day, she took as her mission the fight for a world which would accord to each individual respect, justice, and the material means for a decent life. She was committed to denouncing evil as she saw it, to revolt against the middle-class values she held responsible for the catastrophe of the war. Like her remarkable father, she believed that ideas and ideals were to be lived to the fullest, and she did so, even when her ideas were unpopular. She was convinced that if people exercised their gift of reason, they could change themselves and society for the better, although she came to understand the limits reality poses to human endeavors. Passionately in love with life and the natural universe, she was committed to pacifism, and to an anarchism that was more an aspect of temperament than a political creed.

The major events of the twentieth century are no mere backdrop to Carles's account of her life. Inextricably intertwined with her personal story, they are part of its substance. Thus she offers us the privilege of seeing and feeling our common world history as it concretely affected peasants in the mountains around Briançon in southeastern France.

We know abstractly that in 1914 Europe rushed heedlessly into the first great war, and that France lost a generation of young men in the trenches; in this book, as in the best novels on the war, we confront the devastation wrought on the level of individuals we have come to care about. We watch what happened in the village of Val-des-Prés, and remain haunted by Carles's brother Joseph starving to death in a German prison camp. We are horrified by her sister Catherine needlessly dying in childbirth out of a modesty only her young husband, absent at the front, could have persuaded her to quit for the necessary medical help. With Carles and her family, we live the great hope of the Popular Front government (1936–1938) with its pioneering social legislation; and then through the "Phony War" (1939–1940), followed by German Occupation and Petainist rule; the postwar era; the Algerian War (1954–1962); the Common Front coalition of the parties of the left in the seventies, and the beginnings of environmentalism.

Obviously tragedy is inherent in Carles's story, but the tone is never sentimental, melodramatic, or self-pitying. A born spinner of tales, a close observer of her community and its witty commentator, Carles reveals a marvelous sense of the intricacies and comedy of everyday life. Furthermore, she is always a caring daughter, wife, mother, and friend, who somehow learned to give and receive love and friendship in that harsh landscape. Consequently, her narrative is never wanting in balance and perspective.

The peasant society of the author's youth scarcely exists any longer, transformed for both good and ill by the events of our century, by the forces of technology, politics, and social change. As a schoolteacher, Carles was necessarily involved in that transformation, for one of the fundamental acts of the Third Republic was the passage of the Jules Ferry Law in 1880. To create a citizenry loyal to the new state, it made primary education secular, free, and obligatory; to create the necessary cadre of teachers, it opened secondary education to girls for the first time. Throughout the tenure of this Republic, the elementary school teacher was, as intended, a central, dominating figure in village life, often in competition with the priest.

As a thoroughly secular woman with a family to care for and a clear sense of professional purpose, Carles was typical of this dedicated group. Thus by function as well as by choice, she was an instrument of change. A key phrase in her own awakening to fundamental social and political issues was "it [he or she] opened my eyes." Books and powerful individuals had done this for her, and it was her self-assigned mission to accomplish the same in her peasant society, starting with the children in her classroom. She fought alcoholism, wife and child abuse, superstition, unsanitary living conditions, and the peasant's ingrained distrust of education and books. The standard of living and of farm work undoubtedly was improved by modern plumbing, appliances, and tools; boys and even girls did receive more schooling.

But "progress" also disrupted the traditional peasant economy and relationships, inevitably tinging Carles's pleasure with regret. It emptied the farms and swelled the urban proletariat; it threatened the pristine landscape with deforestation, superhighways, pollution, and a flood of tourists. The telephone, radio, and television ended isolation and drew the peasant population into contact with the rest of France and the world beyond for the first time; concurrently, the new technology ended forever the intimacy and sense of community which grow out of people's need to rely on each other for everything. No longer totally shut off for the six months of their winters, the mountain people abandoned their "veillées," the traditional night gatherings where they whiled away the long winter hours with songs and stories. Indeed, it was here that Carles honed her talent as a teller of tales, as her mother had done earlier.

Although in the French system of education Carles was a civil servant employed by the national government, she never gave up the attempt to explain her pacifist beliefs; to deflate the exaggerated patriotism that leads to murderous wars; to teach her students to question everything and everybody, including their teachers. She urged them to be wary of all political parties, to distrust the agents of power and money at every level. Her iconoclasm did not go unnoticed, but, with one exception, no price seems to have been exacted, possibly because of her qualities as a teacher, and her interest in working in a region hard to staff because it tempted outsiders so little.

During the evening of July 29, 1979, Émilie Carles died in her home overlooking the Clarée River which she had so deeply loved. Catherine Fromm, the librarian at Briançon's Municipal Library, wrote to me: "I knew Émilie Carles well: she was a courageous and funny woman who faced her death calmly and with wisdom; she died of cancer not long after the publication of her book which met with great success in France and throughout the world."

Translator's Note

The present translation is based on the "definitive edition" of Émilie Carles's *Une Soupe aux herbes sauvages*, as told to Robert Destanque (Paris: Editions Robert Laffont, 1988).

The most interesting and difficult problem posed by the text is its multiple tones and textures, often to be found juxtaposed within the same sentence, paragraph, or chapter. I had to listen attentively for the different notes, being careful not to impose a false simplicity on the writer. All her life, Carles remained a peasant woman bound to her people, their traditions, and the harsh land that were her birthright; however, she was also the woman she increasingly became through her education, her profession, her love of reading, and her discussions with Jean Carles and their friends.

On the one hand then, her book, which occasionally has a folkish quality, reflects both the spoken language of the peasant world and the oral tradition imbued in her as a girl raised among people who spent winter evenings telling stories. On the other hand, the book no less clearly reflects Carles's striking intellectual, professional, and literary sophistication. The reader will no doubt notice that the very simple tone of the first pages quickly gives way to the complex tones described above.

The translator's goal is to open a window onto the original text, to communicate its message so faithfully that the reader will not be aware of the translator's mediation while in the process of reading. Nonetheless, the reader must not be allowed to forget the cultural and temporal distance between our world and that of Carles. Thus, even in striving to "convert [that] strangeness into likeness," I worked to "bring home . . . the strangeness of the original," to quote John Felstiner's luminous *Translating Neruda* (Stanford: Stanford University Press, 1975, 5).

Consequently, all units of measure are given in metric; terms of address are reproduced in French: for example, the informal words for parents, "Maman" and "Papa," the French "Madame," with its accent on the second syllable, rather than the English "Madam," with the accent on the first syllable, and the French "Monsieur." Place names are kept in French except where there is a standard English word (e.g., Lyons instead of the French Lyon). Names of newpapers such as *Humanité* and *Le Canard enchaîné* are left in French in accordance with the style of current American journalism; others are translated.

Occasionally, Carles makes a mistake: an author's name may be misspelled (Bérault for Béraud), or as in the chapter entitled "Farewell, Joseph" her pay is given as twenty-five francs, and but a few pages further as fifty. I have not "corrected" the text; a mistake like the former is noted in the glossary, contradictions like the latter are left as is.

The author presents several words in patois which she herself translates directly in the text or in a footnote, well aware that her French readers are unlikely to understand them. Since it seems to me that their presence shows Carles's attachment to her region and her past, I have retained this system.

The word "veillée" has been kept and explained briefly on its first appearance in the text; it refers to a peasant custom which has no match in English.

A glossary is provided to which the reader is referred by asterisks in the text on the first mention of a given word or expression. It takes account of terms kept in French because, for lack of an equivalent in our culture, there is no corresponding word. Also included are the more important authors and publications mentioned in the book. Where a work has not been translated, an English title is provided in the text and the original French in the glossary. Some of the wild herbs mentioned in Carles's introduction seem peculiar to the region; they are described in the text, and further annotated in the glossary as necessary. I have been unable to trace the source of the song in Part One, chapter 4, or the poem Carles taught her pupils (see Part Two, chapter 29).

In the chapter entitled "The Golden Age," Carles includes a lengthy quotation, mainly from Céline's brilliant, bitter, lyrical, and profane novel *Journey to the End of the Night* (1932). Convinced of the correctness of Gregory Rabassa's view that translation is the closest possible reading of a text, persuaded that this would be yet another means to penetrate the consciousness of Carles, I chose to make my own translation and experience her excitement from the inside, as it were. Only afterwards did I read Ralph Manheim's translation (New York: New Directions, 1983); despite its quality, I have decided to use my own version in this volume.

A Life of Her Own

Preface

With the first nice days of spring, when the mountainside is still drenched with melted snow, I like to stretch out on my deckchair on the terrace beside my house, Le Vivier. The sun reaches there early in the day, sketching a play of light and shadow I know as well as the voices of those I love.

The Clarée, that river blessed by the gods, runs by at my feet. Through the branches of the trees, I can make out the clear undulating waters, constantly shifting in color and intensity: tumultuous, calm, roaring, or monotonously quiet. All around me, birds are singing. I speak to them and they answer, and I arrogantly take this concert in as if it were meant for me alone. They are singing a hymn to the sun, the one Rostand° speaks of in these words: "Oh sun, thou without whom things would not be what they are." Left over from the night, the raindrops clinging to the willow leaves glisten in the shafts of sunlight. It is a fairy tale, a paradise. Right before my eyes is the most beautiful place on earth.

A little while later, down by the river, I make good use of my walk, gathering the plants I will need for my soup of wild herbs. I don't have to go far, just around Le Vivier and through the fields along the Clarée. I need only bend down.

This one is rib grass, and over there, wild sorrel, tall *drouille*° with its broad smooth leaves, nettle or salsify, dandelion, lamb's lettuce, a small creeping thistle we call *chonzio,*° a milky plant, sedge, yarrow, *chalabréi*° with its broadly scalloped leaves and white flowers, tetragonia or wild spinach, some *langue bogne*° of the light pink flowers and slim bright green leaves, a

1

sage leaf, and a sprig of chive. Then I add a touch of garlic, a few potatoes or a handful of rice, and I get a rich and delicious soup. To make it come out right, you have to watch the proportions. Not more than a bit of each herb is required; no single one should stand out, for if it does the soup may prove inedible — too bitter, too acid, or too bland. Such is my wild herb soup.

All my life I have lived where I was born, in the mountain country around Briançon. And now I have so many different things to tell, funny or tragic, picturesque or cruel, that from beginning to end, they will serve as the ingredients for another kind of wild herb soup.

Part One

A Tree That
Died for Want
of Sap

When I was six death wouldn't have me. The fact that I'm still alive shows I got off by luck or miracle that day. I fell out of the loft onto a threshing floor hard as cement. To my sisters who picked me up and my father who looked on helpless, I was as good as dead.

It was 1906, in the fall just after harvest when the peasants start threshing the grain — wheat, oats, or barley. In those days I never left my father's side. From morning to night I followed him like a shadow, and the minute he went to the barn loft, I was there too. I wanted to do everything he did; I wanted to grab the sheaves of wheat and throw them down to the threshing floor two stories below where my sisters would spread them flat and start the flailing. Like all accidents, it happened very fast when my father's back was turned. I think he had no idea what was going on. He saw me playing with the sheaves, but it didn't occur to him that I'd want to toss one down just like him. When I threw my first sheaf, I went down with it.

Two stories. I fell like a lump and lay motionless on the floor. Rose and Catherine thought I had been killed on the spot. They picked me up and carried me into the house. That was the day my father was getting ready to fetch the commune's° bull from Maurienne. He didn't particularly react to my fall; for him it was one of life's accidents, not the kind of thing that makes the world stand still. He didn't say "call the doctor" or anything else although my weeping sisters did not know what to do; he just said: "Take care of her, put compresses on her head. I've got to get moving."

Rose, the oldest, not knowing where to turn, asked: "What'll happen to us if our little sister dies?"

"If she dies," my father answered, "go ask the carpenter to make a coffin, and we'll bury her when I get back."

My father was not a heartless man; he was good, generous, and charitable. Of his six children, I was the favorite, but in those days our mountain peasants led such harsh, wretched lives that death could hardly move them; and besides the village depended on the commune's bull for its existence. In that light, a child's death didn't amount to much.

According to custom, the village met at the town hall every August 15 to award rights for that year's bull to the man offering the best price. The whole town was there to debate the stud fees, and whoever got the contract had to honor its terms: he had to purchase and bring back a high-quality bull and then abide by the set stud fee. My father had won almost as a matter of course: he had a reputation for honesty, for know-how, and once he gave his word, nothing could make him back down.

So off he went on foot, he had no choice. In the Maurienne Valley, there is a race of cattle that breeds well with ours. Later on, he would tell me about those trips. He crossed the mountains by way of Névache and Fontcouverte; he skirted the Rochelles at the foot of Mount Tabor before he went back down to Valloir and the fair at Saint-Jean-de-Maurienne. When his deal was made, he returned with the bull the way he had gone, his pockets full of bread and salt. Whenever he was too tired to go on, he simply stopped. He ate his hunk of bread while the bull ate his fodder, and they both slept in some barn along the way. The trip took two or three days. Nothing could have held him back.

As he trudged along those mountain paths, I lay struggling for life. I was in a coma, deliriously babbling gibberish: I talked about the grocer, the cash drawer, squares of chocolate; I said all sorts of things. All the while my sisters were watching at my bedside; and as I rambled on, they wondered: "If she can talk, maybe she won't die?" They tended me as best they could with bouillons, herbal teas, and compresses. Nobody thought to call a doctor — that wasn't the way we did things.

Death was not in the cards for me. Slowly I came out of the coma and recovered. What luck! I hadn't broken anything, and when my father came back with the bull, I was out of the woods. He came into the house and said in a perfectly natural voice:

"You see. She's fine! No reason to bother the doctor."

As time went on, I often heard peasants talk that way. It was not indifference, it was something else. Harsh language may have been a defense against pain. Death struck roughly at children under fourteen. In most families, for every one that survived there was one who died; I've seen peasants bury two in the same week and not show much emotion, especially if the little one was under five. The husband would say to his wife:

"What are you crying for? No one'll miss the kid. Besides, it's one less mouth to feed. What the hell, he couldn't earn his keep, stop crying!"

I remember a story told all over the countryside, that people laughed over because it made fun of the police.

Two local gendarmes on horseback met a peasant on their rounds. He was sitting by the road on a stone boundary marker sobbing as hard as he could. "Well of course," thought the gendarmes, "it's old Grégoire, he just lost his new baby."

"Hello there, Grégoire! Don't take it so hard. You've got other kids at home."

Stung to the quick, old Grégoire drew himself up and answered:

"Oh! so that's what you think! Well, I've only got one cow and she only gives me one calf a year. But this year I won't have anything to sell because the calf just died."

That's the way it was, with peasants often showing more consideration for a cow about to calve than for their own wives and children. The torment of poverty outweighed the aching of the heart.

My mother had died two years earlier, during the summer of 1904. She was struck dead by lightning, right in the middle of gathering wheat at my father's side. She was thirty-six years old; I was four. Peasants carried her down the mountain on a stretcher . . . the sight of my mother lying on that makeshift bed was engraved permanently on my mind, in fact it is my earliest childhood memory. She looked as if she were sleeping, and I was happy for her because I'd always seen her busy from morning till night. I knew nothing about lightning and the damage it could do, I knew nothing about death and its cruelty, and so I called out: "It's so nice Maman is letting them carry her down." People around me said: "Émilie, go give Maman one last kiss." I really had no idea what they meant.

The next day I went to my father in his bedroom. I took his hand and said: "Papa, go get Maman up. It's the middle of the day and she's still asleep." I will never forget how sad he was, or the big tear that began to roll down his cheek. He was bewildered. He took me in his arms and said: "Paouro coco, paouro coco," which meant "poor little darling." My father spoke only the local dialect.

Mother left six children — the youngest, Marie-Rose, was only four months old. Her death was a loss beyond telling. Where we lived, the mother was the keystone, holding the structure together. Overnight, my father was cut to half his size; much later he told me what it had been like, the anguish, the confusion. To help me understand, he compared himself to a tree whose branches had been lopped off.

"I was on my feet, straight as a tree, because a tree stands even when it's dead: its roots hold it up and keep it attached to the ground. Me too. I stayed on my feet since I had children to feed, but I wasn't alive anymore. I was a dead tree, inside the sap had stopped flowing."

Yet theirs was certainly no love match. It was a marriage of convenience, a kind of financially advantageous contract arranged because the families insisted. Had my mother followed her heart, had she been able to choose for herself, she would have married the young man she loved. But that was impossible for a girl in those days, and when my father asked for her hand, she had no say in the matter. She did try to stand up for herself. She went to her godmother — a godmother was somebody, she was important, her authority was recognized and her decisions respected. So my mother asked for understanding and help. It was a waste of time; in her eyes too, the matter was already settled.

"If you don't marry Joseph," she said, "I'm through with being your godmother and I won't speak to you again, ever! And why wouldn't you want him? He's a nice boy, he works hard, he's got spunk and he owns property. He's the best match you can hope for."

It was true. My father had all of those qualities, but in themselves they do not add up to love. The godmother was simply enforcing the law because it was the law: marriageable girls were expected to take the husbands other people picked out for them without a murmur. Usually the men arranged things without consulting anyone. When they met at fairs, they talked about business, they talked about the future. Sacks of oats, breeding hogs, shearing sheep, arranging marriages were all alike — everything got tossed into the same bag.

"Say, you have a girl at home, I've got a son — why don't we marry them off? I've got the farmhouse, you've got the land. So if it's all right with you, let's draw up a contract."

That's what they said; then they drank on it, shook hands, and the deal was made.

For men and women alike, but above all for women, lives were broken by this custom. Almost every girl from around here was condemned to a life she had not chosen. It wouldn't have been quite so bad if it had been only the husband, but a girl practically always married her in-laws as well; moving into her husband's farm, she was at their beck and call. My mother did not escape the system but she was strong-minded, she was not docile and refused to hold her tongue. In any case, she was unforgettable to those who knew her. Tears came to my father's eyes whenever he talked to me about her; he would tell me what an extraordinary woman she was. She had two gifts: she knew how to please and she was generous.

Because of her, the veillées came alive: veillées were gatherings held to while away the long winter evenings, and they were important to us in those parts into the twenties. Afterwards the custom died out, but in my mother's time it was part of daily life. She told stories, she sang, she was always ready to listen. She had a knack for being lovable and doing good turns. This may not seem like much, but in our kind of land, a harsh land where distrust, jealousy, and selfishness were the rule, my mother's generosity was a gift from Heaven that everyone appreciated to the full. Years later, whenever I met people who had known her, they would speak with the same respect:

"Ah, you're Catherine Vallier's girl. What a way to die! Now there was a woman. So gentle, so thoughtful, so funny. Everyone wanted her for their own."

Her generosity was in proportion to our means: my mother would never have tolerated waste, but such was her nature that she couldn't resist helping someone in need. Her sister, for example, was unhappily married; she was poor and had a lot of children. Every year there was a new one, and each time my mother gave her the layette. It was always the same story: when they needed anything, my aunt told her kids: "Go see Catherine, she's got everything she needs." The kids would come over and my mother would give them what they asked for. Inevitably my grandfather noticed these comings and goings and kicked up a fuss, suspecting that she was filching from the household. That is what set them at loggerheads.

For years the skirmishing went on between them. My grandfather was a real old-time patriarch. The house belonged to him, so did the land, and he kept a tight hold on the purse strings. That old peasant knew the price of everything. For him, nothing counted but work and profit. No one had ever opposed his will. My mother did, setting her generosity squarely against his rapaciousness.

It was not always easy; caught between the tree and the bark, unable to intervene, my father had a very hard time. On the one hand, good and charitable himself, he agreed with my mother; on the other hand, he understood his father, a man who had worked hard all his life only to see things from his household given away. Stuck in the middle and unable to do much good, my father still tried, asking them: "What's the use of arguing?" But neither my mother nor my grandfather was willing to listen. They were too different to understand each other or work out a way to get along.

Death finally ended their quarrel. As fate would have it, they died at almost the same time. My grandfather fell off a ladder, broke his femur, and died in June 1904. Forty days later, my mother was struck by lightning during the storm of July 16.

No wonder my father compared himself to a tree still standing but emptied of its life-giving sap. Without his Catherine he was a shadow of himself. And the house, a house filled with six lively children! Overnight, it turned into a body without a soul. That too was a stroke of fate, a harsh stroke.

Still, life had to go on. In situations like that, human fellowship comes to the rescue. Family and neighbors lent a hand and gave my father support. But he found it so awful to be left alone with six children that he did not know what to do. He was lost. The older ones could manage, they were between eight and fifteen and already at work; but the others, the two little girls, were a problem. Most urgent was what to do about Marie-Rose. She was four months old and my mother had been breastfeeding her. So that was taken care of first. Until a wet-nurse could be found, local women with young babies took turns coming to nurse her.

Then there was me. I was four, too little to work in the fields or help out at home. Right in the middle of summer when every second counts, I was an extra burden for my father. He had to find someone to look after me too. My mother's older brother offered to take me in.

"Joseph," he said, "what are you going to do about Émilie? The others are big enough to work with you. They can get along, but she will be in your way. Why don't I take her home with me? I'll raise her and make a schoolteacher out of her."

At wit's end, my father agreed. They got my bundle ready and that same night I went off with my uncle. It was the first time I had ever left home. My uncle was taking me to Guillestre on the other side of Briançon. To me it seemed like the other side of the world.

I don't have a single pleasant memory of Guillestre. My uncle meant well, I suppose; he wanted to bring me up and turn me into something other than a peasant's daughter. He was sincere, I suppose, but I could not get used to his ways or his wife's either. He was a retired customs agent, and to make ends meet he went to all the towns in the Queyras: he would pick up watches to be repaired, leave them with a jeweler in Briançon, and bring them back to their owners a week later.

He wasn't a bad sort; I could have managed with him. But his wife was mean and couldn't stand children. She made my life a nightmare. My aunt spent the best part of her time showing off her jewelry, and she gave me no peace. A spot on my smock, or a rip in my dress, earned me a sound whipping. I remember how I loved to play by the brook — for me it was like playing at home in Val-des-Prés on the banks of the Clarée. But at Guillestre those simple, innocent games, a few drops of water on my clothes, were enough to unleash her fury. She was not just mean, she was vicious. My aunt enjoyed dragging me off to the police station to have them shut me up. Her worst punishment was to tell the gendarmes: "All right, put her in jail, she has been naughty." Why they obeyed, I do not know, but they did, locking me up in a dark room. I have loathed my aunt ever since, along with prisons and the police.

Fortunately, I didn't stay in Guillestre very long. In October my father came to see me, not just like that, for the fun of it, but to buy a cow at the fair. As soon as I caught sight of him I started to yell "Papa! Papa!" jumping up and down and hopping about; as soon as he got close, I grabbed hold of his trouser leg and I wouldn't let go. That moment made such a strong impression that it left an enduring physical memory; whenever I think about it, I can feel the rough corduroy between my fingers. Unable to pry me loose to get my clothes on, my aunt began to fume, for I gave her one hand and then the other, never both at once. I wouldn't let go of my father. Finally my battle-axe of an aunt with her fancy airs couldn't stand it any more. She talked down to my father as if he was some farmhand who did nothing but till the soil, whereas she took herself for a lady.

"But Joseph, surely you are not going to take her to the fair with you!"

My father answered in his dialect, of course:

"What else do you want me to do? You can see she won't let go of me!"

So he took me off to the Guillestre fair. My father was well known for driving a hard bargain, and he had no equal when it came to appraising an animal. He saw defects and good points at a glance. In a cow, he prized handsome withers, slender horns, a silky coat, and a long tail hanging below the hocks. That day, as he went from one lot to another, I dogged his footsteps. Whatever he did, however involved he got with the cows, looking them up and down, feeling them all over, squatting to squirt milk from the udder of a promising animal, I saw only him. Nothing else mattered.

Ordinarily he would have gone straight back to Val-des-Prés, but this time, once his choice was made, he asked the other peasants from the valley if they'd mind taking his cow along with theirs. "I've got to look after the little one," he told them. "I've got to bring her back with me." And so his decision was made, although my uncle tried hard to change his mind.

"But what will you do with her? She is too little for you to look after."

My father would not give in and kept repeating:

"I'm taking her home, I'm taking her home."

Finally my uncle ran out of arguments:

"All right then. But if you are going to take her, at least promise me you will speak French to her and that you will say *vous*.° Do not forget I want to make a schoolteacher out of her, and if you keep talking to her in dialect, I will come and take her away."

And so I came back to Val-des-Prés three months after I left. I had so clearly registered my uncle's words, I was so afraid he'd come and get me, that at first I followed my father everywhere he went. The cellar, the hayloft, the barn, the fields, the kitchen — wherever he was, I was there too. He even let me into the outhouse with him, and that's saying a lot, when you consider how children were brought up in those days. All the while I kept saying: "Papa, don't leave me! My uncle's coming and I don't want to leave you!"

My father took it all; both father and mother to me, he was incredibly kind. He sat me beside him at the table and he chose the best bits of meat for me from his own plate. At night he let me come to his room, took me into his bed, and warmed me, saying: "If I hadn't been there, you'd have died fast." And he would say it in French because after we got home, he tried hard to speak French to me and to say *vous* just as my uncle had advised. I suppose he didn't want them to come take me away, either my uncle or anyone else.

My father often said: "You have to do good turns for bad." He was a believing Catholic and he did not talk to hear the sound of his voice: he meant it. He was not just devoutly observant, he also lived the principles of charity the priest extolled in church. For many people it was all words; for my father it was different, he was in earnest and he never missed a chance to act according to the gospels.

We lived in an ungainly homestead. People called it the "château," without irony or malice, simply because it was the biggest house around. It is still standing, still the biggest place hereabouts, but no one lives there anymore. Once in a while, I open it to put up visiting friends for a night or two. This winter I let some soldiers take shelter there from the cold, not that I'm fond of the military, but it was so cold that I couldn't say no, and I told the captain: "Here you are, take the keys and get your men settled in; they'll be better off there than outside." They were supposed to stay one day and one night — they stayed four. One hundred fellows with their hobnail shoes for four days! They left my house in such a mess! I cried when I saw it.

The place has always been "God's house" — open to every passerby in my father's day, maybe even before, and later too with my husband. One of my ancestors bought it for a song, still unfinished. That deal goes back to the First Empire. From what I've heard, an Italian merchant built it. The fellow made his money in umbrellas and wanted to retire here in Val-des-Prés. Unfortunately he lost it as fast as he earned it supplying Napoleon's soldiers with free shoes and uniforms. It seems they needed them. In any case, he had to sell the house when he went bankrupt and it became the family place.

From one end of the year to the other, we held open house in the "château," with my father offering hospitality to itinerant peddlers, hawkers — everyone who came through the village for his trade. It was a major event when a peddler arrived. That may seem old-fashioned now, but for us in those days — for us children who knew nothing of the world beyond our church steeple, the smell of the stable, and weeding the potato field — the peddler was a show in and of himself. All sorts of people came through: the seed dealers; the men who sold notions and household articles; the tinsmith; the clothing salesman; and the humblest of all who waved his merchandise about on what looked like a candelabrum: I mean the shoelace salesman. They all knew that in our house there was room for them and their horses. My father took in the chimney sweep and lots of others besides; in fact, any traveler was sure to find food and shelter with us. That is what our house was like, the house the village used to call the "château." But no one would have thought of treating my father as the lord of the manor, at most we girls were occasionally called "the young ladies of the château." No, it had nothing to do with titles. My father was an exceptional man; he won respect from everyone, and people revered him for his integrity and his goodness.

Girls my age would say: "My goodness, Émilie, you're so lucky to have a father like that!"

They envied me, and I would answer: "What! Me lucky? I don't even have a mother and you *do*. You call that lucky?"

"It's not that," they'd say. "He's so nice, your father, not like ours. We're scared of ours, but you can tell yours anything you feel like and he listens, he understands, and he gives you what you want. You're better off than us, even if we do have a father and a mother. You can't ever tell them anything; when they go sell wood in Briançon, they come back empty-handed and we just get dry cheese to eat. Besides your papa's not a drunk!"

It's true. My father never went to the café and in our town with its seven bistros, a man who didn't drink — well, that was *not* usual. And the bistro was all there was, the only entertainment around, and those peasants certainly did not deny themselves. Bored and worn out, they saw it as their only recourse. They could play cards at the Mora Café and they could drink. They drank a lot. Worst of all was that people who drank too much did not realize it. They believed that their hard labor gave them the right to drink wine — as much as you please, sir! "A liter in the morning, one at noon, and another at night," they'd say, "that doesn't make me a drunk, and I can still drink a glass or two at the bar." The widespread abuse of alcohol made for a great many alcoholics who in turn made a great many people suffer. It was the wives and the children who paid.

There were terrible stories — I'll have occasion to come back to the subject more than once. Besides, there was the contempt that drinkers felt for nondrinkers. They couldn't refrain from calling them "femmelettes." The word "femmelette" was the height of contempt; my husband was entitled to it and my father too, of course. It meant incompetent, utterly worthless, phony. The whole bit.

My father had the drawbacks of his virtues. I've already said that he was a strict Catholic, an old-fashioned man who had not traveled or read. Nothing mattered to him but work, obedience, and respect for tradition. In matters of principle he was inflexible, and he was wary of change. He was not the only one; all the old peasants morbidly distrusted anything new, as if they were afraid progress would eat them alive. My father belonged to that race of men. But his goodness was so much more important, the great and generous goodness that served me so well. In the months and years after my mother's death, that is what he gave me. Perhaps my view is distorted but for me it is a happy distortion. It was not always easy between us; at times I had to assert my ideas against his, and sometimes his words hurt. But I think that our disputes never cast a shadow over the love I had for him and he for me.

Chapter 2 𐂷

Wolves
in the
Valley

These days, when people talk about Val-des-Prés or the Clarée Valley, they say: "It's the most beautiful place on earth." That is true. I do not know anything more beautiful: the mountains, the river, even the houses, nothing has been touched. Before 1914 and the war, no one cared much about beauty, and this was the harshest place on earth. I lived that harshness, it marked everyone who lived here. The altitude and climate made the conditions of peasant life difficult. For some six months of the year, cold and snow paralyze everything: snow isolates. It did isolate people. In those days, there weren't any snowplows or cars, only horses and mules pulling sleighs, and all winter long we were cut off from the rest of the world. Caught between a long winter and a summer that was always too short, peasants led stunted lives, their time consumed in wresting subsistence from the earth. By the time they were six, children had to do their share of the work in this primitive economy: they had no choice. Their jobs were watching the animals, going to the fields, and doing the household chores. That was the rule. Working hard and looking to grab every penny as if the sky would fall in on them any moment, peasants lived the year round hanging onto their bit of land. It was in their blood and holds true even today for those who are still in farming. Along with stamina and tenacity, the difficulty of their lives nurtured more questionable qualities like selfishness, distrust, and suspicion. Church and patriarchy held them in a tight grasp. It was the Middle Ages or almost; it was a land of mountain people ignorant of everything but work, sickness, and death.

Work and bread, bread and work: nothing was more important. At the end of summer, once the crops were stored in the granaries, the cattle brought in, and the wood cut into logs, the peasants baked their bread. They made enough for six months; it couldn't be done later for according to custom, bread had to be baked in the communal oven, and after November the cold, snow, and bad weather didn't allow that kind of activity.

Those communal ovens were of considerable size; there were several in the commune, one at Rosiers, one here at Val-des-Prés, and another at Draille. On All Saints Day the peasants brought their wood — each family arriving with its loaded cart. Then they pooled the wood and divided it into piles. The first, for starting up the oven, was immense, and each of the others was smaller in turn. The hard thing was bringing the oven up to temperature. There was no problem when it was hot — it had simply to be maintained, but the first person to bake his bread ran the risk of an insufficiently heated oven. That is why when the piles of wood were ready, the peasants drew lots to avoid arguments and inequity. Everyone drew a number; it was the simplest of lotteries with little pieces of paper folded and placed in a hat, and thus the die was cast: "You're number one, you're two, you're three," and so on up to the last pile of wood. Whoever got number one was on duty. It was up to him to light the oven and get it hot; the work was extremely arduous; for ten hours or more, you had to load cord after cord of wood into the oven without ever knowing for sure whether the temperature was right. After that, it was much easier, as the oven would work smoothly.

Tradition decreed that number one, "the loser," take charge of the process. It was his job to announce the date and time for starting the oven, and the next day or the day after, he baked his bread just as he'd decided. The others followed. Those were utterly exceptional times, holidays almost, at least for us children, since bread wasn't the only thing they made. The women took advantage of the oven to turn out cakes, tarts, and cabbage pies. They threw themselves into the task wholeheartedly, each joyously shaping her dough as she pleased before it went into the oven.

I remember that during those days my father was everywhere at once, at the kneading trough, the oven, the hayloft. Besides making our family's bread, he served as baker for those who couldn't do it for themselves. In a village, there are always people unable to work, the old, and the sick, and my father took care of them. That he prepared their dough and then baked it was entirely in keeping with the way he did things. We helped him, my brothers and sisters and I, as well as we could. He did the kneading, and we made up the loaves. When they rose enough, we placed them on large boards covered with bran and then carried them over to him. Usually he was doing what was called *escouber* in the local dialect: that is, he swept the embers with pine tree branches, took the bread shovel, and, as we handed him the loaves, flung them expertly into the back of the oven. The bread was done in an hour's time.

This bread was meant to last the whole winter, and we carried it to the hayloft where we spread it out on huge hanging trestles, and we'd go fetch it up there as needed. Obviously, it was as hard as wood; to soften it ahead of time, we'd hang a few loaves in the sheep pen, just above the sheep. The heat and humidity softened it to a point, but it was a far cry from fresh bread and from one end of winter to the other, we ate it stale. We used a special knife, yet it was so hard to cut that it shattered into fragments that scattered to the four corners of the kitchen. But it was good: that bread had an extraordinary smell, and what a taste! My sisters and I fought over the crusts, sucking on that bread with as much delight as if it had been cake. Dunked in café au lait, it was a feast.

Once the bread was made, it was winter. The first snows come early around here. Winter brought radical change into peasant life. Today, with central heat, television, cars, and all the rest, there is practically no difference between seasons, but in those times, it was night and day. Cold rooms were closed off, wood provided the only heat, and stoves were still a rarity. As a shield against the cold, families confined themselves to the common rooms: the kitchen with its fireplace, and the stable where the warmth of the animals maintained a bearable temperature.

Winter did bring a certain respite into peasant lives, yet beyond milking and animal care, a thousand things remained to be done: repairing harnesses, keeping tools in working order, sharpening blades, spinning wool. You might say that the time for crafts arrived with winter. Everyone had his own: cabinetmaker, shoemaker, saddler, wheelwright, blacksmith, basketmaker, weaver; some even knitted socks. There was no lack of work, but life was totally different, it was calmer, more relaxed. During the summer, at harvest time, peasants ran every which way, fighting rain and storm without a moment's breathing space. With the end of November, the frantic pace eased and they felt calmer. Time itself was different, we didn't go running after it anymore: it belonged to us.

People lived according to the rhythm of the day and ate early. After evening soup, families got together for the long evening's watch. Kindred spirits formed groups, each person bringing along his chair, his piece of work, his mouth to speak, and his ears to listen.

Veillées were held in the stable — the stable was a world unto itself. In one corner were the cows, in another the sheep, with the donkey off some-where. There were the smells, the heat, and then the only light came from a single lamp hung from the rafters. A distinctive atmosphere reigned, with people forming groups according to categories: the women were in one cor-ner, their hands in constant motion knitting or spinning wool; the men in another, smoking their pipes and listening to the younger ones among them. People chatted, sang old songs with everyone coming in on the chorus, and told stories. In wonder and in terror, I would listen to those tales from an-other time, from the days when nothing frightened the wolves who attacked the flocks and gobbled up the foolhardy.

First Wolf Story, Told by My Father

"My great-grandfather had a bone to pick with one of those fellows, a lone wolf fierce as all get-out. It was on a night like this, during the veillée, when he had a sudden urge to take a crap and went out to the *luou*.[1] In those days, it was a more isolated and primitive place than it is today. It was a simple hole in the ground with a board on each side for the feet. You never stayed there very long, especially in that season. He wasn't settled for more than a minute or two when he felt a huge hairy mass fall on his shoulders. His heart leaped into his mouth, his hair stood on end, but he had the presence of mind to grab the animal's front paws, hold them tight around his neck and race to the stable as fast as a jackrabbit. Talk about ghosts! Old Grandpa with that beast on his back and his pants around his ankles like an accordion on its side. It was a howl! But they didn't take time to laugh, not right away. He let go of the wolf and the animal started to leap around in the cow's food rack — he didn't know what was going on and nei-ther did the cows. So everybody grabbed whatever came to hand: hoes, pitchforks, scythes, tool handles, and they finished him off. There stood old Grandpa with his dicky sticking out in the open, shaking so hard he couldn't get his pants back up. With the animal dead, they could all laugh, and the women who'd never seen such a fine pair up close kept on chuckling, and the others went right on making fun of him. That whole business lent a touch of variety to the veillée. All the same, old Grandpa had a close shave."

---

[1] *Luou*: literally, "the place." This is the familiar term for outhouse. — AU.

Second Wolf Story, Told by a Woman

"You know, Joseph, not all wolf stories turn out so well. I don't know if you remember little Marie, the girl who used to live over in Calla. She didn't have your grandpa's luck. You can just imagine, around there nobody gave any thought to wolves. The houses are all sort of close up against each other, and even so, wait till you hear this! Marie lived alone with her baby, and every evening she'd leave the veillée to give him his bottle. Afterwards, depending on how things were, she'd come back and spend the rest of the evening with us or she'd stay home and go to bed. Nobody paid any attention. So this time when she didn't come back, we weren't especially worried. But the next morning, it was another story. Marie's neighbors happened to hear the baby crying. That was unusual so they went to see what was going on. They knocked, they called, and since no one answered and the door was locked, they had to break in to see what was going on. The baby was alone, in his cradle screaming for food. Since Marie's bed wasn't slept in or anything, they knew straight off she hadn't gone to bed. She'd disappeared the night before. Right away the men organized a search party, and since it had snowed during the night, they went around in circles for a long time before they found her — well, what was left of her. It was the wolves. They'd pulled her out of the village, beyond the houses on the edge of town, into the Casse woods. The only things left were bits of torn clothing and traces of blood; they dragged her there before they gobbled her up."

Third Wolf Story, Told by a Woman

"We used to call him the fiddler. He played at all the weddings and the young would dance to his squeaky fiddle. Later on, in the middle of the night, he'd go home, always taking leftovers and bits of pie for his family. One night, on the way back from a party, he was attacked by a pack of wolves between Val-des-Prés and Rosiers. Talk about your surprise meetings! But he didn't lose his head either. Without missing a step, he threw them all the tidbits he'd picked up at the wedding, but they didn't amount to much, a mouthful for those wolves. Then the old fellow thought of his violin. Talk about your ideas! But he didn't want to run, so he said to himself: "If I do that, they'll jump me." And keeping up the same pace, he started to play. He played whatever popped into his head, he got so much noise out of that violin that some strings snapped. It made such a racket that the wolves moved off. But not for long: a minute later they came charging back, they'd figured out his game, and the more he sawed away on his fiddle, the closer they came. Somehow he held out till he got to the chapel at Rosier, and he just had time to open the door and slam it shut. Since it didn't have a latch or a lock, he spent the whole night holding it closed while the wolves scratched at it with their paws and pushed it with their muzzles, more and more furious as time went on. That old fiddler didn't go free till the wee hours of the morning, so he's another one who can say he was scared shit-less."

I have heard so many stories like that; it is as if the wolves really had an effect on peasant lives. Otherwise, why talk about them so much? Obviously that wasn't the only thing they talked about, but wolf stories came up like the chorus of a song. I bring them up here because even today the wolf's presence and all that goes with it have not entirely died out in the villages of our region. The fear persists, whether or not there really are any wolves around. At the slightest hint of danger, wolves come to their minds. I remember when I was teaching school here in Val-des-Prés — I'm talking about the forties — one of my pupils was a little girl who came all the way from Alberts. It's a tiny hamlet, three kilometers away, so small there weren't enough children to justify a school. Well, her father would never let her come to class alone; for fear of wolves he chose to pay me for her room and board. In these parts, people all have sheep, they're all shepherds, and for them the wolf is the Evil One: he steals sheep.

A few years later, wild dogs attacked the sheep. In spite of the newspaper articles and news bulletins, no one around here would believe it was wild dogs; all they talked about was wolves. One day a peasant rushed down the mountain all excited: he'd caught sight of a wolf. "I saw one! I saw one!" he yelled all through the village; everyone believed him and that time too the men set off to scout for wolves. When they got back, they had caught an animal, but it was a wild dog, not a wolf.

My father didn't have a second trade. Unlike the other peasants, he was neither cabinetmaker, tanner, nor anything else. During the winter, he did all sorts of things around the house, but only for himself. He was a farmer, and since the soil was stingy and did not feed his family, he was both farmer and smuggler.

There is one thing I want understood. My father was neither a bandit nor a thief. Nobody thought it was dishonest to smuggle sheep between here and Italy. It would never have entered my father's head to do any dirty business, but in the peasant economy of those days, you had to have several strings to your bow to provide for your family. Then again, there was a deep-seated hostility to the state in all peasants, even a man of my father's strict principles. Most of them respected tradition and authority, but they never missed a chance to get around the law if they could. Also, for mountain people, the state was first among thieves, and in their eyes, there was no harm in putting something over on it. So being an excellent shepherd who knew the region like the palm of his hand, and fluent in all the patois spoken on both sides of the border, he went to Italy every year to buy sheep and bring them back to sell in France. It brought in a good profit. Excursions like that were possible only in the spring after the snow melted, and he didn't go alone — he got other peasants like himself to help out. Those trips were real expeditions. To avoid the customs men, they had to take impossible routes, going along the ridges and through passes no one would risk in the normal course of things. He told me all about it:

"It was quite a business; everything had to be worked out so people would hardly notice. Up here, the minute you take one step off the beaten track, the whole village picks it up and, let me tell you, smuggling stories are no joke, because if you get caught, you've had it. The customs men don't only seize your flock, you're also liable to be fined and you may very well end up serving time in prison. You had to figure everything just right and fool every-one you knew, so loose tongues wouldn't cause trouble. Those trips had to jibe with fairs, at least some regional fair. You see why? You'd leave empty-handed and come back with a hundred, a hundred fifty head, and you had an answer for all the questions coming at you: 'I bought them at the fair at such-and-such a place,' but the stories had to jibe. So that's what we'd do, my pals and I, we'd make a careful plan — every detail, the dates and the routes — and we'd stick to it unless something happened out of the blue. That's why we never got caught. I'd leave home and I'd say: 'I'm off to the fair and I'll be away for a few days,' or else I didn't say anything at all, and I left for Italy by way of Montgenêrre and Clavières. Once I got to Italy, I didn't have to worry; I'd meet my sidekicks and we'd go shopping. That could mean a long trip — it depended on the year. There were times we found our hundred or so animals right away, other times we had to go way up the mountain. One year I went as far as Rivoli to find sheep, it was a long haul, more than a week — that's a lot. We had another trick up our sleeves, three or four of us took shifts, so each of us would be gone for the least time possible, and we'd pull a fast one on those customs men. They guessed something was going on. Your mother — well, her three brothers were in customs, you know, and they were dying to get their hands on us more than anybody else. No wonder! They were sick and tired of hearing their superiors say: 'So, you let Joseph alone because he's married to your sister.' It got them hot under the collar, and I think they'd have done anything to catch me red-handed. They were hilarious! After I got back, your mother would tell me about their visits — they took turns stopping by at the house. The first one would say:

"'So where's Joseph?'

"Your mother would answer: 'Why he's up there cutting wood.'

"'Oh,' he'd say. 'So he's cutting wood. You mean to tell me he's always cutting wood?'

"'Yeah, sure, he's in the woods, we need wood,' she'd say.

"The next day, one of the others would come by, and he wanted to know where I was, too.

"'Oh, so he's in the woods. Funny thing, isn't it, he's still in the woods.'

"Your mother would shrug her shoulders; she knew they couldn't do a thing, they couldn't know the when or the where or anything. When it was the third brother's turn, there I was: I'd done my shopping, I'd brought the animals to just above Plampinet where my pals took over.

"'Oh! So Joseph's here,' the brother would say, goggle-eyed.

"'Yeah, sure I'm here!' I'd say. 'Where'd you think I was?'

"Then he'd go report to the customs office: 'No, nothing doing with my brother-in-law, he's home — I went over there and I saw him.' That's all he could tell them. And the whole time, my pals were moving the flock along. The hardest part was the border. There were customs men looking for us with their dogs, well that was a godsend, because the barking warned us off and we'd stay on the Italian side till they all left. Then we'd take the plunge, at night if we could, and keep moving on the French side but right along the border, just in case. We went by way of Les Acles, by way of Les Thures at the foot of the Rochilles du Thabor, made a detour as far as the Névache mountain, and at that point a third pal would take over the flock. He'd come back down through the Guisane valley, Monestier, by way of the Buffère Pass. After that it was child's play, you just had to make your entry through Briançon, and there, like I told you, it only had to jibe with some fair in the region."

They used that ploy for years. My father was the one to take the initiative and put up the money. In the fall, he'd go off to the fairs and meet his friends — he chose them for their competence as mountaineers and livestock dealers, and together they'd plan their operation.

"Good, we're all agreed. I put up the money, I get you twenty head, and you take over from me at the Dormiouze Pass."

"O.K."

They shook hands on it and the deal was made.

My father spoke of those times with feeling — they were his youth. I think he missed the journeys over the mountains. At that season of the year, nature is in full bloom — you have to see it to get some notion of what it's like, flowers everywhere, the grass bursting forth — there is absolutely nothing that compares with walking in nature there. He must have missed his endless discussions with Italian peasants, and also those long trips back at night, urging the flock along as he looked for a place to cross over where the customs men would not appear simply because they couldn't imagine anyone else coming that way.

"I really had to stop," he'd tell me, "it was getting too dangerous. That last time out, they almost had me. It was at Vachette, I ran into the customs men, and that once we'd been held up and there wasn't any fair. You realize what that meant? What could I tell them? Nothing. It was a woman who got me off. She came over and before the customs men could say a word, she asked me:

"'Hey, Joseph, did you see my man at the St. Crépin fair?'

"She was a smart one. I never found out why she did it, but she struck a light in my head: there certainly was a fair at St. Crépin. When the customs men came circling around the flock, I was ready for them. The one in charge said:

"'Come on now! You couldn't get here from St. Crépin in such a short time'

"'Sure I could. Why not?' was my answer. 'I bought these animals in the stables last night, I left at sundown and we walked all night.'

"The other customs man took his turn and said:

"'Just look at this one and that one over there — these sheep don't come from St. Crépin, their fleece is much too long.'

"'Bah,' I told him. 'I don't know anything about that, all I know is I bought them at the fair in St. Crépin.'

"They could think what they liked, they couldn't prove a thing. Italian wool or not, I was saved. But it was a close call, so close I decided on the spot it was time to quit. Do you have any idea of the risks I took? Let alone the money I put up for the others — all my savings, and no way could my sidekicks pay me back till we sold off the animals in the fall. It's true I doubled my stakes every time, it was all profit, but I was too frightened at Vachette to take the risk even once more. If it hadn't been for the goodness of that woman, I'd have earned a stay in jail. I considered it a warning from heaven and I stopped. That business had gone on for more than sixteen years."

Chapter 3

Tied Down on a Mule

Work was life. I say "was," but is anything more important today? Certainly not. You just have to read the papers or look at the news, that's all they talk about. Over a million people are looking for work, and our leaders have only one word on their lips: unemployment, reducing the rate of unemployment! Our society wants it that way. As I see it, a man without work, who cannot choose his work, is less than a man.

A peasant whose crop fails or who loses his livestock is a ruined man. Those things happen fast, it takes almost nothing. In 1906 there was a terrible drought, the grass and water were gone, everything was dry and the animals were dropping like flies. My father was killing our sheep one after the other — you wouldn't believe how skinny they were — before they fell sick, and we would go from door to door in Briançon to sell them. A leg here, a shoulder there, so it wasn't a total loss. For those who had no livestock, or didn't think of killing them until too late — what was there to do? Nothing but cry their eyes out. In the circumstances, peasants could only grit their teeth and tighten their belts or else steal or beg. Stealing — well all right, but begging or merely asking for help was a different matter. It would never have entered anyone's mind to ask a neighbor for something, that never! They called it self-respect, pride. I do not: I call it stupidity, but that's the way things were.

For a man, work was the only way to avoid destitution. In those days there were no unemployment payments, no family allowances, no social security, nothing at all. When the day came that a man was out of work, for whatever reason, he was driven to the worst extremes.

In the village there were two men living that way, permanently poor, father and son. People called them the bearded guys, they hadn't shaved for years, they were unkempt, they were ugly, and they were filthy as sin. Those two had given up taking care of themselves. They were so poor . . . well, they did have a little land, but so little! They were so deprived that they never had enough money to light their place, not even with a plain oil lamp; and that's the way they lived, going to bed before it got dark and getting up with the sun. Destitute as they were, those two, when you wanted to give them a hand or help them out, you had to be as clever as a Sioux to bring it off. I remember my father getting them to accept some hemp shirts. They had nothing to put on their backs, they were dressed like bums, and the one thing of value they owned was a donkey, but what a donkey! She was such a skinny, foolish-looking beast that I wondered every time I saw her how she managed to stay on her feet. She was tiny, and when the old fellow was on her back with his feet touching the ground, you'd have thought it was a caricature of Sancho Panza, but an effeminate, repulsive Sancho Panza. Well, those two men living like medieval serfs accepted those shirts from my father. I don't know how he went about it; certainly they gave him something in exchange since they did not want to be indebted to anyone.

One day the schoolteacher called me aside. She'd made a ratatouille and had some left over, she even had a lot left over, and since everyone in the village knew the bearded guys didn't always eat their fill, she wanted them to have the benefit of her food.

"Émilie," she said, "you know them slightly, so take them this ratatouille, they'll be pleased."

I went, but I couldn't tell them the ratatouille came from my house — that they surely would not have believed because we all came from around here. So I told them the truth, I told them: "Madame Roman sent you this ratatouille."

"Huh!" the father answered in patois, "What do I want with her damn ratatouille. Take it the hell back!"

He wouldn't have anything to do with it, I was obliged to carry it back to the schoolteacher and of course she didn't understand, she was hurt and furious. But for those men, there wasn't any choice, they'd rather go hungry than accept charity and have people find out. That was the mentality around here, and they shared it with the peasants in the valley.

More recently, there was the story of the man who hanged himself . . . I do not intend to wallow in what is called miserabilism, that's not the point, it's a matter of speaking candidly. It would be more criminal still to hide this poverty. In the spring, the forest ranger found a man hanging in the Rosier woods. The old fellow must have strung the rope around his neck just before winter, and when the ranger came across the body it was not a pretty sight. Frozen a hundred times over, chunks eaten out by animals. They cut him down and carried him to the town hall. He wasn't from around here, nobody knew him, they searched him to find out who he was and where he came from. They found a notebook in his pocket — a little notebook bound in black oilcloth, and fourteen cents. That's all he had on him. In the notebook, the man had recorded all the places, all the shops and companies where he had asked for work: "On the so-and-so I went by Manosque to such and such a place, no work . . . on the so-and-so I went by Gap, no work, on the so-and-so to Largentières, no work." There were a dozen entries like that, maybe more, each with the same annotation: "No work."

This is one thing that has always revolted me; I cannot accept a man's not finding work when he wants to work. How can they talk about progress or humanity? How dare they talk about Liberty, Equality, and Fraternity?* It's hot air! So long as a man cannot choose his trade, all the rest is hot air. . . . Well, this man from out of nowhere, who didn't know anyone around here, decided to hang himself without a word, without looking for help, rather than beg for work in vain and live without being able to satisfy his most basic needs. He too had his pride, a damned thick layer of pride, to reach that point. Later on we found out that he did have family, a sister who could have helped him, but he refused to be a burden, either to her or anyone else. He would rather go deep into the woods, in secret, like a thief.

That man's story is not uncommon; suicides were frequent, especially among men, and there were many more then than today. In our cemetery there has always been a potter's field, the corner for the drowned or the hanged. That is where they were put; they were so hardened, so proud that they never complained, never made the slightest mention of their poverty, but when they couldn't bear it any longer, they hanged themselves or jumped into the water. Sometimes they left a word of explanation, sometimes nothing, and each of us was left to imagine what had prompted the act.

I know another example of a man who had no alternative because he couldn't find work. It's even more appalling because this time it's about an old man, who had worked for the same company all his life, from age twenty to seventy, fifty years of "good and faithful service." When the contract was up — and it was the company that broke it — they even awarded him a medal, one of the first bestowed in France for work well done. It was so shabby! When he walked away after a glass of bad champagne and a handshake from the boss, he had nothing left but that gilt medal. There was no such thing as a pension in those days; once the old man was fired he had no means of support. That good and simple fellow started out by visiting each of his children in turn, thinking: maybe they can take me in, they're young, they can't do everything by themselves, I can help out, that way I won't be a burden. It was all in his imagination, but even so he went. . . .

He was discreet, he was discretion itself, he acted as if he wasn't asking for a thing, saying he was passing by, just like that, for a visit. All he wanted was a place to settle down, a bed, a bowl of soup in exchange for handyman jobs that would be useful in a household. Finally, he was obliged to give in and face facts: whenever he dropped in on his children, he saw that they couldn't make ends meet. He couldn't be anything but a burden. So he turned around and came back to his home region and began to look for work. Since he was skilled at dressing grape vines, he found a place on an estate. There were seven kilometers to walk morning and night between house and job. At his age, you tire fast, and you're less productive than the young. So, in spite of his experience, his new bosses didn't keep him on; at the end of the first week they told him:

"Given your age and all the things you have to haul around, it's too much for you, we can't keep you on."

They said "thank you" and paid him his wages. When he got back home, the old man decided to kill himself. He left a note saying: "I'm out of work, I'm too old, my children have problems of their own, I'd be a burden to them, the medal they gave me for my work won't fill my stomach, so I'd rather do away with myself." He hanged himself too.

Dramas like that were so very frequent in the mountain villages. I believe that all peasants dragged around the specter of destitution, that they dreaded its sudden apparition in their own lives. An illness could decimate their flock, rain destroy their crop, fire reduce their house to nothing. This fear that had always been in them was the root of their stubborn perseverence at work, and their greed for profit.

My father did not escape that law. For generations, from father to son, they had been peasants in his family, they were people for whom land was everything. From childhood on, every day and every act of his life had no other purpose than preserving the patrimony and making the family land bear fruit. For him idleness was unthinkable, on that matter he was adamant to the point of intolerance. Only the sabbath interruption was tolerated, but even so! There were Sundays when we went off to work like any other day. The minute mass was over, we whirled as fast as a storm, exchanging our Sunday clothes for old shoes and work dresses, and went off to gather the hay, tie up the wheat into sheaves, harvest the lentils. No one could escape the immutable code of work: from the time you were very little you had to be useful and to produce. I lived that experience, just like my brothers and sisters. And yet I was my father's favorite, I can even say he was deeply attached to me, but that didn't make the slightest difference. For him, there was no contradiction; he really didn't see any, of that I am convinced. Set against his goodness and generosity was a monkish strictness. That's the way he was, those were the two sides of the same coin.

When I was five, my father tied me onto a mule and I set off, all by myself like a big girl. And so I started on my way, very much against my will.

Like most families in Val-des-Prés, we had land and a chalet at Granon. Granon is a mountain above the village; we used to climb a steep path through the forest to get there. In the summer, when the grass was mowed, dried, and raked, we would tie it in bundles and bring it down to the village on the back of a mule. It was endless, arduous work, especially for the animal that went up and down from morning to night. During the day my father or one of my brothers made the trips, but in the evening, when they came down for the last time and the mule was unloaded, there was still work to be done. But the *miaule*[1] was at the end of his tether; after two or three trips, sometimes four, all he yearned for was his stable, fodder, and sleep. My father didn't see it that way; he wanted to save time by sending the mule back up so when morning came it would be on the spot ready for work. There was a stable up there, and one of my sisters was waiting in the chalet. Getting that animal to climb back up to Granon was a problem. He was worn out and unwilling to move, and it was out of the question for him to go up by himself or for my father to take him. So my father would pick me up, set me down on the mule's back, and fasten me securely with rope. I was tied like an ordinary package so I wouldn't fall off if I fell asleep. Then my father would slap the mule on the rump and we'd start off. It was night-time, and to get all the way up there you had to allow two solid hours.

Today there is a road, but in those days it was a simple mountain path; it was very steep and that animal was in no hurry. Every time it branched off, he'd halt and wait. He knew the way, but in his mulish head he must have been saying: "If I can, I won't go any higher, I won't take one more step," and he'd stand stock still. Peasants coming down the mountain would get him started again. They'd hit him with a stick when they came by and the mule would set off again at the same tired pace. I just let him carry me along,

---

[1] *Miaule*: mule. — AU.

sometimes dozing, sometimes waking, with the forest all around me, the larch trees, the firs and the deepening night. But I wasn't afraid . . . all I wanted to do was get there and go to sleep. When we finally reached the top — it could be any hour depending on the mule and his whims — it was darkest night. He would stop at the chalet door and bray until my sister came out to untie me. She took me in her arms and carried me inside. Often I didn't have the strength to eat, I was stiff and sore, I hurt everywhere from the ropes that had cut into me — shoulders, legs, the small of my back. My sister put me to bed and I slept like a log.

Chapter 4

A Family Portrait

Someone said to my father: "Joseph, your youngest, the one with the wet-nurse, isn't coming along like she should. That woman's neglecting her — she has barely enough milk, she feeds her own first and all yours gets is what's left over. You might drop in there before Marie-Rose gets too run down."

It wasn't long after my mother's death. My father was still a stricken man, incapable of seeing things clearly. When he heard the news, he accepted it as one more stroke of fate. Rather than take up his staff and go see what the situation was, he resigned himself to the worst and wondered if it wasn't time to order a little coffin. My two sisters were the ones who rebelled. Against his despondency — all he said was: "If she dies, we'll bury her," as he did for me a little later — they set their resolve.

"Well, before you talk that way," they told him, "see how she is and what's going on with the nurse."

The wet-nurse had neither a bad reputation nor a good one. She was an unwed mother from Névache, about ten kilometers from where we lived, and when my mother died and they had to find somebody to take care of Marie-Rose, she was the only one who offered her services. She had just had a baby, she had milk, and she was willing. So my father left for Névache. When he reached the wet-nurse's house, he thought our sister wasn't doing either well or badly, maybe she was a little puny, but that's all. She was not at death's door as held by honey-tongued mountain folk who enjoyed peddling such news. . . . People are dreadful, they can't help taking a wicked pleasure in spreading bad news. Nevertheless he wanted to get to the bottom of things, and insisted that the young woman give Marie-Rose her breast on the spot. He stayed until my sister had taken her fill and was smiling sweetly. My father told the girl:

"If you don't have enough milk for two, buy some, for goodness sake, make bottles if you have to, but don't let her get weak and die of hunger, we're not down to our last penny!"

By the time he left, the matter was straightened out. After all, maybe that talk was slander. Maybe not, it was hard to know. However, from that day on the rumors about the girl stopped circulating and Marie-Rose filled out normally. I don't dare imagine how it would have turned out if my father had followed his first impulse, and had not gone to see the wet-nurse. Today that probably seems unbelievable, yet that is the way things were; as I've already said, a child's life didn't amount to much.

That being understood, children — well, there were so many around here! Far more came than were wanted. Before the 1914 war, you could count six or seven youngsters to a family. That was a minimum — many had ten or more. No birth control or anything. From the time they were married, women had a baby practically every year. Not far from here, a record was even set, through the feats of a person I'll call "that irresponsible man" rather than name him. He married his first wife when she was eighteen or twenty and kept on getting her pregnant until it killed her. She had thirteen and died in childbirth at the age of thirty-three. Then he took a second wife and had ten more with her. A sum total of twenty-three kids! That may be a record but it is also a crime when you think of how they had to live. As soon as they were old enough to go off to work, he turned them out of the house.

Milk was a problem too. There were those who had cows, and then there were the others. Not owning a cow was a sign of great poverty, it meant you had to buy milk, and for some people that could not be taken for granted. It was not exceptional that my father and the wet-nurse, in their own different ways, could conceive of a little girl starving to death. Children really did die of hunger. That monstrous thing happened to a local woman in a bad marriage where the husband drank and there was nothing in the house. When I say nothing, I mean the essentials: bread, wood for heat, and milk, of course. The woman had children and she fed them as best she could. Usually she sent her oldest girl to buy a few cents' worth of milk (I no longer remember how much it cost), and the days when things were at their worst, when there wasn't any money left in the family purse, the girl took her bottle to be filled anyway. The most heartbreaking part of the story is that the little girl went to her cousins to get milk — much later on she told me what had happened. These cousins were people who had everything they needed, and lacked for nothing. One evening she came to their stable with her bottle and the husband was there. He was a decent enough sort, so he didn't argue about filling the bottle, but his wife, who was in her bed in the adjoining room, heard the noise. She asked:

"Who's there?"

"It's little Julie," her husband answered.

"Did she bring money?"

"No."

"So don't give her any milk."

Like the big simpleton he was, the fellow obeyed: he took back the full bottle and emptied it into the pail. "To think what I went through when I heard the glug-glug of the milk being poured back," Julie said when she told me the story. "It was as if he was taking my little brother's life away. That night when I got back home, there was nothing to give him but a bottle of sugar-water." Well, the boy didn't make old bones; since things went from bad to worse in the household, the sugar-water bottles came more and more often and one day the child fell sick and died. Perhaps he didn't precisely starve to death but he was so weakened, so undernourished, that a simple cold could have carried him off to the grave.

When Marie-Rose returned home, she was very behind for her age. At two years old, she wasn't walking or talking, but that had nothing to do with milk or food. Of us all, she was the person most affected by our mother's passing away. Overnight she had been torn from the maternal breast to go off among strangers. For almost two years she had lived outside the warmth of family life. A wet-nurse is no substitute for a mother; some of them are certainly good, but that was not the case here, for while Marie-Rose was housed and fed, she was deprived of what was fundamental.

I clearly remember her return. To teach her how to walk, my brothers and sisters and I would join hands in a circle all around the kitchen. It was a game, she was delighted and learned fast. But you had to watch her all the time, not because she was retarded, on the contrary she was quick and mischievous, but she was totally devoid of experience and, above all, she had not the slightest sense of danger.

At home, except for the summer months when we were outside all the time, we lived close beside the chimney corner. All day long there were stout logs burning in the fireplace which was used for heating and for cooking. The fireplace was rather tall — about the height of a man — and over the embers in the hearth, the soup pot was permanently hung from the chimney hook, with polenta or stew cooking just beside it in casseroles placed on a three-legged brazier. It was primitive, but we were used to it.

Like all children, Marie-Rose was fascinated by fire. It was our job to keep it going and she wanted to get close to the flames just like us and move the logs around over the embers. This was strictly outside her domain, and every time she went too close to the fire, we would say: "Careful, Marie-Rose, you can get burned, don't go near it," and she'd listen. One evening, however, she got so close that her dress caught fire and burst into flames. My older sister was there, saw what happened, reacted correctly, went to grab a blanket and got back in time to roll it around the child and save her, but both of them were burned on hands and legs; the burns were not deep but still they had to be taken care of. Sending for the doctor was out of the question. Why do that? For burns we had a remedy far more effective than any medication a pharmacist or a doctor could prescribe: the potato. You cut potatoes and applied the slices to the burned areas. My sisters screamed with all their might, but they were more scared than hurt.

My father was frightened too. Within the hour he left to buy a stove in Briançon. When it was installed, we spent hours looking at it, lost in admiration, entranced with its "modernity." At the time, there were probably very few of them in the village. As far as I'm concerned, it was the very first I had seen. I remember it well: it was a fat, triangular, potbellied stove with three apertures. We put it into service right away; my father got it going and we set it up for cooking with the soup pot on one opening, the stew on the second, and the kettle for hot water on the third. It was truly a marvel. For me that stove was a revelation, not in itself but for the change it represented; I can say that it was the first major change I witnessed. Later I would see others: the first cookstove, the first light bulb, the first bathtub, the first automobile, the first tractor; but of all those new inventions that altered peasant lives, the Thierry stove is even today the most impressive. It was comical and warm, exactly like a friend, and what's more, you could get close to it with no risk of catching fire.

But aside from the stove, our ways hardly changed. We led our family life according to unvarying age-old principles. It was a patriarchy and all that goes with it. At the top of the pyramid was my father who ruled the house with an iron fist, for all that he called himself a dead tree. He was the master, and his power was even less open to challenge than it might have been because my mother was no longer there as a counterweight. He had all the rights, and the one limit to his power was his own sense of equity. Today they would call it discretionary power. I have no wish to pass judgment; my father never took advantage of his authority; on the contrary, he was an even-handed person in all domains. He didn't talk much. Long speeches were not a family custom. "Good day, Good night, Do this, Do that, I'm leaving, I'm back" was our most usual language. . . . With me, my father was more open, he'd confide in me — oh, nothing much! But still he told me a little more than he told the others. It was the same thing with feelings, within the family we rarely expressed affection — the same for kissing each other on the cheeks. We kissed our father twice a year, on his birthday and on New Year's Day. That's all. The rest of the time we would greet him, calling him "Father" or "Papa," and we were always respectful when we spoke to him. Physical contact between him and us was restricted to punishment. He was not cruel but we were entitled to it like everyone else. That was the rule; children were beaten much more than they are today. I for one have always been against physical violence, but at home, for the slightest mistake, voluntary or not, and for the slightest breach of the rules, we got slapped on both cheeks or spanked with nettles. No one challenged this order of things.

After the father came the eldest brother. So François was someone special, he was the heir, the second in command. François was no shining light; it was difficult to grasp his character, he was full of himself, and a braggart. He was eleven years older than I, and for a little girl like me, it was a considerable difference. In my eyes, he was as important as a grown-up, I stood in awe of him, he was always at my father's side, he was his assistant, played the heavy, and never once missed the chance to remind us that he was the eldest. It was vanity, I suppose, but it worked. We were afraid of him and we respected him every bit as much as our father.

Rose-Marie was the eldest girl; she had a foul disposition, none of us escaped her sarcasm, and we were always at odds. She was nine years older than I, still a girl but almost a woman, and she took her role very seriously. She loved authority — she wanted to be in charge and never let us forget it. It was her nature to be hot-tempered and often unjust, and she was always quick with a slap. If our mother had still been alive, things would have been different, but Rose-Marie was the one who ran the house; primarily engaged in making stew and keeping the place in order, she almost never went out to the stable or fields.

Right after her came Catherine, two years younger than Rose-Marie and not at all like her. I have rarely seen two people in one family with such dissimilar temperaments. Catherine was an exemplary worker and everything she did was done thoroughly. She wasn't interested in pleasing the crowd, in putting herself forward, or winning respect; with her everything was inward, like a smouldering fire, like a sleeping volcano — one could sense it. Just by looking at her. Her gaze was somber and direct: you sensed she was like that, all of a piece. But she was ferociously shy, untamed; for her only one thing mattered, her work. She did not stop until it was done — and well done.

Joseph was the youngest brother. He was a nice boy, all sweetness and, since we were only four years apart, more of a kindred spirit than the others. We had the same tastes, the same friends, and the same games. Like Catherine, he was completely intent on what he was doing. I always saw him work like a man, going to the fields, taking care of the livestock; later on he would learn the shoemaker's craft.

Then came me and my younger sister Marie-Rose. She was appealing but always in a flutter. My mother even had a seventh child, a girl named Marie-Colombe, but there's nothing to tell about her, she died a week after she was born in the chalet at Granon.

On the whole, we got along well, we were what they call a harmonious family, and except for Rose-Marie we liked each other. I remember us all at the kitchen table at mealtime. My father let us chatter away; he accepted our vitality and our youth, he liked them. Presiding from the middle of the table, he was the one who served us. Through this ritual act, jealousy and recriminations were avoided. He would get up, and go around the table, giving each of us our share. Any protest would have been seen as a challenge to his authority and his sense of justice. That was unthinkable. Only for me did he make an exception on the days we ate ham or meat; since I had trouble swallowing fat, my father would put my share on his plate along with his and "tidy it up." Invariably, as he cut the fat away from the lean he would tell the others: "Since the fat's no good for her you can't complain, I gave you all your full share, what I give her is only off of mine." No one made a peep, but that kindness led to jealousy, you could feel it.

Every Saturday my father inspected our shoes. In those days, we wore stout hobnail boots for everything all year long — in the fields, at school, and for play. Those boots were meant to last us a year and more, without a trip to the shoemaker, and so my father looked them over every week. He'd replace the nails that had come off, and when the heel or tip began to wear down he would put on heavy hobnails. You might say they toughened our shoes, because with those hobnails in place there was no way the soles could be punctured. Did I ever suffer with those thingamajigs! I was condemned to wear boots passed down from my elder brothers and sisters, shapeless old clodhoppers that battered my feet. It was inevitable; I was the fifth in the family and those shoes were so sturdy, in such good condition, that there was always a pair to finish off. Not one pair was ever bought especially for me; not until I was twelve and making my first communion did I have the right to a pair of shoes in my size.

And so we went from one end of the year to the other dressed as soberly as we were shod. The boys wore what we used to call "Lafonds," trousers of heavy corduroy or blue duck according to the season. Nothing could have been sturdier than the cloth their shirts were cut out of. And we girls, summer and winter, wore dresses out of serge, a heavy material almost impossible to wear out. Straight cut and absolutely plain, the dresses were kept clean and undamaged by the smocks we wore over them. That's how we went about our business at school and on the farm.

Work in the fields often came ahead of classes. Our peasants had no idea what schooling was about, they had mistaken notions and didn't see what use it could be to learn and improve your mind. Like their ancestors, they thought that to raise a calf or tend cows you didn't need to know how to read and write. My father first and foremost. He was almost illiterate. As for Jules Ferry's law that had made secular schooling obligatory and free, he didn't understand its importance or its implications. He had been taught by clergy, the kind who told peasants: "You don't need any schooling, you'll never be anything but farmers"; and since those were holy words, they were believed. Occasionally in those days we still heard songs like this one:

> "Why should you bother to leave the farm?"
> Said the man as he stopped them on the road.
> "How does it help to be a learned man or marm
> When there's land to be tilled and hoed?
> And what will all that learning do,
> Will it make fully ripened corn and wheat?"
> "It makes our hope spring up anew,"
> Answered all the children sweet.

When we were in school — my brothers and sisters and I — that was still the way people thought. They had a morbid distrust of school — school took away their farmhands — so in self-defense they said it was a waste of time, and you only learned nonsense; but it was obligatory so clearly they had no choice.

Outside of class time, we worked in the morning before we went and in the evening after we came home. On the farm we raised just about everything that can be grown around here. Grains like wheat, barley, oats, or rye, and potatoes were the staple of our diet and hardly ever sold; they were strictly for us and our animals. We also had a kitchen garden for our vegetables, and my father raised lentils for sale. They were famous all over the district and even beyond. My father had a green thumb, he knew how to grow them, and above all he knew how to pick and sort them better than anyone else, so when he was done, there wasn't one pebble left among them.

We would sell them in Briançon, in the market, or to the private individuals my father had built into a clientele.

We raised animals too. The sheep and everything that had to do with the sheepfold were my father's domain and at the time, around 1910, he had some sixty head. Then there were the cows. We had a rather nice herd and it was up to us children to look after them. We had to milk them, clean them, see to the fodder and the litter. All of that fell to us.

At the end of the summer my father would buy the pigs, one or two depending on the year. We fattened them for several months and killed them around Christmas. Most of the peasants in Val-des-Prés were in the habit of picking up their pigs around April, but my father said that wasn't advisable; according to him it made more sense to avoid the extra burden in the summer — he said there was enough to do without the extra work of fattening pigs. It's quite a job to fatten pigs, you have to gather the greens, cook them, add potatoes — and all that to save a few cents. So he wouldn't go along, he preferred to buy them in September. Sometimes he went to the fair, otherwise he got them from a merchant who came to the house. One year the merchant arrived with his herd and stopped by to make a sale. In the middle of the lot was a piglet who came up as high as the table, but was he ever skinny! So skinny he didn't look anything like a pig. All the others were markedly smaller but they were constantly nibbling at him so he had hardly any ears left, he was covered with sores and bleeding all over. It's a shame to see an animal like that, and of course the dealer wanted to get rid of him as soon as possible. I can still see that man with his stick and his blue shirt, standing in the courtyard opposite my father who was listening to him. He said in patois:

"Come on, Allais, take my big fellow there, it'll be a good deal, you'll see."

"No way!" my father answered. "He won't do at all."

But rather than lose heart, the dealer kept at it; knowing my father, he understood there was a chance to persuade him. All he had to do was keep trying.

"You can't do that to me, Allais! You see how he is, at the rate he's going this fellow won't make it to Névache, the others are biting him like all get-out, it's awful to watch!"

My father tried hard to hold out, but he had a reputation for never having the last word, everybody around here knew it and so did the merchant. He didn't miss his mark, my father took the pig, he bought it and settled it in the stable. He took such good care of the animal that when we killed it, it was heavier than a cow. Dead, it weighed over 250 kilos — a genuine record — and on that day my father was all smiles. "You see," he told us, "I didn't make such a bad deal after all."

"Pig's Day" — that's what we called the day for hog slaughtering — was absolutely exceptional: the whole family came, all the closest relatives, it was the chance for a reunion with uncles, aunts, and little nephews and nieces. Everybody fell to work, the woman preparing the bouillabaisse or the aïoli sauce, the men taking care of the pigs. And it always came off just around Christmas and New Year's Day in the bargain, so there was an end-of-the-year atmosphere and, sometimes, unexpected gifts; besides, killing the pig was a major event. We children were right up front and we didn't miss any smallest detail.

In Val-des-Prés, my uncle Auguste was the official pig sticker. Uncle Auguste was a character. Besides the fact that he had a reputation for never missing his mark, he liked the ladies, he was one of the boys, and he was a joker who found time to do tricks so the children would have fun.

While he was setting up and getting his instruments ready, he never failed to call us over, and when there were enough of us around him, he went into his act.

"Come on up, come on up," he'd say, "and look at this marvel that's going to play tricks on me if he can."

All during Uncle Auguste's patter, the pig never stopped his horrible shrieks and in spite of his securely tied feet, he kept jumping up and down.

"Oh yeah! He'd like to play a nasty trick on me, I think somebody'd better hold him by the tail, otherwise! . . . Okay, you, over there, come here, grab his tail and hang on tight while I settle his hash, but be very careful: if you don't hold on right, I won't get him."

We took his story about the tail as gospel truth. There was always one of us to grab it and hold on boldly as Uncle Auguste slaughtered the pig with one thrust of his knife. Right afterwards as the porker uttered his last cries and finished draining, my uncle would walk around him to inspect the ears, shaking his head like a man with a lot of worries.

"Good God," he'd say, "what ears on that pig! In my whole life I never saw such dirty ears — I'll have to go all over the countryside to find me an earpick, I can't do a thing with that animal as long as his ears look like that. I have to clean them with an earpick. There's no other way."

It always worked. You got fooled only once, never twice, but there was always some simpleton who'd run off to ask for an earpick all over the village. Everybody was in on the secret, and everyone would say:

"Oh, no! I don't have one of those — why don't you go next door to the neighbors and see maybe they have one."

Uncle Auguste cut up the pig and made blood sausage the very same day. After that we managed as best we could. Making up the pork specialties was no small affair, it was as important as could be; the sausages and hams we got out of our pigs were the basis of our diet all year long; that is to say, we had to do it right or else it was a disaster. When a ham spoils, all you can do is throw it away or bury it, even the dogs won't touch it, and it's no use anymore.

Fortunately my father was good at it; even though he wasn't a trained pork-butcher, he knew what to do. For the hams, he began by soaking them in brine for two weeks, then he let them drain and dry, and once they were good and dry they were rubbed with garlic, salt, pepper, and juniper before they were sewed tight into hemp cloth. They were hung in the hayloft for a while, and then put in the seed bin° for protection against air and flies; that way we were sure they wouldn't turn rancid.

For the sausages, my father had bought an appliance and I always saw him make his sausage with that particular device. It was a bulky, archaic machine with a crank arm, but he managed all the same. He made everything himself. He'd go to the slaughterhouse in Briançon to buy what we called the odds and ends — liver, heart, and other cheap cuts of meat that he'd clean, put in boiling water and then scrape. He even let them freeze outside for three or four nights. In his opinion, that was the only way to get rid of the odor, and he also said freezing made it easier to slice the meat thin. Next he would shape it on a broad wooden board called a *chapouelle*, about forty inches long, wide at the center and narrow at the ends, and then he would stuff his sausage with his appliance. He made two kinds: one with cabbage that we called the household type, and a leaner sausage without cabbage that we dried. We lived on those meats all winter long.

Chapter
5

Learning
to
Read

During the first days of August 1914, we were all at Granon, right in the middle of the harvest. When we heard the bells, we all wondered why they were ringing like that. Everyone in our countryside knows the sounds of the bell. You think: Well, there goes a baptism, or Well, there goes a wedding, or else, It's a funeral. They're easy to recognize. But the sound that day was nothing of the sort. It was different. Maybe a fire? But where? What fire could set off all the bells at once? They were ringing one after the other.

At first we heard the one in La Vachette, then it was Alberts, then Plampinet and, of course, Val-des-Prés. And they went on and on. We had time to imagine all the things that can run through your head at a time like that. All but the right one. It was the local policeman who announced the news. He came all the way up with his bugle, telling everyone he met:

"It's war!"

"War! What war?" people asked, totally unprepared to hear the news.

"You know, war!"

"But who with?"

And looking smug, like a person sharing secrets with the gods, he said:

"With the Germans! The Germans declared war on us."

It did not seem real, the word itself did not sound real; we had to say it over and over among ourselves until it became a word that held some kind of shape. "War. War." We looked at each other, we were so far away from such a thing. You have to know Granon to understand: it is a plateau on the mountaintop, with fields and woods as far as the eye can see, and the sky above. All of us were in the fields in the middle of bundles of hay and we had our own war — the one we were fighting against the threatening storm. We had more important tasks than figuring out what a military war might mean. Even my father did not understand; his was the generation of 1870,° and '70 was far off, part of another era.

It was only the next day or the day after that the war began to show its true face. When the call-up orders and the travel orders arrived in people's homes, they began to grasp the reality of the war. All able-bodied men received their travel orders: before anything else, war meant separation.

In those early days the village was completely disrupted, nothing was the way it used to be; in a matter of hours decisions had to be made: finish reaping such and such a place, forsake another. Everyone was out of doors, talking, asking questions — it was the world inside out. I think that is precisely what happened. War had burst on us like a cannon shot, turning our world upside down and, one by one, the men were going away. The optimists did not take it seriously; cracking jokes when their orders came, they'd say:

"So here it is. A vacation smack in the middle of summer, our first ever. Better make the most of it."

To hear them talk, war was nothing much, a huge joke, and you were better off if you looked at the bright side. But there were others, the worriers, who saw the dark side of everything. For them, war — or simply going off in the middle of harvest — was the end of the world and they wanted nothing to do with it. Delaying, they put off their departure until the last minute. Finally they all left. There were cases of men who went off and hid in the woods, giving in only when their wives threatened to tell the gendarmes. Not one family in Val-des-Prés was spared. In the space of a week the village was radically changed, with not a man left between the ages of twenty and forty. They were all off to war.

August 2, 1914. I was just fourteen. I had grown up in the meantime, and I can say that I grew up at school . . . yes, I think I can say that. It made all the difference between my brothers and sisters and me. I loved school; I loved to study; I loved reading, writing, learning. I felt at home the moment I started school, and I blossomed.

I began when I was five. It was the normal age. In those days, there was no *maternelle*° or any other kind of preschool; you started at five and left at fourteen or fifteen. The cleverest managed to wangle their certificate,° the others had to be satisfied with the notorious "knows how to read and write" inscribed on official documents. That's the way it went. I liked school right away. How can I explain? It was as if I had been a sponge deprived of water until then. Was I a particularly gifted child? I really don't know. One thing is certain: I had a natural aptitude and as soon as I learned to read, I devoured any and every book that came my way. It must be said that my choice was limited in a village like ours, but I always had a book in my hands. I would read everywhere I went, as I was getting out of bed, in the kitchen, and at recess.

It made my teacher sick to see me reading while the other children were at play, it drove him crazy. He'd come over to me from behind and snatch the book out of my hands.

"Go play with the others," he'd say. "You have plenty of time to read later."

I'd cry, I'd stamp my foot, I'd demand my book back. His wife had to intervene, she was more understanding and she would say:

"So give back her book, she's not hurting anybody."

And I would tell him:

"You know perfectly well I can't read at home, there are too many things to do, this is the only place I have any peace."

At last, he'd give it back and I would be caught up in my reading again.

I read everything that fell into my hands. Oh, there was nothing especially wicked. *Jim, the Rebel Peasant,*° *The Devil's Pool,*° and other books on the same order.

Another place I loved to read was the stable. I would keep my sister Catherine company while she looked after the cows and I read to her. The nights she sat up waiting for the cow to calve, I stayed with her. She would be seated on her stool knitting while I read her whole chapters, stories, or tales. She loved it and I was in seventh heaven.

I had told my teacher the truth, because outside of class, my father didn't give me much time for daydreams. On that score he was inflexible, school or not you had to "produce." During the noon break Joseph and I ran all the way to Draille at the other end of the village to tend to the sheep. My brother took care of the fodder while I went for water. When it wasn't the sheep, there were droppings to gather for kindling, or else pine nuts, and it was out of the question to come home with your basket half full. The worst chore was going for water, you had to get it in pails from the Clarée, and that turned into a real skating rink in winter when it froze, not to mention the slope: I had to take one step forward and two back, it's a miracle I didn't fall in. When we finished, we ran home for lunch and at one o'clock we were back in school. We started all over in the evening.

In spite of the chores, in spite of the exhaustion, I have wonderful memories of those years. There was no boredom, no sense of time dragging.

When I got into bed, my body was worn out but my head was full of images and I fell asleep making up stories or planning for the future. The next day I would set out renewed. My reading, the pails of ice-cold water, the stable smells, the sensation of growing and learning more every day — for me those years are like the memory of an enormous cake you need only bite into: it was inexhaustible. The few stones in my path hardly mattered compared to all that was good. I kicked them out of the way without a second thought.

I passed the exam for my primary school certificate at the age of twelve. "Brilliantly," as they say: I was number one in the district. In a region like ours, people hear about such things. I was entitled to congratulations from the inspector and the principal and I was called in with my teacher. They wanted to know if I was going on.

"Going on with what? School?"

I could not have asked for more, but it wasn't for me to decide, it was up to my father to say whether or not he was willing. Knowing him, the teacher told the inspector:

"Certainly not. Her father has his land, he is a widower and he keeps them all working; there is not much chance that he will let her go on to school in Briançon."

"How come?" the inspector said. "He has no right to say no, this child is gifted, she is intelligent, and does remarkable work. He has to let her make her way in the world."

The next day a delegation came to see my father at home, the principal and the teacher who arrived with the support of the inspector from the academy° who had sent them off with the words:

"Tell him he has no right to keep a youngster like that at home, it would be a crime."

My father let them have their say, he took his time answering.

"You know, as far as I'm concerned, I'd rather she didn't go on in school, there's no reason for her not to do like the others, she has to earn her keep."

The principal couldn't do anything but repeat the inspector's arguments:

"But you have no right to keep her home, you have no right to talk like that, Monsieur Allais. Your little girl does remarkable work and if she goes to school you will be helping her get a good position in life."

"That's possible," my father answered. "That's possible, but how could I manage to send her to school? I don't have the money."

The principal thought to herself that my father was half-convinced. She said:

"Monsieur Allais, since you are a widower with six children, we will ask for a scholarship, you have a right to it and that way there will not be any problem for you."

"In that case, yes!"

And so the matter was settled like a cattle deal when they reached an agreement, shook hands on it, and said: "Done." The scholarship argument had been enough to convince my father. For me it was fantastic that he'd said yes. I was sure he'd never go back on his word once it was given. When the next term started, I would go on to the secondary school in Briançon. I was completely happy.

That was the year of the centenarian. Such a thing had never been seen, no one in Val-des-Prés remembered hearing about any centenarian. The mayor and everyone else agreed to give a party.

The centenarian, born in 1812, was a character. I knew him well, I used to see him pass by every day for he'd go out behind the house to gather his bundle of firewood. Rain or wind, good weather or freezing, nothing kept him from going off into the woods; with his *gouillette*[1] he'd cut off small branches, coming back at night with his bundle of firewood. He did that for twenty years, invariably dressed in an old-fashioned hemp shirt, wide open and showing the white hair of his chest, and a black fish-tail jacket. Old people around here used to wear that kind of clothing, but by 1912 it was already so outdated that it looked ridiculous. He could not have cared less, and went around picking up his wood in that get-up. He went bareheaded and unkempt, and didn't feel either cold or heat. He had another obsession: over twenty-five years ago he had chosen a spot in the cemetery where he wanted to be buried. Every afternoon, he stretched out there on the ground and settled down for his nap. He slept there for a quarter of a century, telling anyone who looked surprised:

"This is where I'm going to be buried, so I want to warm my place."

When he died, they respected his wishes and put him in the hole they dug on that very spot. He was 102.

In the meanwhile, the commune paid him tribute, the commune and the French Republic, since the subprefect° took the trouble to come in person for the occasion. We went out to greet him, I can picture us schoolchildren walking along the road to La Vachette behind the band, dressed up in our Sunday clothes, and me in my new shoes. It was like a story from Daudet,°

---

[1] *Gouillette:* a knife shaped like a pruning hook used to trim small branches. — Au.

with the road winding along the Clarée, the budding trees, the sun, the flowers, and the air that's so special here, limpid, transparent mountain air. We came together in open country, there were words of welcome, the mayor and the subprefect exchanged courtesies, and on a sign from the principal, we sang:

"A people is strong when it knows how to read, when it knows how to read a people is great."

All the village folk were invited. Enormous tables had been set up outside for the banquet, with our centenarian presiding from the middle, proud as a pope. The celebration went on all day long. After the banquet we got the speeches and the congratulations. I was part of it, of course, one of the happy few called on to recite in front of Monsieur the Subprefect. It was up to our principal to distribute the roles in advance; she had chosen the prettiest recitation for her niece, the second best for the "maid of honor," the third for me. I remember what my speech was called, it was "I Don't Like Arithmetic!" and I remember the stage fright all three of us felt, our jitters made us fart and we trembled like leaves. Besides, there were prizes. First prize for the best recitation was a box of candied fruit, and fate willed that I was the one who carried it off with my "I Don't Like Arithmetic!" I did it so well that when I finished everyone around the table started to chant in cadence: "First prize, first prize," so the principal had no choice but to give me the box of candied fruit meant for her pet. I was also entitled to congratulations from the gentlemen, and kisses, and everything, but when I got home it was a different story. My sisters had their noses out of joint! You can't imagine how jealous they were.

"You've kept us waiting to go cut hay at Granon; Father has gone ahead and what with all your uppity airs we're late, so come on, hurry up, it's enough already."

They were mean, they made faces, and that box of candied fruit stuck in their craw. They teased me so much that they got exactly what they wanted: they made me cry.

Around that time cracks began to show up in the "château," in a manner of speaking. With the passing years, we had all grown up and we were not children any more. Until then we'd been a tightly knit family: through good years and bad, we'd managed to overcome our hostile feelings and silence our sibling jealousy. My father had a great deal to do with it, but he too was growing older. After my mother died, my father aged overnight as they say. At fifty-five, he looked sixty-five or seventy, and as we grew up, each of us asserting individuality, his authority weakened. And so there were days when the house was really too small for us all. You could feel it. Tension and bickering were on the rise and it was hard for my father to keep things on a steady course. The fact that I was going on with school provoked divergent reactions among my older brothers and sisters.

"School? What for? Why her?" François and Rose were the most virulent.

François was the first to leave. He went off for his basic training. In those days it meant three years in the army; three years is a long time, but in any case no one in the house was under any illusion. Underneath his superior airs, François was an indecisive man who clearly did not want to inherit the farm or shoulder responsibility for it. You can sense things like that. He would have had to show some initiative but he never did; instead he always remained in my father's shadow, doing nothing more than he had to. When he left for the army everyone knew he was leaving us for good. It was not "so long" but "goodbye."

With François gone, the covert war setting Rose against the rest of the family expanded abruptly. It was Catherine who set off the explosion; they were only two years apart, and inevitably there was not a single day without a confrontation between them in the house. They quarreled over nothing, household matters, anything at all; it's natural, their characters were so very different and each wanted to run things her own way.

When it erupted, the crisis was incredibly violent. It was like water in a dam that gives way all at once, carrying off everything in its path. Nobody was spared. On that day, Catherine who was patience itself lost control, she had reached the limit of what she could put up with, and calling my father to witness, she said: "One of us has got to go. It's either her or me."

My father looked sick, it was the first time in his life he'd been confronted with a situation like that and he hesitated. As for the rest of us — Joseph, Marie-Rose and I — we knew what we wanted, we liked Catherine better than Rose and since my father stood there undecided we began shouting: "Catherine will stay. Rose will go."

There was nothing left for her to say so she packed her bags and went off to find a job in Lyons. The day she left Catherine said: "Now I can take care of the house."

And Joseph: "Nobody wanted her around. It's very simple, we'd rather work harder than have her constantly underfoot. She was really too difficult."

We had thrown off the tyranny of the older children and the change was considerable, with the house recovering something of its former ease. There was more work but we couldn't have cared less, we were free to do it

the way we wanted. That was the year I went to secondary school in Briançon while Joseph began learning the shoemaker's trade. It was not the height
of happiness but, even so, we were happy, we liked what we were doing, and
there wasn't a cloud on the horizon.

Still, I had a kind of presentiment. It was vague, but I couldn't help
feeling threatened. By what? I had no idea and I tried to be reasonable. I'd
tell myself that we had a right to this commonplace happiness. Learning a
trade, having the people you love around you, were nothing out of the ordinary, every human being has the right to expect such things. But I couldn't
help it and I lived in fear.

In April 1914, Catherine married. The groom was our neighbor, the
dairyman. Without any question, it was a happy occasion. For once it was a
love match and not a marriage arranged around money. In spite of that, in
spite of my sister's happiness at marrying the man she loved, I did not manage to share in the celebration. I could not help being apprehensive and I was
visibly glum.

"Good heavens!" my aunt Colombe remarked. "What's the matter with
you, Émilie? Your sister's getting married, she's got a man who's as nice as
can be, she's happy. You mustn't look like that. Have a good time."

"No, that's impossible. I don't know what's the matter, I don't know
what's going to happen, but I'm afraid for her, I don't think she'll be happy."

"Well, stop talking nonsense."

I told my father the same thing. I knew I was hurting him with that
kind of talk but I couldn't help it, I couldn't hold back. He tried to reassure
me:

"Why say that? You mustn't believe things like that. She's got every
reason to be happy."

It's true. Catherine had every reason to be happy. She was married to
one of the finest men in the commune. He was named Joseph like my father.
He had a trade, he even had a steady job making milk and cheese, and his
house was right next to ours. It was a perfect marriage from every point of
view: for my sister, for my father, and for him too.

They spun the perfect love in those first months and knew great happiness. Early in July, they went up to Granon where they'd rented a chalet and
they settled down for the summer. He collected the milk and made his butter
and cheese. With the leftover whey he fattened pigs, and my sister Catherine
helped out. They were a sight to behold. They stayed together all day long,
you would always see them together; they were truly in love and my sister
was already expecting a child. For her, the "untamed one" as we used to call

her, constantly on the defensive as a girl, love was a revelation. She threw herself into it with the passion and determination she brought to everything she undertook. I had never seen her like that. She was radiant, and so was her Joseph. Their happiness spilled over on all sides and touched us all. It was wonderful.

Chapter
6 ✍

They Died
for
Their Country

War sounded the death knell of that happiness. When Joseph was called up, he did not have a moment's hesitation. He was of the race of men for whom duty is sacred. But Catherine wouldn't hear of it: when he set off down the mountain, she hung on to him to keep him from leaving. They dragged each other along the path from Granon to the village, she pulling back, he pulling forward. Clinging to each other like two poor wretches aware they are condemned to separation, they reached a spot called "the wolf's basin." They were desperate. They had been married for four months. He tried to reason with her:

"Look here, Catherine, let me go. I have to leave or they'll come get me, they shoot deserters, do you want them to shoot me?"

Catherine wasn't listening; she clung to him like a drowning woman to her life buoy. It was as if she'd gone crazy, shouting:

"No, no. I don't want you to go, what'll become of me? They have no right to do that to us. I won't have it. I won't!"

They were a sad sight, it was sad to hear them, but in the end she had to let go. Joseph left to join his regiment and Catherine stayed up in Granon alone. She had the dairy on her hands, it wasn't easy and she knew very little about it. We helped her as much as we could, taking care of the pigs, making the butter and cheese. It went on that way to the end of summer. Then Catherine closed the dairy and moved back to live with us until the baby came.

She had her first pains in April 1915. After Joseph left, she was only a shadow of her former self. She hardly spoke and she worked like a robot, dragging around like a soul in torment, without desire or will. Catherine was emptied of substance. On that day, sensing she was ready to give birth, she took to her bed and, pulling up the covers, shut herself into a kind of delirium, repeating her husband's name over and over: "Joseph. Joseph. Joseph."

She was totally uninformed. Exactly like me, exactly like most girls. Catherine had no experience of sexual matters. They never told us anything here; there were a few mothers who instructed their daughters, but it was rare. Besides, given her upbringing and her extremely shy temperament, my sister could not imagine unshrouding her nakedness to anyone. Neither my aunt Colombe, certainly an experienced woman, nor the midwife from Briançon could convince her to lift the covers. Writhing with pain, Catherine tightened her lips and bit her tongue, but every time one of the two women came over to the bed, she held the covers tight, saying:

"No, no, no, I won't! Let me be!"

And the unbelievable, the unimaginable happened. For forty-eight hours those two simple women were incapable of noticing that Catherine's water had broken. When they did, it was too late, but the little one had not emerged. The doctor was called and he agreed it was too late and said the only thing left was to rush her to the hospital.

My father and I spent those two days eating our hearts out with worry. Hearing her screams and supplications was unbearable. My father did not know where to turn, he was utterly miserable; like Catherine, he had no experience of these things. I had no say in the matter, my rights were limited to making herbal teas and keeping quiet. And still! It was so obvious that something had to be done, but the midwife and Aunt Colombe would not stand for any encroachment on their territory.

War had come to the hospital too. All the doctors had left for the service. What irony! Only army doctors were left and there were no specialists or gynecologists or anything. They performed a Caesarean section and pulled the little one out but he was already dead. After the operation everything went from bad to worse, infection set in and Catherine came down with puerperal fever. What exactly went wrong? We never found out. Was it too late to do anything for her? Didn't they know how? Or didn't they have what they needed? For thirteen days she raved in delirium on her hospital bed and then it was her turn to die. She was twenty-two years old.

It was one of the darkest periods of our lives. It was hideous. Every day that same trip to the hospital and back. To make it worse, my brother Joseph had just been called up and had left to take his basic training and get ready to turn into cannon fodder in the trenches. Only my father, little

Marie-Rose, and I were left at the "château." To save money on an ambulance, we brought Catherine home on the mule-drawn cart, shut inside her casket. My father did not say a word. He walked on, straight as a ramrod, apparently insensitive to fate's blow.

Oh, that dignity! There were times I'd have given anything for him to slough it off, to become a little more human. I remember a conversation I had with him on the question of dignity; I even dared tell him what I thought, how excessive it seemed at times, whether his own or the respect he accorded the dignity of others. But either he did not understand me or he did not want to understand what I was saying. He had a special way of looking at dignity and everything connected with it — honesty, loyalty, candor. He told me:

"In life, you must forge ahead and never have any reason to reproach yourself and then no one can reproach you, and in the end, when you go, you leave an irreproachable memory behind."

I don't know whether I'm quoting him word for word, but that was the spirit of his teaching. During those dreadful days, he was dreadful too. Oh, that return journey from Briançon to Val-des-Prés. It was so beautiful, all around us nature was bursting with life, and there I was, fifteen years old, with my whip in hand, and a father as hard as granite, walking along like a robot. Ideas were knocking around in my poor head, but there was something I could not swallow. What it was, I didn't know, but it felt as if an iron collar of fear and resignation held me tight, while deep down inside a seething force told me to refuse the old order.

The funeral was dismal, no one was there. Who could have been? Under wartime austerity, even correspondance was difficult. I thought of my brother Joseph who loved Catherine so much; and I thought of the other Joseph, her husband, who was not there either, who did not know anything. When the funeral was over my father grew even harder. We were scarcely out of the cemetery, scarcely back at the house, when he went to the stable and called me:

"Émilie."

I found him saddling the mule.

"The manure has to be loaded and spread right away. Get at it."

I looked at him without understanding; I'd hardly had time to take off my mourning clothes and my shoes.

"But Papa!"

"Don't give me any 'but Papa.' Are you waiting for her to come back maybe and do it for you? Now that she's gone she won't be doing it anymore. I'm counting on you."

For the moment I made no effort to understand and I did not answer.

It was too much for me. His face wore such a savage mask. I took the mule by the bridle and set off to load the manure. I made the first trip hauling it to the field at Draille. I dumped, I spread, and I went back for the second load. I don't know how many trips I made that afternoon. How can I describe those hours? It was like a road to Calvary. When it was over, I didn't know where I stood; I saw in my head everything we'd just lived through in a few days: Catherine's delirium, the doctor, the hospital, the casket, and my father's face. No doubt about it, I could not swallow all that.

With Catherine dead and buried, what would happen to the man at the front who was waiting for news? We sent a telegram, but he didn't get it until much later. Meanwhile he'd been wounded, they'd carted him from aid station to hospital, and weeks had gone by when he found out that his wife and baby were dead. During that time we were receiving his letters to her, there was one almost every day, it was unbearable. I opened one. He wrote:

My dear Catherine, I'm wounded but it's not serious, as soon as they take care of it I'll be coming home on leave for a rest, I'll stay with you and our baby, is it a boy or a girl? Not that it makes any difference, we'll be happy."

I never opened another and we waited for him to come back. When he arrived, my father said:

"Do you want the key to your house?"

Joseph didn't move a muscle, he spoke simply: "No. What's the use? We were too happy there, I don't want to go in without her." And he added: "Besides, what good would it do? I'm not coming back here. Ever."

In point of fact, he never did return. He went off to the front and did all that he could to get himself killed. People who knew him and were with him in the trenches told us he acted like a madman. Every time they asked for volunteers for dangerous jobs, he was first on the list. By sheer dint of exposing himself, he achieved his goal: witnesses saw a shell blow him apart, head flying one way, arms and body another. Thus concludes the story of my sister Catherine and her husband Joseph the cheesemaker. To think that for once it was a love match.

I was still far from rebelling. I could not imagine that other people had chosen to say no to war. No one I knew had questioned the rightness of the French cause against domineering, barbaric Germany. Every Sunday the priest inflamed the French to combat in his homily. He justified their patriotism and condemned the cruelty of their opponents. To hear him, you would have thought France was God's treasured child while Germany was the devil's own land. *Poilus*° had no duty more sacred than tearing the guts out of the *Boches*.° I am not exaggerating, that's the way it was.

In the middle of the winter of 1916, my brother Joseph materialized. There is no other way to describe it, he materialized out of nowhere, nobody was expecting him. He'd managed to wangle a leave and his visit was like a ray of sunshine for me.

He tapped on the pane and waited outside for me to open the window. His first words were:

"Émilie, don't come close and don't touch me, hand me some trousers, a shirt, socks, and a sweater, but don't you come out."

I got out what he asked for.

"Throw them here," he said, and through the window I watched him change. He put his army togs into the water of the *bachal*,[1] and only then did he come inside. He had more to say:

"Émilie, I don't want you to touch those things, I'll take care of them tomorrow, I don't want you picking up any lice."

That is what he did first thing the next day, cleaning his belongings with patience and care, examining every seam for nits, pulling them out and squashing them one by one.

I found Joseph changed. He'd been gone hardly a year, but he was more solemn than before, even more serious . . . with sorrow written in the depths of that seriousness. He told me the war was hounding him, that you couldn't forget it just by coming home on leave: life in the trenches was a vermin less easily routed than lice and fleas.

He was the person who opened my eyes. During his few days at home, he spoke mostly to me and of course he talked about the war. For us in Val-des-Prés, except for the men going off, there was something abstract about the war, whereas Joseph had seen it up close, living the life of the trenches on the front line, and he'd come back full of bitterness and resentment, desperate and sad.

"You see," he'd tell me, "all that stuff the teacher told us, about patriotism and glory — well, it's nothing but nonsense and lies. He had no right to have us sing 'Wave little flag.' What does it mean, anyway! Can you tell me?"

I did not know. I did not see.

"Émilie, if you do teach some day, you must tell children the truth,

---

[1] *Bachal:* the hollowed-out tree trunk into which spring water flows. AU.

because it's very simple, the guy on the other side, the German, certainly has a plow or some work tool waiting for him back home. After the war, he and I, if we're not dead, if we haven't lost every shred of our human dignity, we'll have to get back on the job fixing up the ruins left by the war. But the war, well, neither he nor I will get anything out of it. When it's all over, the profits will be in the hands of the capitalists and the guys rolling in money from selling their weapons, the career soldiers will have the stripes and promotions they've won, but not us, we won't have anything to show for it, we won't have won anything. You understand?"

So many words, so much rebellion left me dumbstruck. I had never seen him like that, he'd been gentleness incarnate.

"You understand, Émilie? And when all is said and done, what's going to happen when they decide it's enough? We'll be the turkeys, us in the trenches, me and the man on the other side. No, war is *not* what they told us, it's monstrous, I'm against it, a thousand percent against it. I have not killed anyone and I am not going to kill, I won't have any part of it, and the only thing I ask is that they don't kill me either because I didn't do anything to them."

" . . . "

"You understand?"

I think I understood why he was talking like that. He had suffered too much. His words expressed his revolt against the suffering and the injustice.

"You understand?"

I nodded my head. Deep inside I was afraid Joseph would use the same language in front of our father who would not have put up with it. His sense of duty, his respect for law — that was his whole life. Joseph knew it too and he told me so, he had no intention of discussing it with him. Telling me lightened his burden.

"Because you're young, you want to be a teacher, you must know the truth."

We went around the farm together. He realized the work it represented and tears came to his eyes. I had seventy-five sheep, eight cows, I made the butter in a hand churn, I took care of the hay and harvests, I was sixteen years old.

"What! You, the student, you with all that hard studying to be something more than a peasant, how can you do all this? Émilie, if I come back, I promise you'll go back to school. Money won't be a problem. I'll work, I'll manage, but I swear to you that you'll finish, and you won't just be a schoolteacher, you'll be a professor."

On the fourth day, when he was obliged to go rejoin his regiment, Joseph was already absent without leave. He told me:

"To go back, I've got to get past the gate at the station without letting the gendarmes see me."

"Joseph, that's crazy, think what could happen if they catch you. You might be court-martialed."

"What!" he said, recovering all his vehemence, "what more can they do to me? I've just spent forty-five days in the trenches without washing, without sleep, practically without food, in mud up to my belt, with vermin, fear, cold, and non-coms standing over us with loaded pistols aimed at our heads. What more can they do to me? Nothing can be worse than that hell. They'd do me a favor if they shot me, remember that, Émilie."

My father and I walked out with him, but he did not want my father along. At the level of the Vivier he stopped and said in patois:

"Papâ na vou nin! ["Be off, Papa!"].

My father turned around and left without looking back.

"You know why I sent Papa away? I don't want him to see me cry, it would be too painful for him — and for me too."

"But, Joseph."

"No, Émilie. I know I am seeing this place for the last time. I am sure I will not come back from this war."

Words like that . . . they're hard to swallow. I said: "Joseph," but I couldn't add anything else. My throat was tied in knots.

"Let's get going."

I kept him company as far as Briançon. He jumped the barrier and took his train for the front.

Chapter
7

And the Wind Would
Carry Me Off
Like a Bird

With Joseph gone, I saw the house in all its wretchedness. It was empty as never before. That night I gave way to dark thoughts. and I missed the two years that had just slipped by when all of us were together. It's true we squabbled, but at least the house was alive. Now I was alone with my father, who closed up tighter with each passing day, and Marie-Rose, who was still a child.

Still those two years had not been easy. I split my time between Val-des-Prés and Briançon, and more than once I'd been forced to grit my teeth and bend to the wheel. I was the only one who knew what I was aiming for; my brothers and sisters did not understand why my father let me go on studying. It made no difference that the scholarship came through just as the principal had promised; the fact that I was going to a secondary school stirred up jealousy.

My oldest sister was the most openly and violently opposed. One day when the principal came to see my father and argue once more to let me stay at school — it must have been for the fourth year — Rose, who was present for the discussion, screamed:

"Oh no! I won't have it. She is not going to be a schoolteacher with me a maid in middle-class houses."

It could not have been clearer. With the others, it was less obvious, subtler. They weren't mean, they just saw it as a way to escape farm chores. They even said so:

"It's not right for her to sit on a bench all day with her arms folded while we knock out the dirty work."

In one sense, they were not wrong: they were stuck with whatever I did not get done. That's why I polished off my jobs every chance I had outside of school time. I'd get up at five in the morning to work in the fields. I hoed, I harrowed till seven before I went back to the house where my father was waiting for me. While I was at work, he got everything ready: my basket, my city shoes; I changed my clothes and left for Briançon. In good weather I walked: seven kilometers in the morning, seven at night. I studied on the way so I wouldn't lose time. I had improvised a schoolbag that I wore suspended around my neck; it was like a desk and I could set my books on it.

At noon, I'd make myself at home in a park to nibble my lunch. It was always frugal: a hard-boiled egg, a few slices of sausage, a piece of bread, a bit of cheese, and water from the fountain. At two, I went back to school and in the evening, when I got back, I set to work again.

With two years of that life, I earned my *brevet** in 1916. Then everything was thrown upside down and there was no question of returning to Briançon to prepare my *brevet supérieur.** We even turned down the scholarship they awarded me. From then on, after Catherine died, I was the only woman in the house and the fortunes of the "château" weighed on my shoulders. The situation was incompatible with school.

I harnessed myself to the job. I became a peasant woman to the exclusion of everything else. My father, Marie-Rose, and I worked to the limit of our capacities. We were not the only ones with problems — the war touched every family.

The army had requisitioned the mules so that every time you wanted to plow or cart anything there were problems, and you had to manage with the few nags still around. They were old beasts the army wouldn't take, they were hard to drive, and they had to be borrowed. It made for endless trouble.

Before he left, Joseph taught me to plow. The hardest part wasn't so much dealing with a mule or a yoke of cows as holding onto the handle. I was not tall. I remember we had an ordinary plow, the swing type, with a handle designed for a man. It was far too high for me. When I cut furrows with that contrivance, I got the handle in the chest or face every time I hit a stone. For me plowing was the road to Calvary. One day I was struck so hard that I let go and the animals bolted. I'd been knocked half senseless for the moment. My father, following in my wake, blazed into a fury and came at me with the thick handle of his wooden rake raised high, ready to strike.

"Off with you! Off! Catch them! Pick up that plow immediately!"

There was as much rage and despair as pain in the tears I shed, but I picked up the plow handle and straightened the furrow.

And so the months followed one upon the other. I had no sense of time: a year could have been a day or ten thousand years, it all seemed alike. The only thing that mattered was work and weariness, weariness and work, to the point of exhaustion. I hardly had any time to think about myself, or even to think at all. Yet sometimes I went on making plans. I had not completely given up hope of taking up my studies where I left off. I'd tell myself: God almighty! This war's got to end. François will come back, so will Joseph — this nightmare can't last forever.

I often thought back to Joseph, to what he told me when he was home on leave: when he came back, he would take my place, he would pick up the plow handle and I . . . My dreams were simple in those days, nothing more than a balanced sharing between Joseph and me, restoring life to the house and the smile to my father's face, letting me finish what I had begun.

Why had Joseph told me: "I'm sure I won't come back"? I was obsessed with those last words of his, they hurt and I could not forget them. For me too, death was unacceptable. Accepting Catherine's death meant accepting injustice, and that I could not swallow. With his stories of the trenches, with his bitterness, Joseph had given me a glimpse of a world I did not know, a world of refusal and revolt. For me, it was a new language but I sensed that he was on the right track.

1916. 1917. The war went on. It dragged on endlessly. I saw three main stages: first the men leaving, then the emptiness, and finally the return. But most of them came back feet first. Here and there, death notices reached the villages and we picked up the habit of calling them by the new name they'd earned: "Dead on the field of honor." A pretty name indeed, it reminded me of my worker with the long-service medal, the one who hanged himself. They came back with their lovely decorations but they had no use for them. They were dead in the prime of life, irretrievably gone.

1918. Suddenly there was no news from Joseph. Until then he'd written regularly, at least one letter a week. The passing months brought nothing. We imagined everything, including the worst. Since victims' families were generally notified in case of death or injury, there was reason for hope. Five or six months later when we were so doubtful of everything that we even avoided mentioning his name, the postman brought us a letter. I recognized his handwriting on the envelope immediately, and for a moment I felt so sure I was looking at the writing of a ghost that I was incapable of moving my hand to take it and open it.

"Come on, read it," my father said.

The letter read as follows:

Dearest family,

I've been a prisoner of the Germans for five months now, this makes the fifth letter I've written, but I haven't had an answer. I feel as if everyone's abandoned me, but most of all, the hunger hurts so bad that I'm asking you to send me a package. You have no idea what the suffering is like, please, I beg you, send as many packages as you can or else we'll all starve to death.

We hadn't expected that letter; Joseph was alive. But it was so terribly sad that we were sick at heart. We would have been upset at less: hunger was not a part of our experience. From that day on I sent off two packages a week, one by mail, and another bigger package by train. We were naive to think they would reach him. The Germans didn't have anything either and they rifled the contents along the way. Joseph wrote:

Dear Émilie, you know, I just get the empty wrappings of your packages. I wet my finger with saliva and pick up the few crumbs left in the folds of the paper, I sniff it too for the smell of the good things you put in. That's all they leave, but please, I beg you, keep on sending me things. If by some chance one happened to reach me intact, what a feast we would have. Our hunger is so painful.

There were times when his letters turned harsher, more cynical:

If you saw me the way I am right now, you wouldn't recognize me I'm so skinny, I must weigh less than a bag of feathers. I say to myself that if I went up to Granon on a windy day, the wind would carry me off like a bird. . . . Do you have any pigs this year? I think of them often and how lucky they are to eat their fill — I'd like to be one of them when Papa takes them their feed.

Those letters hurt, but Joseph was alive. He was a prisoner and he was hungry, but he was going to come home to us. It was just a matter of months, weeks perhaps. In that summer of 1918, the war was drawing to an end. You could feel it. Men were coming home to stay, and François had already announced his return. It was said the Germans were at the end of their rope, the Allies victorious on all fronts, and the armistice imminent.

In those circumstances, after my years spent devoted to the farm alone, I grew increasingly impatient to return to school. I'd already applied twice to my academy for a job, but they had answered that I was too young to have children in my charge. I applied again. But there were no more openings. After an absence of four years, the demobilized schoolteachers were coming home and there was a surplus of temporaries. That too was a sign that the war would soon be over.

With my father's consent, I began to look for a position in a private school. Given my brevet, I was eligible to work as a study hall monitor; that way, I could study and pay my expenses. This had always been understood between us. It was François who helped me out, now that he was back from the war. He had served as a stretcher bearer, and made friends among the chaplains during his years at the front. He wrote to one of those priests in Paris who was likely to help me find what I was looking for. It was September: I still had a few days left to bring in the crops, and then I would set off for Paris.

During those last days, I worked like mad. I wanted everything left in perfect order so my father would have nothing to worry about. I never felt tired, I was everywhere at once, with the wheat, the rye, the oats, up to the last minute. The night before, my father had said:

"Émilie, you're not leaving the potatoes."

"No, they'll get done."

And I left with Marie-Rose early next morning to gather the spuds. Together, we filled fourteen sacks. Pulled out of the ground, loaded on the cart, and delivered to the house, all before noon. It was man's work, but I was so excited by the idea of going away that I could have done anything.

After that, everything went fast. I packed my suitcase in the afternoon, and took the train for Paris in the evening. For the first time, I was leaving the region of Briançon. I was eighteen years old.

Chapter

8

Just As It Was
in the
Middle Ages

I was thunderstruck when I arrived in Paris. Until then, the only things I knew about the city and its bustle were the rummage sales of the Grande Gargouille° and the fairs on the Champ de Mars; so for me the sight of the capital's streets was the revelation of a world I could never have imagined.

One of my first cousins came to meet me at the train. He was a middle-aged man I knew only by name, a retired customs agent who had lived in Paris for quite a while and knew the city well enough to guide my first steps. He was the only person I had to call on for help, since except for François's letter of introduction to his priest, I wasn't sure of anything.

We took the metro. My cousin lived on Montmartre; he was married, with two daughters who were already grown, and ever since his retirement, he'd been the concierge in a middle-class building.

"We don't have much room," he told me. "It's not like in the country, all the houses are too small and the rent is too high, but I'll do what I can to help you out. My wife's hard to get along with, you know, so the sooner you make your own living arrangements the better — for you as much as me."

"All right, tomorrow I'll see Abbé Josse. He's supposed to find me a place in a boarding school. It'll take two or three days, and then I'll have somewhere to stay."

"Good. Otherwise we're going to have problems."

There wasn't much warmth in his welcome, but I didn't care. I couldn't get over what I saw all around me on the metro and the streets. There were people everywhere, dressed to kill, and walking as if they'd just heard their houses were on fire. I had never seen anything like it and couldn't keep from remarking on it to my cousin:

"Doesn't anybody here work?"

"Why do you say that? Of course they work, and they work hard."

"But they're all wearing their Sunday best."

My cousin couldn't hide his smile. My remark may have seemed naive to him, even idiotic, but since I only put on proper clothes for mass I didn't mean anything impudent.

"That's the way they do things here," he answered. "First of all, most of the people you see don't do messy work, they have jobs in offices or stores; the others have clothes for commuting to work and change when they get to the shop."

"But they never stop moving around. Do they have time to work?"

"You know, Émilie, living here is nothing like Briançon, it's big here, you've got to go a distance to get anywhere; there are millions and millions of people, when some go off to work others are coming home, so it never stops and you get the impression they're out for a walk when they really all have jobs."

I was amazed. The feverish pace, the traffic, the noise, and the smells affected me like alcohol. It all made me drunk, and tired me more than lugging my fourteen sacks of potatoes. Paris reminded me of an immense stage with thousands of people spending all their time walking around. It was so different from our life in Val-des-Prés, working the land from dawn to dusk in our clogs and blue serge dresses.

I could not help thinking back to tales of home, to what my life had been until then. My whole girlhood came to mind, the winters, the storms, the droughts. I told myself that all those things were done and gone, that I had turned a new page, and was entering a new world. Gone the pure white silence, gone the muffled sounds of the snow, gone the little peasant girl fetching pails of icy water from the Clarée River.

I thought about my father, about everything I'd learned from him, his ideas on integrity, dignity. But what exactly was his dignity? I asked him once if he didn't think there was a limit to dignity, and he calmly answered no. That reminded me of the man who used to stop by the house every month and got a five franc piece from my father. The man had been one of his friends when they were young and smuggled sheep together. Each time he came, he insisted on signing an i.o.u. before he put the coin in his pocket and my father bowed to his wish, even though the man was illiterate and could only write a cross for his name. That little game had gone on for years and one day I couldn't contain myself any longer and asked:

"But, Papa, why do you have him sign that slip of paper? It's worthless. And besides, why do you lend him money if he'll never pay it back?"

"I lend him those francs because he needs them."

"But he doesn't give you back a cent."

"That's because he can't."

"So why all those useless i.o.u.'s piling up in the desk drawer?"

"That is because if he didn't sign them, he wouldn't take the money. He'd say to himself: 'Joseph has lost confidence in me; he thinks I won't pay him back,' and he wouldn't take my coin any more."

Around the same time, it was well before '14, he'd been involved in a controversy with the mayor of Val-des-Prés. It wasn't the first time. Old rivalries had always pitted the two families against each other, but this time it was a matter of stolen wood and my father was in the wrong. Like many men in the hamlet, he made ends meet by chopping down trees that he cut up and sold. But he committed "dry wood offenses" only; he would never have felled trees in their prime or damaged the forest.

This time, he went off to the woods by moonlight and cut down a specimen he'd spotted earlier. Whether by chance or not, the mayor had seen him and the next morning lost no time in reporting him to the forest ranger:

"An offence was committed last night. I heard a tree fall, I kept an eye out and saw Joseph Allais taking it home. Officer, you'll have to write up an official report."

The ranger came to see my father at the house. He was not a bad sort, we were even on reasonably good terms, but he did have to write his report. He said:

"Joseph, I know you're a widower, you've got six children to raise, and when you take wood you always do it right. I know all that so I close my eyes, but this time I'm obliged to report you: someone saw you last night and he informed on you."

"Go ahead," my father answered, "Do what you have to do, I understand; if you don't, you'll have trouble and you have a family too. No need to draw pictures for me, I know who turned me in. It's not the first time he's played a dirty trick on me, and it certainly won't be the last."

There's another wood story about Marion Jambet who had his own problems with the forest ranger and then got stuck with the name he invented. His real name was Albert, he had six children, and was not very bright. He often went into the forest for wood, but he lacked my father's scruples and chopped down trees in their prime. This time he decided to take advantage of a new ranger who didn't come from around here; he thought the time had come to fell a beautiful specimen he'd had in mind for a long time. That Albert thought he was smart and he set to work with a will, taking no precautions. When the tree was on the ground, he stopped to catch his breath and turned around to find himself face to face with the new ranger.

"Well, my friend, I think I've just caught you red-handed," the ranger said.

Albert collected his wits immediately, telling himself: "Pooh! What difference does it make? He doesn't know me," and when the ranger asked his name, he answered "Marion Jambet" without hesitation, thinking: He'll have to do a lot of chasing around till he finds me again.

"Where are you from?"

"Why, from Plampinet," he said, thinking: But who's he going to send his report to?

He was really naive to think that the ranger would merely send him something in the mail: like all people new on the job, the ranger was out to prove himself. The name sounded odd and the fellow had acted suspiciously, so he went right down to see the mayor of Névache.

"Do you have anyone named Marion Jambet in your jurisdiction?"

"No, indeed," the mayor answered.

"Still, the fellow swore it was his name and that he lives in the village."

"What does he look like?"

"I'd recognize him anywhere. He's tall and blond and he has very long legs."

"There's only one man who fits that description: it's Albert."

It didn't take them long to figure out the hoax, and the fellow was charged and fined. He got out of his fix all right, but the name stuck and since then everyone's called him Marion Jambet.

Another case. More tragic. It might have finished with a young man dead. It was a miracle he escaped with his hide. There was a young woman, Zéphirine. They were young, in love and wildly passionate. He was doing his military service with the Alpine Chasseurs° at the fort, and at night he would ski down and join Zéphirine in her bedroom while her father was hanging out in the local bistros. The old fellow had a reputation for going home dead drunk and only when the last café closed its doors, and then he had just enough strength to fall into bed. One night he came home earlier than usual, and when he saw skis standing against the wall he immediately understood what was going on. In those days, soldiers were the only ones to use those contrivances. No one ever found out what went through his head. Without a second's hesitation, he went down to the cellar, grabbed a cheese dish cover — those covers were cast iron, the smallest weighing around five kilos — and tiptoed back upstairs. In the bedroom, Zéphirine and her soldier, living it up with no other thought in mind, were far from imagining that her father might catch them by surprise. By the time they heard him, it was too late. The old man was there, and bashed the young fellow while he was trying to pull his boots back on. One blow was enough to drop the lover and split his skull. The man Zéphirine picked up was lying motionless at death's door, bleeding profusely.

After the initial shock, the old man came to himself and told his daughter:

"Get me the bottle of rum from the kitchen."

He laid the wounded youth flat, massaged him, pulled his teeth apart, and forced him to drink. By the time the whole liter went down, the soldier uttered a few groans.

"He's not dead," the old man said. "Tear up some cloth for a bandage."

Without a word, Zéphirine made the bandage, and her father took the body, loaded it over his shoulders, and walked out into the night.

He went straight to Fort de la Cochette. It was a damned amazing feat, at night, with snow falling, the ascent, the weight of the body plus the skis. When he got there, he dropped his load at the sentry post and stole off, saying:

"I just found him on the mountain, he got hurt skiing."

That story could have gone much further. But it didn't. They took care of the soldier in the hospital, and when he came to, he confirmed the accident theory. The surgeon wasn't fooled:

"Your skull is split from ear to ear, with hairs and a piece of beret in your brain. It could not be from a fall."

"It is, it is. I fell on the mountain."

He always told the same story, so there was nothing to do but believe it and the whole thing was buried and forgotten. He died of that "trepanation" later on, but he never once talked about that night and the cheese cover.

That was the way peasants worked, settling things among themselves; it was an old law everyone respected. "Hard, hard, hard": such was their life, and such was mine until that time. I realized that I had never been young, but that too was the law. There was no dearth of examples. Take the aptly named Angèle, a veritable angel who spent her whole life serving her lout of a cousin. She started out as his servant, and he finally married her so he wouldn't have to pay her wages anymore. He too was a drunken clod, and she took everything without complaint. She was even-tempered, gentle and smiling, always pleasant. Every night she waited up for the drunkard who came home after roaming the countryside with his cart, invariably stopping at every bistro along the way. And when he appeared, usually after midnight, she'd take him under the arms and somehow manage to get him to bed; she'd make him comfortable and then feed him soup by the spoonful like a baby. By day she earned money to run her home working for other people: she took care of widowers and old men, doing their housework and laundry. She did so much wash that her hands were misshapen. Clarée water is unforgiving if you're not careful, it's rapid and freezing cold. Angèle's hands were red and swollen, they weren't hands anymore, they were paddles. Her smile and her goodness never left her. Angèle! A lifetime of uncomplaining submission.

And then there was that mountain flower whose parents forced her to marry a fellow who was so mean that around here we called him "the unlicked bear," after the tale about the mother bear who licked her malformed cub into shape. He terrified her from the start. Meeting nothing but blows and threats from morning to night, the young woman's only refuge was insanity. She'd leave the house in any weather and wander along the paths and in the woods talking to herself. When she met children, she'd talk to them about the dead among whom she lived increasingly in her flight from the living. I remember, one day she took me by the arm and told me:

"You know, I've just seen your mommy and she asked me if you were a good girl."

She really frightened me that day, and I screamed:

"No, that's not true!"

Even so, her husband gave her no peace, and when he was in heat he went after her in the woods, pursuing her insistently until she yielded to his superior strength; just about anywhere would do, he'd pull up her skirt and then leave her there when he was finished. Harmless madness and all, that woman had eight kids.

I think there are no words strong enough to describe that brutish life. The Middle Ages, perhaps, but I wonder whether people were not more civilized in those days. The story of Marie and Joseph may well be the model, since it illustrates perfectly the conditions of peasant life around here before 1914.

Marie was the only child of poor peasants. She was of marriageable age and was living and working with her parents until a suitor appeared. That was an illusion. Those people lived in a tiny mountain village, completely isolated from the rest of the valley, with a single mule path for its only link to the outside world. They lived in one room, animals and people together under the same roof. The room was divided in half by a curtain, with the kitchen-bedroom-living room on one side, and on the other the stable with the sheep and cows.

Marie finally did get married, to a boy from the village, and on the wedding night the young couple came into the single room. The beds touched, and when the young man cautiously tried to draw close to his young wife, the girl, who didn't know a thing, began to scream:

"Papà, qué José que me tocho! [Papa, Joseph's touching me!]."

The father sat bolt upright in the next bed:

"Marie, I hear you. You want me to get up?"

The young man gave up and kept still for the rest of the night. He began again the next day, and the day after that, and each time the girl, no more knowledgeable than the night before, started screaming in the dark.

"Papa, Joseph's touching me."

And the father would answer: "You want me to get up and get the club? I'll show that rascal a thing or two."

And so weeks and months rolled by. With winter coming, the young man decided to leave. "Since I don't have a wife, I might just as well be off." He took his bundle of belongings and went to work in Marseilles. When springtime came, the father told Marie:

"You ought to write to Joseph, tell him to come back, the rush'll soon be on, there'll be lots of work."

The husband took some convincing, but he did return. He figured that with the spring and the work in the fields, he'd be able to lure his wife off to a secluded spot and make her understand what he wanted. In fact, just after he got back, he went to mow the grass. He told the family:

"Today I'll mow the high field; it's far and there's lots to do, so to save time I won't come down to eat. Marie'll bring me my basket."

At the appointed time, the young woman arrived with her husband's lunch. They were alone and it was child's play for Joseph to persuade his wife to do as he wished. And so it was that they made love for the first time, a few months after their wedding.

Chapter 9 ⚘

Farewell, Joseph

Abbé Josse was perfect. He welcomed me, gave me addresses of boarding schools, and told me to come back if I did not find what I was looking for. But I found something immediately. The school, called the Institute of Notre Dame de Chavilles, was run by nuns who did not wear habits, and its students were daughters of the aristocracy and the middle class.

The nun offered to take me au pair. That was not unusual.

"It is the practice here," she said. "Since you will be working on your brevet supérieur, it will be as advantageous to you as to us: you will get food and lodging and we will take care of your wardrobe."

The word "wardrobe" is something of an exaggeration. The ladies gave me a nightgown and bathrobe immediately: they were indispensable to my rounds in the dormitory. Later on, they told me, I would have handkerchiefs, towels, and other such trifles. I accepted on the spot; I think I would have accepted whatever they offered, the important thing was to have a place to study in peace.

In return, I had a full schedule. I was to take charge of classes for the very little girls, supervise recess and dining hall, accompany the young ladies on their evening walk and keep an eye on them in the dormitory. This routine kept me busy from seven in the morning to ten at night. Then I was allowed to think of myself and work, but I had to do it by candlelight since that was the time they cut off the lighting gas. Those were the rules.

It was November 11, one month after I came to Paris. From my father and Marie-Rose, I heard that once again there was no news from Joseph. They told me in their letters that all the men were returning home to their villages — all but Joseph. I did my best to reassure them, writing: "As long as the war goes on, it's to be expected; but as soon as the armistice is signed, Joseph will be released; since he's in enemy territory, it's certainly hard for his letters to get through." That language kept up their hopes, and I must say that at the time we did not doubt he'd return.

Nevertheless, on the day the bells rang out in Paris to announce the end of the war and the victory, I was so uneasy at Joseph's absence and silence that it was hard for me to be happy. I asked myself: Why doesn't he write? Why are the others coming back, but not him? Why?

Paris was on holiday. All of France, even my boarding school, was seized with an explosion of joy. Every one of the young ladies was stricken with the virus of patriotism, and for twenty-four hours discipline was shattered.

"Mademoiselle Allais, Mademoiselle Allais" — the Mother Superior came running through the halls — "We are going out, we have to get ready, tomorrow we are going to town, we will watch the parades and cheer the poilus. I want no exceptions, no one is to be sick."

I had no choice. That's what they paid me for. So on Victory Day, I went into the streets of Paris with my young ladies. It was wild, there were dizzying mobs of people. At every intersection, every public square, music, crowds, dancing, hugging, kissing; soldiers and civilians mixed in together. It was an explosion of collective joy with the attendant screams, laughter, garlands, parading soldiers, and I — in the middle of all that — was paralyzed. It was sheer torture. I longed to scream with them, I longed to kiss those soldiers and clasp them in my arms. But that was impossible. The thought of Joseph kept me from being happy. My frame of mind had been exactly the same on Catherine's wedding day: I was afraid something terrible was going to happen. It was irrational, but beyond my control, and you could see it in my face.

The principal came over to me and said:

"Come on now, Mademoiselle Allais, you must not look like that. Do what everyone else is doing, enjoy yourself! That brother of yours will come back, he will."

The very next day I decided to act. The situation could not go on that way. But what was I to do? Anything but remain passively resigned like my father. The people around me gave what advice they could: some told me to wait a while longer, delays were to be expected, things were in a mess everywhere; others, on the contrary, urged me to take steps. I did not hesitate for long. I took my courage in my hands and set off. It was a Thursday.

I did a whole apprenticeship. The endless waiting, the forms to fill out, the indifference of clerks behind their counters opened my eyes to the administrative universe: unwieldy, passive, and, in many respects, inhuman.

Through all those offices, all those files, all those anonymous fingers running down columns in search of a serial number, my brother was turning into an abstraction. His shadow would emerge from a drawer only to go back in a moment later. This game of hide and seek, hope and disappointment broke my heart. But what could I do? I was not the only one hurrying along corridors in search of a missing soldier; mothers, wives, and sisters struggled around me against the impossible silence, hoping like me for a miracle.

Every time I went to those offices, I left sick at heart. I finally gave up believing in miracles, I told myself it was useless to hope, Joseph was dead and would never come back among us. But that I could not write to Val-des-Prés, nor could I talk about it to anyone. As they said at the ministry, so long as nothing is official, there is still hope.

Every morning one of my students would come to my office saying:

"Mademoiselle, I took communion this morning so your brother will come back quickly."

Such ingenuousness did not leave me cold, but I do think I was already having doubts about many things.

Somehow or other I got through the winter. I lived like a nun, cloistered behind the walls of the boarding school. Mass, classes, preparing homework, correcting papers, iron discipline, and a schedule accounting for every second left me little time for dwelling on my worries. I liked that, I needed it, and I did the work of several people for a pittance. After doling out shirts and handkerchiefs, my good ladies had finally decided on a salary, the huge sum of twenty-five francs per month — not as much as you'd give for charity, but so be it, it's just a detail; my head felt too heavy, my heart too anxious to worry about myself.

The news came at the beginning of June with the curtness of a government office form. No regrets, no condolences, nothing but a death notice with last name, first name, middle name, serial number, and a brief sentence specifying date and place. Joseph died in his prison camp; the supreme irony is that he died of starvation on the day of the armistice, on November 11, at the very moment France was singing and dancing in the streets and the public squares.

I wanted to know more and in spite of my sorrow I went to the ministry one last time. I do not know why I did it, even today I wonder why; there were only macabre details of no interest. Yes, he died of hunger, there was a doctor's notation: hunger and exhaustion. They had buried him in a common grave with a few of his comrades in Avesnes.

When I got back to the boarding school, I was in a state of collapse. The hardest task was still to come: I had to give my father the news. I did not want to write or send a telegram, I wanted to go to Val-des-Prés myself to temper the shock. When I informed the principal of where matters stood, she answered:

"Mademoiselle Allais, you must offer this sacrifice to our Lord in His goodness."

I was beside myself at those words, and I could not contain myself any longer:

"Please," I said, "don't talk of offering sacrifices, and leave the good Lord out of it. If there is a good Lord He doesn't know what He's doing; after what we've been through, it's a horror."

"You do not know what you are saying, Mademoiselle Allais."

"Let me alone! You're not the one who has to tell my father the news."

I slammed the door and left for Briançon. I had my train ticket in my pocket and three miserable francs in my wallet. The trip was a horror, I was in mourning clothes, bereft and despairing. When I reached home, I did not have to say very much; seeing my clothes, my father understood immediately. He merely said:

"I expected it; we didn't have any news, we saw the others come home, and when they were all back, for me it was over. I knew he was dead."

A few days later, a fellow from La Vachette sent me a few details through a third party. He and Joseph had been in the same camp, they had met and talked. He also wanted me to know that he should have come himself, but that those moments had been so painful, he did not have the heart. Here is what I learned:

Joseph was in such poor condition that the man had not recognized him at first. He was so weak he couldn't do a thing for himself, and other prisoners were carrying him to the john in their arms. He looked like a ghost and it was Joseph who recognized the man from La Vachette and called out:

"Hey! Mondet, you don't recognize me?"

"No, I don't. Who are you?"

"Come on, I'm from Val-des-Prés, we made our first communion together. My name's Joseph Allais, don't you remember?"

The man remembered him at once, but he couldn't tell Joseph that he was altered beyond recognition, he was so thin. He was sick to the nth degree, he'd picked up all the diseases of filth that linger in those camps, diarrhea, dysentery, and he didn't have the strength to fight anything off.

Those last pieces of information could not increase our sorrow, nor could they detract. Besides, we did not know what to do with our tears: how do you weep for a dead man who has eluded you until the end? Even his corpse had evaporated; with all the application forms and the searching, we never did manage to find out exactly where he was. As for Avesnes, there are five of them in France. The only thing we had left of him were our memories and an enamel plaque standing against the cemetery wall.

July 1919. Summer. No matter the mourning or the sorrow, we had the land and the animals to look after. I exchanged my city shoes for the peasant's clodhoppers, my hands picked up the patina of old tool handles again, and I plunged back into the warm smells of the stable to milk the cows and tend the ewes.

Once in a while François came by to lend us a hand, but he was increasingly aloof. The connections he'd made during the war were useful, and he was a sexton now in Briançon, dividing his time between his church, his priests, and his bachelor's set ways. Yet with Joseph dead, the question of his return came up again: would he like to take over the paternal farm? His life was as carefully ruled as the lines on music paper, and the fields our mother had left him were all he needed; with his cart, his mule, and one or two cows, he got by selling his milk privately in Briançon. Besides, since he was all sugar and honeyed attention with the old maids of the parish, he collected tips and New Year's gifts. With one thing and another, he had more than he needed to live in comfort.

In October, I set out once more for the boarding school of Notre Dame de Chaville. It was less than ideal, but I had no choice. I could have looked for something else, but I decided to go back rather than try my luck in a new institution. I had no illusions, I knew I was exploited with my nightly vigils, my classes, my Thursday and Sunday outings and the fifty francs a month they gave me. But I was used to it, and besides, only one thing mattered, I had to get my brevet. That is what I concentrated on in the months that followed. I worked like a slave, seeing no one, hardly ever going outside the boarding school walls and, in the spring, I earned my brevet supérieur with distinction and congratulations from the examiners. I had just completed another stage of my life.

I returned to Paris the following year. This time I decided to forsake my ladies of Chaville, they had exploited me enough and I needed a change. I certainly did not have much knack for choosing. The director of the Jeanne d'Arc de Gagny boarding school had a bad reputation. She deserved it. Caught in the fire of her sarcasm from day one, I was forced to defend myself. A few pointed, no-holds-barred discussions plus support from the house chaplain made it possible for me to keep my job and work under relatively acceptable conditions, and I had no problem getting my teaching certificate in June. Now I could request an assignment in the public system, but I had different ambitions. I remembered Joseph's words. Before he went back to the front, he had said:

"I promise you'll finish school, and you won't be just a schoolteacher, you'll be a professor."

I had not forgotten, and I enrolled at the Sorbonne for a *licence*° in Italian.

I did not want to go on with the cloistered life I had been leading for the past three years or to be exploited by the nuns. My diplomas gave me reason to look for a position matching my ambitions, and I found it at Nogent-sur-Marne in a private establishment run by two sisters. One taught French, the other English. They welcomed me with open arms and offered me 400 francs a month to prepare their pupils for the brevet. It was beyond my hopes. No more monitor duty, no more walks, no more extra duties on Thursdays and Saturdays. I taught my courses and had the rest of my life to myself, so I could organize my time as I saw fit. Just one drawback: I had to find my own housing, but again fortune smiled on me. As luck would have it, I landed with people completely different from any I'd known before. There I would meet the man who opened my eyes to the world once and for all by his ideas, his authority, and his example. Like Joseph, he would teach me that war is a disgrace and that to take up arms to kill one's fellows is far more shameful still.

Chapter 10 🪶

Thou Shalt Not Kill

Before the war, my sister Rose had gone with a certain Maurice Vernon. It hadn't come to anything but Rose had remained in touch with his friends. Also, one of my cousins had married his brother Clément. Both men, libertarians and draft evaders, had left France, but my cousin was still living in Saint Cloud. When I reached Paris in 1921, I moved in with her. She'd agreed to take me as a boarder.

At the time, my cousin was living with Joanés Cuat, who was also a libertarian draft evader. It was through him that I would discover a world as yet unknown to me: the world of anarchism. From the start Jo made a strong impression on me. In every way, he was the opposite of the peasants of Val-des-Prés; he had clear, reasoned ideas on people and society and, most important, he had chosen his life. Joanés Cuat was a free man. I admired him right off, first for his ideas, then for what he had done. Just like my father, he believed in bringing his thought and acts into consonance, but their worlds were radically different. He told me his story himself. I was twenty-one and he was eleven years older.

"You know, Émilie, most people don't know what it means to be a deserter. They think it's cowardly, and if they think so, it's because they don't know any better and they haven't thought it through. How can you expect them to think when society doesn't give them the means and even does everything possible to keep them from thinking? From childhood on their heads are stuffed with false ideas; they hear about heroism and patriotism, but it's all hot air. Émilie, when you're in the classroom, you've got to remember, the civics lessons and all the baloney are put in to lull the conscience. Nothing is as vulnerable as a kid; he believes everything you tell him, too bad if it's a pack of lies. Desertion is refusing to say yes to human stupidity. Sure, they all went off to war, they fought in the trenches, and they risked their lives. But in the worst-case situation, there's always the chance that you'll make it through. How many died? A million, they say — it's true it's terrible, but millions upon millions came home. On the other hand, if you desert, if you go underground, you find you're alone and that's bad enough, and then, if you get picked up, it's the firing squad for sure. You are refusing the system when you desert, you are saying no to the whole setup. You are saying no to the rich guys who decided on the war, you are saying no to the arms dealers, you are saying no to the colonels who play servant to the rich, and you are saying no to the priests who give them their blessing. War is state-sponsored savagery, and its first victim is the man who goes off to serve, the workers and the peasants, the people like your brother who go off to fight because they do not understand.

"Well, for us, with our ideas, there was no reason to comply, and we didn't. Because there are people who are against it in words, but the minute things get a little hot, they're the first to shout about sacred union. The Vernons, me, and a few others, when we saw the war coming straight at us, we decided not to serve and we made our plans. The ideal thing was to leave France, to go away and start life over in a country where there's no danger of turning into a serial number. It isn't easy for a workingman to leave, you need the means, you need money, so we chipped in to buy tickets for the Vernon brothers. We agreed they'd go on ahead and get settled, find work, and send us money as soon as possible so we could follow them. Clément left his wife and baby behind, and I stayed too. We did what we said, they left for America and we stayed here. In the meanwhile, we had to live. For me, there wasn't any problem. I have a trade, I could wait. There was only one danger: war could break out sooner than we thought, with me still on the spot — that was the only fly in the ointment. But for her, for Clément's wife, it was a different cup of tea, she didn't have anything, no means of subsistence, and she had her baby to raise. She began doing day work, and she found out that cleaning people's houses with a baby is no sinecure. Her ladies were constantly at her:

"'Look at that,' they'd say. 'Look what your brat did! He just messed on my carpet.'

"And just like that she'd lose her job, she lost them faster than she could find them. One night I went to see her, she was beside herself, she'd just lost another job and she was desperate. You're either comrades or you're not; I couldn't leave her in such poverty while I was living high on the hog. After all, we believed in solidarity, we were going to leave to join our comrades together, so I offered to look after her and the kid, I told her:

"'Look here, Maria, from now on you won't do day work anymore; I'm moving in. You'll do my laundry and the cooking, and I'll earn enough for the three of us.'

"So that's what we did. We didn't live together, we formed a community, out of respect — not for morality: that's just another bourgeois hang-up — it was respect for the comrades. Clément Vernon was my pal, it didn't enter our heads to betray him or deceive him, but tongues began to wag, and Clément's mother was first in line. Right away she saw evil where there was nothing to see, and she lost no time writing to America to tell Vernon that Maria and I had shacked up. She wrote in her letters:

"'Whatever you do, don't send them any money, because if your wife comes over there with Jo, the three of you will be living together.'

"Clément believed her, he followed her advice and didn't send anything. When war was declared, there I was stuck in Lyons like a damned fool, with my mobilization orders on the way. I packed my bundle and took off for the mountains. The first thing I did was hide out in the Saint-Claude forest since I know my way around it; I understood the risk I was taking, but I didn't hesitate for a second. I was ready to face anything rather than take up a gun.

"I held out as long as I could, hiding, living in the woods like an animal, and then I set to work, organizing my life. There is a degree of fellow-feeling among libertarians, after all, and I managed to get myself a new identity. I took over the papers of a Swiss citizen and became Paul Robin. Overnight, Joanés Cuat was dead. Not completely. The risks were still there because the masquerade was pretty crude, but even so it offered protection if I met up with the gendarmes. They just better not be too curious.

"I heard about Maria, I knew she'd taken refuge at a sister's in the southern Alps. Officially she was the wife of a draft evader, and according to law, she could be prosecuted as an accomplice. I decided to join her. For weeks I walked along the mountains till I got there. We didn't start living together immediately, it took even more adversity and blame to bring us to that. Clément's mother kept at us, and so did the war. One day Clément's little girl died. She fell into a well and she was already dead when they found her. The mother-in-law accused us, Maria and me, of killing her to get her out of our way. That isolated us from the comrades even more. There was nothing left to hope for, they'd never send us tickets for America. That's when we realized there was only one thing left to do and we did it. We fell in love."

I thought it was an extraordinary story, especially since the person telling it to me right there in the little apartment in Saint Cloud was still wanted by the authorities. As he said, Joanés Cuat may have been dead, but it was such an artificial death, such a precarious situation, that every day, the merest nothing could unmask him and bring him before a military tribunal. In 1921, Jo was still liable to the firing squad, the amnesty law was still far off, and yet he was leading a thoroughly normal life, I mean from an anarchist's point of view. He worked for Renault, subscribed to libertarian journals, spoke out frankly and did not hide his ideas. It was through him that I discovered anarchist literature and La Fouchardière's° *L'Oeuvre*. They opened my eyes because *L'Oeuvre* was really something, a newspaper for working people, much less partisan than Jaurès's *Humanité.*° To me, *Humanité* seemed to wear blinders, while *L'Oeuvre* was a breakthrough. It was a treat. It was a world that had done with my education and my habits. It was the world upside down, but an upside-down world that seemed far more right side up than the one proposed to me up to that time.

Jo and his friends respected religious belief; what they found intolerable was the power of the church and the church's collusion with the state and with war. When they spoke that way, they were only working loose the last remaining stones of an already shaky structure. As a little girl at catechism and school alike, I was diligent and learned easily. My gift for remembering Bible history made me the priest's favorite, he held me up as an example to the others and I was proud of it. In those days, everything having to do with God and the sacraments was taboo. I believed the church's teaching, whatever they told me: the Holy Trinity, the sacrifice of the mass, remission of sins, holy communion, hell, and heaven; and the day of my first communion I was as if carried away by faith and love of God.

Later on, the reality of life dulled my fervor. The war, the priest's patriotic homilies, what Joseph told me about the trenches, and, above all, death—his and Catherine's, both so absurd—had shaken the structure. The worm was in the fruit, as they say. Long before Jo opened my eyes, I had said to myself: But if the Good Lord exists, how can He tolerate such abominations; if He is infinitely good and infinitely just as they say, how can He accept injustice like that? It's impossible!

But given my isolation, all those ideas had just come and gone. Gone? Not entirely, they were buried deep inside like seeds ready to sprout.

And then there were the Bertalon brothers: they were a revelation, too. When I first heard of them, I went out of my mind, I was so proud. They were from the mountains around Briançon, two men from my part of the country who had set an example and were still doing it, since in 1922 they were far from the end of their work. For eight years they had been in hiding, for eight years the gendarmes had been looking for them and they were still holding out.

"You see, Émilie," Joanés Cuat would say, "in situations like that religion has its good side. For the Bertalons, religious principles made them choose draft evasion. They're Protestants, and from the time they were little, they were taught: 'Thou shalt not kill,' and in '14, when their orders came, they decided to go underground, saying: 'We will not kill.'"

What I found most exciting about the Bertalon story was the village rallying around them. They did not have to go very far for shelter, they stayed right in the region. By day they hid in caves, and by night they came out to work their fields and their neighbors's fields too. The moment a gendarme's cap came into view, the person who'd seen it would ring the church bell and the two brothers would go back up the mountain. That's how they were never caught, the whole village joined together and no one failed to respect that solidarity. Women, children, old people, all of them pulled on the bell rope at the slightest alarm. It seems that since the brothers lived out of doors all the time, their faces were as black as prunes, thin and etched by wind, sun, and cold. Later on, they would give themselves up, but they held out for thirteen years, from '14 to '27. They were put on trial — I'll get back to it later — but I'd like to relate the older brother's reply when the military judge said:

"Come now, Bertalon, think about it, if every Frenchman had acted like you, what whould have become of France? The Germans would have completely overrun us."

"Monsieur le Président,° the Germans would never have come into our mountains, our rocks are no use to them. Why would they have come? To share our miserable life and our winters? The earth here is so hard nobody would want any part of it."

For me, Jo's life, the Bertalon brothers' lives, and all the ideas revolving around them were like an oxygen balloon. The life I'd been leading in Paris for the past three years had not been fun, and I often lost my bearings. Because of those men, I took heart again. I sure as hell needed it. What with the classes I taught in Nogent and the courses I took at the Sorbonne, running back and forth, lunches on the fly with a penny's worth of bread and a mug of cocoa, I overdid it. Since I gave myself no quarter, I fell sick and the doctor who examined me didn't beat around the bush.

"Mademoiselle Allais," he said, "staying in Paris even one day longer is out of the question. You must go back home immediately."

It was a hard blow, but the evidence was irrefutable: I had lost ten kilos and I was always tired. My lungs were affected.

"What can you expect?" the doctor added. "You've always lived in your mountains, Paris air isn't good for someone like you."

"But doctor, I can't leave my class, I'm getting six students ready for their Brevet, I have to finish out the year."

"No, it is out of the question; in your condition you can consider yourself free of any responsibility. Your health is at stake."

So I packed my bags and left. My ladies at the school in Nogent took it well; they wrote me excellent recommendations and wished me luck. The die was cast. Since I could not continue with my studies, I would be a schoolteacher. When all is said and done, that is what I had always wanted.

In June, I applied for a job in the public school system. I asked to be placed in three *départements:*° Seine-et-Oise, Seine-et-Marne, and the Hautes Alpes. I was offered three assignments and I had to choose. I opted for the Hautes Alpes, it was natural for me to stay close to my father: he needed me, and besides, the doctor had said, "Stay in your mountains as long as you can; the air you breathe there is irreplaceable."

Chapter 11 ✒

"It's When You Spits"

When my assignment came, I had to look at a map for some idea of the place I was supposed to go to. I had never heard of the village: Réalon-les-Gourniers. I did find a Réalon near the town of Savines, but no trace of any Gourniers. Oh well, I thought, when I reach Réalon, I'm sure to find Les Gourniers, so I packed my suitcase and left.

When I got off the train at Savines, there I stood on the railroad tracks without any idea of where to go next. I entered the only bistro around and asked the woman who ran it how to reach Réalon-les-Gourniers. She was a kindly person, and looking at me as if I'd appeared out of nowhere, she said:

"So you're going up there! Well, it's in the mountains. How to get there at this hour, I really don't know."

She looked embarrassed. At that point, an old fellow who happened to be in the bistro came over to me.

"To go to Réalon, you h-h-ave to ph-ph-phone Missus Pé-Pé-pé-Péron."

The little old fellow with the stutter was such a surprise that I almost burst out laughing. I looked up Missus Péron's phone number and called. When I got her on the line, I told her who I was and what I wanted.

"Well," she said, "outside of the evening bus, there's no connection, there's only the bus that comes down in the morning and goes back up at night; if you don't want to wait, you'll have to use a private service."

In those days, there were no taxis or anything of the sort. The only solution was to find a carter who would agree to haul me and my suitcase. The stutterer referred me to a man with a horse and wagon who might be willing to take me all the way up. I found the old fellow in his stable and asked if he could drive me to Réalon-les-Gourniers.

"Réalon-les-Gourniers?" he repeated.

"Yes, I'm the new schoolteacher and I'd like to get there before evening."

The old fellow scratched his head: "That depends," he said. "Do you have a lot to carry?"

"No, just my suitcase."

"Well, in that case, I can take you, you and your suitcase, but when we start climbing, you'll have to get out and walk, you know."

I accepted his conditions. The old fellow saddled up and we set out. It was a tiny two-wheel cart, a kind of buggy, with a plain bench to sit on.

Fortunately the fellow had warned me, the path climbed without relief and we walked behind the cart more than we sat on the bench. It was an extremely arduous trip, twenty kilometers on a seemingly endless twisting path. When we came in sight of the village of Réalon, and were passing by the cemetery, the old fellow said:

"Just look at that! It's the end of the world up here; there's lots as stay and never come back down."

That idiotic sentence didn't mean a thing but it was too much. I burst into tears. The fatigue, the remoteness, and the fear of the unknown had left me vulnerable to the slightest irritation, and that "never come back down" had upset me far beyond what the old fellow could have guessed.

"Oh, young lady," he said, "don't pay any mind to what I said. I didn't mean to hurt you, I wouldn't have said a word if I'd known."

"It's all right, don't worry. I've got the blues and if that's all you can think of to cheer me up, things are in bad shape."

The old fellow didn't dare look me in the face after that. He said:

"I didn't say it to be mean, and besides, we're not there yet, you know. Les Gourniers is still higher and it's even more isolated."

That blow almost made me laugh, but he was right, the higher we climbed, the wilder and dryer the countryside looked. Crossing the timber line, we entered the zone of alpine meadows where nothing grows but grass for sheep. I told myself that if Réalon was the end of the world, Les Gourniers was still worse, and my heart skipped a beat when I caught sight of the first houses in the hamlet from a bend in the road. I'd expected a mountain village, but I had never seen one like this before. It was a sort of cluster of black stones set between sky and earth, without a single tree, with nothing but tufts of grass between the rocks. The closer we got, the more the desolation and poverty of the village stood out. No doubt about it, the old fellow was right: we were at the end of the world. Beyond the houses, there were only pastures and snow-covered peaks and the path that stopped short at that point.

The carter left me at the side of the road. When I paid him, he turned his horse around and galloped off as I stood alone amid the houses. Everything was closed tight and silent, the village looked abandoned, and for all that I was used to the ways of mountain peasants, I have to say that my chest tightened as if I were making my way into an unknown world for the first time.

I leaned my suitcase against a wall and decided to knock on doors until someone answered. I had to know where to find the school and the key to unlock it. At the third or fourth house, a woman opened the door; she looked me over, took the time to listen to my question, and then as if she couldn't believe her ears, answered:

"Oh, the school! The school! Come along."

Leading me across a square, she brought me to a tottering structure.

"There it is," she said.

She opened the door, let me in, and added:

"See for yourself."

I was faced with the most miserable of rooms. Dampness had eaten through its bare walls, and for furniture there was nothing but a bed of wooden planks with a sack of hay for a mattress, a table, a chair, and a wood-burning stove. It was all falling apart, and I couldn't help saying: "But, what am I supposed to do?"

"Oh, you'll manage."

"Is there a grocery store?"

My question seemed so ridiculous to the woman that she shrugged her shoulders: "Well, of course not, you have to go down to Réalon to do your shopping."

I was aghast at such a minimal existence, but she was right, there was nothing, no grocery, no butcher shop, no bakery. I hadn't been brought up in the lap of luxury, but suddenly I was reduced to the level of absolute zero. The woman was still standing there and I asked her:

"What can I buy in the village?"

"Nothing much, we don't make anything here, maybe a bit of butter, but you can't count on it."

That's where I began. I went to a farm and the farmer's wife consented to grant me a little butter. But what butter! The peasants had strange ways of doing things in Réalon. Because they were isolated, they kept milk four or five days, skimming off the maximum, so they started out with very rancid cream and that's what they made into butter. Even so I took that bit of rancid butter, but that's all I had for dinner. There was no question of going back to Réalon, I didn't have the heart for it, and so I had no choice but to return to the place set aside for my lodging. For the second time I took stock of the disaster. The doors of the neighboring houses had closed up again and I was alone. I said to myself: If that's what it's like to be a teacher, I might as well change trades right away, it's worse than being a monk in a Trappist monastery.

What was to become of me without heat, without bedding, without bread? There wasn't even a telephone. To calm my nerves, I left that room to take a few steps along the mountain stream. I sat down on a rock and I think I was really on the brink of tears. I remember, I was still clutching the butter I'd bought at the farm.

"Mademoiselle, what's wrong?"

I looked up; a young man about twenty years old was standing in front of me. He was the prototypical mountaineer: hair almost blond, gawky-looking but solidly built, with a likeable mischievous twinkle in the corner of his eye. He repeated:

"What's wrong, Mademoiselle?"

I wanted to make some gesture to show how disconcerted I was, how disappointed, but what gesture could have been strong enough? So I said:

"Look, I've been here for less than an hour and I'm desperate. What am I supposed to do with that?" I showed him my packet of butter. "And over there," I pointed in the direction of the school, "how is a person supposed to live in a hovel like that?"

The young man smiled at me, and at first I thought he was making fun of me. He asked:

"You're not from around here?"

"Of course I am, I'm from the mountains just like you! I come from Val-des-Prés, I'm the new schoolteacher. In all my life I've never seen such deprivation. I've come for a few days of substitute work, and all I have is a suitcase with nothing in it. If they'd only told me it was the end of the world up here, I'd have been ready, but I don't have anything, and there's nothing, no coffee, no tea, no bread. What am I going to eat?"

"Oh, if that's all," the boy said, "I'll help you out. I'll go down and pick up a few trout for you under the pebbles."

He went down into the stream and a few moments later he was back with six or seven trout, beautiful trout, that he handed me as a gift. I gathered a few sticks of wood and went back to the school. I lit a fire and cooked up a few of them with the butter. I ate them like that and then I went to bed.

The woman who welcomed me had said: "For school, just ring the bell, the kids'll come."

So the next morning, I rang the chapel bell and waited for the children. I waited a while and even rang the bell again once or twice, but no one came, little or big. It was as if I were absolutely alone in the village and I said to myself: What kind of place did I fall into? What do I do if nobody comes? Am I among savages or what?

I made up my mind to take a walk around the village and I stopped a woman walking by with two little girls. I told her:

"You have to send these children to school."

That simple woman looked at me as if I'd dropped from the sky:

"Well, you know how children are."

I answered as vigorously as I could:

"What is that supposed to mean? School is obligatory!"

"Hmm. Well, y'know it's not a good time, they got so much work, the cows, the sheep, the hay, they're all at it."

"And those two, are they yours?"

"Well, yes."

"They're school age, both of them, you have to give them to me."

"Well, the little one's just five."

"So, you'll give them to me?"

"If I have to. You can take them along."

I went back to the schoolroom with the two little girls. I was boiling with rage and indignation: the apathy of those people was beyond me. Those two girls weren't a big catch, but it was a beginning, and I could start class.

Getting them to talk was another story; it was certainly the first time they'd been face to face with someone they didn't know. They stared at me, surly and tight-lipped, as if I were about to eat them.

"All right," I said, "we're going to start. Do you know the letters of the alphabet?"

Neither one said a word or moved a muscle. They were like a cement wall.

"Fine!"

I turned to the blackboard and drew an 'o' and a 'u' with chalk.

"You see that?" I said speaking to the littlest one, "That looks like the moon, it's an 'o' and the other one's a 'u.'"

Total silence. I started my demonstration all over and at the end I asked: "So you understand? What is it?"

And since there still wasn't any answer, I asked her:

"What do you say to the donkey when you want him to stop? Back home where I live, in Val-des-Prés, when you say 'o' the horse stops, when you say 'u' he starts off again — so what do *you* say to make him stop?"

The little girl looked at me for a moment, then she opened her mouth and let out a great big "Brrouuu."

That is the only thing I could get out of her. Outside of that one resounding "Brrouuu," neither child unclamped her lips. During recess, I realized that the little girl had told the truth, the peasants of Gourniers said "Brrouuu" to get their animals moving, it was the only word they had to stop them and to start them off again.

After recess I came back into class with my two youngsters. I wrote on the board the two syllables "vo" and "mit" and asked the bigger girl to read them for me.

"VO-MIT."

"You know what that means?"

"It's when you spits."

I sat down on my chair. I was dumbfounded. I thought: Well, they won't choke on a vocabulary overload in these parts. Then and there I gave up trying to teach them any other rudiments of language. I picked up a book and read them stories till the end of the day.

That evening, I finished my last trout in butter, and the next day, I rang the bell again. This time nobody came and I gave up the idea of hunting children down and bringing them back. Since I was to have a medical checkup and go to a teachers' conference, I packed my suitcase and left for Gap. My only alternative was to see the inspector and explain the situation.

That was how my stay in Réalon-les-Gourniers ended, for I never went back. When I told the whole story to the district inspector in Gap, he agreed with me; there was no point in sending in a substitute when all the children were committed to the autumn's work. He offered me other substitute jobs to tide me over until he could find me a regular position. As luck would have it, my first appointment was for here, in Val-des-Prés. For the first time in my life, I was going to teach in the classroom where I had learned to read and write myself. The appointment won me a certain amount of jealousy. The nastiest reaction I met was when I went to pick up the key to the school. The receptionist in the mayor's office looked at me as if she couldn't believe her ears when I explained that I wanted the key. I must say that woman drank more than was good for her, and she was pretty tight already. She kept repeating:

"The key? The key to the school? What for?"

"I've just been named as schoolteacher."

"What! You, the schoolteacher? That's impossible! It's scandalous. You think we don't know what you were doing in Paris? You were a street-walker, everybody knows that. You won't ever be our schoolteacher here, not on your life, and I won't be the one to give you the key to the school."

She slammed the door in my face, leaving me standing there in the street. This was one stinging humiliation; even though I knew the woman was an irresponsible drunk, the insult was hard to swallow. A little later the mayor and one of my uncles set things right. They gave me the key to the school and I received an apology, but I was not completely reassured. I have always been frightened of meanness and calumny because you can never predict where they will end. All the same, when I arrived at school the next day, the youngsters behaved beautifully. I couldn't be sure of that ahead of time. The class I was facing was unlike any other: these were children who had always known me, some of them used the "tu"* form when we talked, and I didn't know how they would behave with their new teacher. As it turned out, everything went nicely. When I walked in, I was greeted by the ritual "Good morning, Mademoiselle." It must be understood that in our villages respect for the schoolmaster was virtually religious. That day, the children of Val-des-Prés used the "vous" form when they spoke to me, and gave me their closest attention. From then on, I never had any problems with them.

Chapter 12 🖋

Beware
the Loose
Woman

In January my new assignment came; I was appointed substitute in La Monta, a little village at the far end of the Queyras Valley.

In 1924, the trip through the Queyras was a real expedition. The sun almost never reaches the deep, narrow corridor that we also call the Gorges du Queyras. In winter it is one of the coldest spots of the region and usually gets the most snow.

There was just one road winding around the mountain, and in that season, sleighs were the only means of transportation. The Queyras sleigh was a world unto itself; even today it makes me think of the covered wagons the American pioneers used to go west. Of course, there weren't any Indians or outlaws, but the cold and snow were appalling enemies. At any moment a blizzard or an avalanche could jeopardize the trip, and it is more than thirty-five kilometers from Guillestre to the terminus in Abriès.

For all my knowledge of the ways and customs of the Briançonnais, this was the most picturesque of journeys. The two horses advanced through the deep snow at an even pace, and from the coach we could admire the landscape at our leisure as we struck up an acquaintance and chatted. You came into contact with all sorts of people on that sleigh. In every village, we stopped at the café or the inn, and every time some people got off and new ones came on. It was an uninterrupted parade: soldiers, gendarmes, peasants, notaries,° priests, and, of course, me, the schoolteacher going off to take up her post at the far end of the valley. Everyone was in high spirits. Some knew each other and conversation went at a steady pace. I was young, naturally playful, and did my share of joking.

But what bitter cold! The sleigh was an open coach, with no roof, and people got whatever protection they could. For legs and body, you could manage — we had blankets and hot bricks — but for ears and nose, it was torture in spite of our caps and scarves. I wonder if it wasn't the biting cold that moved us to chatter like magpies. At every stop, we'd rush inside the inn for a cup of coffee or a burning hot grog. Before diving back into the cold, we'd get new hot bricks in exchange for ours that had cooled, and we set off on the next stage of the trip.

It took the whole day. Leaving Guillestre at 11:00 in the morning, we reached Abriès at nightfall. Before I left Val-des-Prés, I'd written to an old lycée° friend, Yvonne Richard. She'd had no luck; for years she tried to get her Brevet; she gave up after two or three failures and went home to live with her parents in La Monta. I attached great importance to my letter, since I didn't know anyone in the village and I understood that the room allotted me by the administration would not be set up or heated. Yvonne Richard and I had spent a lot of time together, and surely she would have taken care of the essentials.

But Abriès was not La Monta. There were still several kilometers to go. No one thought it was a good idea to travel that road at night. Besides, how could I have done it? I'd have had to find someone willing to take me. So resigning myself to a delay, I decided to find a room for the night.

At that very moment, I came face to face with a great, ungainly oaf holding the bridle of a mare almost a story high.

"Pardon, are you Mademoiselle Allais, the new schoolteacher?" he asked.

"Yes," I answered, wondering privately who he was and what he wanted.

"I have come to take you on to La Monta. I have come at the request of your friend Yvonne Richard, and with your permission, I shall load your suitcases."

The fellow took my baggage and carried it behind the mare to a kind of hut mounted on a sleigh. The mare was already something else — she was monumental, but the sleigh was outrageously comic with that plank shanty on top, its stove pipe poking out and smoking like a steamship funnel. And with all that, I had fallen in with a chatterbox.

"It's lucky that you have come now, Mademoiselle. Just one week earlier, you would have faced death in my taxi."

"Your taxi?"

"Well, yes. That is what I call it, it is my taxi-sleigh; it would be out of the question to travel in this weather any other way. It offers the most up-to-date comfort on the mountain, far more comfortable than the one you took from Guillestre. I can assure you that there is no further risk."

"Oh fine, there's no further risk."

I was puzzled. I wondered whether I wasn't dealing with some lunatic and if I could trust him. But it was nice inside the cabin with the stove roaring.

"What I mean," the fellow added as he went on getting me settled, "is that last week I was almost burned alive in there, but the roadworkers saved my skin."

"So now you say it can't happen again?"

"No, I have perfected it. It used to have just one door, and the other day, when I turned over, the taxi rolled onto the door side, and there I was, all alone with the stove smoking as hard as it could, and no way could I get out. Snow blocked up the door, and had it not been for those roadworkers, I would have ended up smoked like a fox in its den. When I rebuilt the cabin, I put in two doors, so there is no more risk — if one door gets blocked, you have the other. Let us get going. Giddyap, Long Legs!"

"Long Legs?"

"Yes, Mademoiselle, that is her name, you've seen that rump! There is not another like her for getting through soft snow, and besides she knows her road, so there is no danger of tumbling into a fissure."

"Still, you did tumble over the other day."

"Oh that. It wasn't Long Legs's fault, it was the wind."

We started out. You could not see ten feet ahead, but the fellow seemed to know the way and so did the mare. The trip took two hours and he never stopped talking. Two hours to cover the eight kilometers to La Monta. When we arrived, Yvonne Richard was waiting for me. We kissed each other and she led me to the lodging reserved for me: one room, on the small side, unpretentious but clean, and most important my friend had lit a fire and made up the bed.

La Monta does not exist any more. It is one of those villages razed and burned by the Germans in their impotent rage of 1945. Today, only the cemetery is left. Back in 1924, life in La Monta was a closed circuit, open only as much as necessary to the world below, to Abriès, but self-sufficient in the main. Its rustic economy was based on cows, sheep, potatoes, lentils, a little wood, a few pigs. Each person worked for himself and respected his neighbors. I felt comfortable right away. I'd never known such kindly people, they were the polar opposite of the peasants in Réalon or Val-des-Prés. From the first they proved obliging and straightforward, and whenever they saw me they'd come over to say: "Mademoiselle, if you need anything, don't stand on ceremony, just ask."

They sold me whatever I might need. Any time someone went down to Abriès, he stopped by first: "Mademoiselle, is there an errand I can do for you? What do you need?" Such kindness was natural in those friendly, spontaneous people, but they also must have been sensitive to my own intense need for acceptance. Almost all of them came to talk to me about their children. An Italian laborer who had settled in the region brought his son to meet me. The youngster was a strapping fifteen-year-old, a good head taller than I, and already sporting a mustache. The boy was behind the others because knowing only Italian, he'd learned almost nothing. His father came because he'd heard I spoke the language — that's true, so my two years at the Sorbonne had been good for something at least — and he wanted me to work with his son. I agreed since it was my nature to be helpful. On principle, I have always lent people a hand when I could, and there was ample opportunity in those mountains, in those villages turned in upon themselves.

I've already mentioned the respect aroused by the schoolteacher, a respect intensified by the fact that he or she was frequently the only representative of what, in all humility, I call knowledge. That is why peasants would come to the teacher for advice, but knowledge could provoke distrust as well and another authority could oppose the schoolmaster's: the priest's, for example. I shall have occasion to speak about that later, but at La Monta, I found acceptance with the whole population and, I think, affection.

While I was in the Queyras, I could not look after my father and the house. By now, the "château" was a big, empty dwelling. I had gone off sick at heart, leaving my father and Marie-Rose behind, lost and bewildered. Characteristically, my father had not said a word of complaint or reproach. In the course of the years just gone by, he had accepted the fate meted out to him and, as he grew older, he did indeed take on the dry toughness of old tree trunks struck by lightning. More than ever the soul of honor, but increasingly distant as well, he went on doing his work without faltering. My sister helped out, she was his only companion, but at twenty, Marie-Rose was beginning to strain at the leash. The day I left, she walked me to the station, and just as we were about to say goodbye, I had the impression she was going to tell me something. She never talked but I'd sensed she had problems; I even said to myself: You're worried, little one, and asked:

"Is anything wrong, Marie-Rose?"

"Oh no," she answered, "only I was thinking I'd really like to come up and spend a week with you."

"Sure, why not? Just write to let me know ahead of time."

Marie-Rose could be very sly when she had a mind to it. Ever since she was little, she'd been thoughtless, with no clear sense of responsibility in the face of life's realities. She drifted with the tide of events, but once she got an idea in her head, she could be stubborn, relentlessly dogged until she found a way to do what she wanted. So she didn't let me know — she just appeared one day in March.

"But I told you I'd come see you," she said.

"Yes, but you should have let me know ahead of time."

"Goodness!" she answered, "I felt like coming, and this way I can take cheese back to Papa — I came on the milk wagon."

To reach La Monta, she'd worked out an arrangement with the carter who went back and forth between Briançon and Ristolas. In that part of the Queyras, they made cheeses known throughout the region for their exceptional quality; they were really very good and every week the fellow came to get them for the dairy in Briançon.

"And how about Papa?" I said. "You left him alone."

"For a few days, it's not so terrible, he knows perfectly well I'm coming back."

I should have suspected something right then. But I didn't. Maybe I was too taken up with my own concerns to have an inkling. So I looked on Marie-Rose's visit as something unexpected and pleasant on the whole. It was only later, at Easter vacation, that we had it out together and I discovered that she'd come to La Monta to tell me about her problems but hadn't dared. Marie-Rose was six months pregnant and did not know which saint to turn to.

"But why didn't you tell me since that's why you came?"

"I don't know, I couldn't, it was too hard to say. Anyway . . ."

"Anyway what? It's too late to do something about it now."

"But there's Jacques."

That is, the Jacques who was responsible for her pregnancy, and Marie-Rose had only one thought in her head: to marry him. I was against it; Marie-Rose had no reason to expect anything good from that young man, but she persisted as only she could, always finding arguments in her efforts to convince us:

"You'll see," she'd tell us, "I'll make him over the way I want as soon as he leaves his house; he'll change, I know he will."

I didn't believe those fine words; in my opinion, he was a bad lot and that's the way he'd stay. My father was much more sensitive to my sister's arguments; for him, a son-in-law, a man in the house, were everything, and besides, there was the shame. It was my turn to reason with him:

"Since the baby's there, we have to keep it and raise it, but why let her get into such a bad marriage? She'll suffer all her life — she's better off an unwed mother who's happy than a woman tied to a drunk. And shame, if there is any shame, is no one's business but ours. If you think that brat is capable of taking care of the farm, you're wrong, and if we need a man in the house, he's not the one."

My father listened to me. He seemed to understand and accept what I was telling him, but I sensed his vulnerability. For him, for a man with his ideas, an unwed mother was unbearable. Nevertheless, throughout that Easter vacation, I was so categorically firm that I was sure there would never be a wedding. The baby, yes: it would be a little Allais boy or girl; the husband, no. When I left for La Monta, it looked as if the matter was settled once and for all.

After those few days in Val-des-Prés, I returned to the little community of La Monta the way you return to a second family. Teaching school was a real pleasure for me; I had about twenty pupils between the ages of five and fourteen, divided into four groups. Once I finished correcting papers and preparing lessons, I had a lot of free time outside the classroom.

Idleness is the worst problem for people without ties to the place they live. I couldn't spend all my time in my room reading and dreaming, I had to keep busy, use up my energy, so I offered my services at every opportunity. In a village like La Monta it was hard for a schoolteacher to avoid being involved in people's lives. That's what I liked, socializing, the pleasure of knowing this one and that one, talking with them and comforting those in need. When that happened, my peasant instincts took over, I wanted to work with them.

There was a pupil in my class whose mother was expecting a baby. She had five youngsters already, and she was still so young. . . . She was killing herself to make ends meet, ruining her health because she didn't stop from morning to night. I couldn't resist, and one day I told her:

"You know, I think I could help you out, I have some time on Thursdays° and Sundays. And if you'd like, I could watch the flock or mow the hay for you."

My offer surprised her. It wasn't in line with local custom and she hesitated slightly before she answered. She finally agreed, and Thursdays I went off with the flock. I liked those days out in the fields; those hours close to nature with the flowers, the wind, and the animals took me back to my early years. Other times, I helped the husband with the haying. He'd get the *trappes* ready — they were net bags made with heavy twine — while I raked up whatever was left. It did me a world of good and that woman spoiled me like crazy. She insisted on paying me back, and made up bags of food the likes of which I had never tasted — she cooked me the regional specialties, dishes the way they do them in the Queyras, much subtler than anything we knew in our valley. Accustomed as I was to my father's sausage and lentils, I thought it was marvelous.

In the depths of winter, I decided to organize an evening of entertainment at school. I persuaded the whole village to pitch in and I worked like the devil to make it turn out perfect. The mayor himself made a round table and a few props, and all the inhabitants of La Monta, young and not so young, helped prepare the festivities. It was a total success. The peasants were so delighted that the following week I had to start all over for those who'd been unable to attend the performance. We'd acted little sketches, and every one of the young people had a part, not just the schoolchildren, but all the local young people, my friends and Yvonne Richard's, and in the evening I brought over my record player and records and we danced.

The very next day the priest went all over the village raising a hue and cry, telling everyone it was scandalous, and that the school festival was a pagan celebration that had ended with an orgy. Going from door to door, he threatened to refuse absolution to any of his flock who allowed their daughters to frequent the loose woman. The loose woman was me. Most people just laughed. The priest's influence in this half-Catholic, half-Protestant village was not the same as before the war but, all the same, he was jealous of my success with the festival and he did his best to discredit me in people's eyes.

In July I had to leave. I packed my suitcases and said my goodbyes. One last time I walked through the sloping streets of the village to greet the men, women, and children who had shared my life for six months: my first six months as a schoolteacher in a mountain village.

Chapter
13

Three Stories
Plus
One More

1910. The scene takes place during recess in the Val-des-Prés elementary school. Charlotte and Félicie are playing in a corner of the courtyard. Charlotte is seven, Félicie is eight, they're best friends and almost always together. Suddenly Armand appears. He's a churlish boy from the older pupils' section and he commands respect with threats and blows. He heads toward the little girls and yells: "Charlotte." His hand is raised, and in his hand a stone — a heavy, sharp-edged flintstone — about to be thrown.

Catching sight of him, Charlotte tells Félicie: "Félicie, Armand means to hit me with a stone, you get in front, he's got nothing against you, he won't throw it at you."

Reasons are beside the point. Félicie doesn't argue, she takes up a position between her friend and the boy. Seeing the maneuver, Armand gets more threatening, and tells her:

"Shove off, Félicie, because if you don't beat it, you'll get it."

"Why? I haven't done a thing to you," says Félicie.

Armand threw his stone. Félicie sees it coming in time to turn away so she won't be disfigured; the stone strikes her from behind on the crown of her skull. It hits so hard that the little girl collapses. She's bleeding profusely and when she runs her hand over her head, she feels through her hair the hole made by the stone. There won't be a doctor or anything, and Félicie will barely escape a rebuke for goading a boy. The teacher will cut away the hair around the wound as best he can and he'll improvise a bandage. After a while Felicie's wound healed as best it could. It might just as easily have become infected.

1919. Julie is twenty. She's pregnant and forced to get married under the worst conditions. Unfortunately she comes from a family of atheists, her father has never given her any religious instruction, neither mass, nor catechism. Under pressure from her in-laws, Julie is obliged to make her first communion to get married. Every day, she must walk through the village under the wing of her mother-in-law to be, and face people's jeering looks and mocking smiles. Every day she makes her way into the presbytery to listen to catechism from monsieur the priest. For Julie there cannot be a worse public humiliation. For that is certainly what it is: watching her walk by and laughing at her is a way for everyone to satisfy some old, private grudge. Julie is alone against everyone, it is not even a matter of saving face, it is nothing but a farce.

1924. Someone tells me: "Talk about the fuss she made! Why she managed to stir up the whole village. Think about it, what with brewing all that time, it had to burst sooner or later. Makes you wonder why she married him in the first place if she throws him out when he's in the house, or won't let him in when he's outside. She's all the time threatening him with her broom handle, makes you think he's not a man but a real wet hen—it's the world upside down. Still, she came by it honestly. Her old unlicked bear of a father killed that nice wife of his, terrorized her till she went stark raving mad. The daughter is his spitting image, only worse, since even *he* pulls in his horns when he's around her. She's really not afraid of anything. That evening she didn't want to let her husband into the house. She yelled so loud the whole neighborhood could hear:

"'Get lost,' was what she said, 'I'm fed up with your half-wit's face, and I'm warning you if you come in here I'll break your back.'

"As usual, he knuckled under and didn't say a word; he was worse than a battered, beaten dog. She wrapped up the scene by slamming the door in his face. He was sure to spend the night outside. The first thing he tried was to go persuade his brother to come over. He did, and knocking on the door he called out to that Josephine woman. When she saw who it was, she jumped down his throat:

"'What are *you* doing here? Go mind your own business! Why help that fathead brother of yours? You better watch what's going on in your own house. You with ten kids, and maybe not one of them yours.'

"*He* didn't let out a peep either, he couldn't calm her down and just went away.

"For his second try, the husband brought in his wife's father, and so the old bear made the next attempt to reason with her. Even that lout thought it was out of the question for a wife to keep her husband out of his home. But she was unimpressed and she didn't leave him with a leg to stand on either.

"'Who do you think I am?' says she. 'Don't take me for your old lady. *I* know what I want, and no revolting old man like you is going to come around and tell *me* what to do.'

"She yelled so loud the whole village knew everything. Her voice carries, and her husband kept at a good distance the whole time, leaving the other two to negotiate for him, but since it didn't work, he came forward to say:

"'You got no right to act like that, it's my house and I got the law on my side, I'm going for the gendarmes, and then we'll see who has the last word.'

"'So go get your gendarmes! You think they'll scare me? You'll see the welcome I'll have waiting. You can bring the Pope too for all I care.'

"The third person he brought was the mayor.

"'Josephine,' he says, 'you have no right to keep your husband out; open the door and let him in.'

"'Humph.'

"'Josephine, you're making a public nuisance of yourself. I am asking you to stop.'

"'Shut up,' was her answer. 'What's it to you anyway? Who do you think you are, talking to me like that?'

"'I'm the mayor.'

"'Mayor of what? *I* don't know you, so go put on your sash of office if you're the mayor; then we'll see.'

"He went home to put on his sash. Can you imagine such a story in a place like this, with people who'd been at school together! When he came back wearing the sash over his shoulder, she went on:

"'Just look at the representative of the law! Well it's certainly well represented by a freak like you!'

"'Josephine, will you stop this disgraceful behavior!'

"'What are you talking about! What disgrace? You're the son and grandson of men who were hanged, so you want me to give you rope to hang yourself, don't you! You want me to send it to you, or do you have it all ready? You collect rope in your family, so go hang yourself with your sash and leave other people alone.'

"It was so funny that no one gave another thought to the husband who was still expecting things to be worked out for him. But old Josephine wouldn't hear a word of it and faced them all down, so he couldn't do anything but put up with it."

1925. One day a farm woman from Casset goes to tend her poultry in the coop. It's Félicie. She meets three men on the way who laugh and make fun of her. One of them is Armand the cheesemaker, the dreadful boy who once hit her with a flint that left a permanent scar on her crown. Félicie wonders why those three fools made fun of her. It doesn't take her long to find out; scattering her mash, she notices that her three finest ducks are gone. She retraces her steps immediately, the three men are still there, insolent and mocking. Furious, Félicie says:

"What's so funny? Are you the ones who stole my ducks? I'm afraid the answer's yes."

"Us? Of course not," Armand answers. "When do you suppose we did it?"

"Why, last night; you were seen, and now I can put two and two together — last night, someone saw you through the window, one keeping watch on the road, the other above, while the third must have been doing in the ducks."

"Félicie, you don't know what you're talking about. You gotta have proof."

"A fat lot of good it'll do you, because it won't bring you luck. I don't want to know which one of you three set it up, all I know is that he'll die before the year is out."

Félicie doesn't know why she said such a thing. It's anger; she's angry enough to say anything that comes into her head.

Several months later, Armand's body is found, his skull fractured in two places. He's wearing his beret, and his bicycle stands beside him against a rock.

No one ever found out exactly what happened. The accepted explanation was accidental death. But how did the accident happen? On the one hand are the facts, on the other, conjecture. The facts are, first of all, that the cheesemaker was found by his son, that the son loaded him onto his cart and brought him home. The facts are also that it must have been ten o'clock at night and that the cheesemaker's wife and son waited until he stopped breathing to notify the mayor at three in the morning. In the meantime — seven hours, that is — the cheesemaker lay stretched out on his bed, with his wife on one side and his son on the other. No one was informed except a doctor at the end, and all he could do when he came was certify the death and grant permission for burial.

Theoretically, the case was closed at that point. Armand the cheesemaker had died accidentally, in accordance with Félicie's prediction. However, when the mayor saw the condition of the corpse at three in the morning, he was suspicious. He scratched his head and asked himself some questions. There seemed to be no explanation for the double head wound, but he didn't say anything either; he respected the doctor's conclusions and did not alert the gendarmes. As Armand's cousin, he was the one to go order the coffin in Briançon the next day. Since he forgot to bring the dead man's measurements, he called the village, and as luck would have it, Félicie picked up the phone. The mayor asked her to go to the dead man's house for the measurements.

When she arrived, right there were the two men who'd been with Armand the day the three ducks were stolen. Félicie went in, she crossed herself and she made the sign of the cross over the dead man as custom decrees; only then did she look the two accomplices straight in the eye. The two men were as white as the plaster wall behind them. Félicie didn't say a word, she asked for the measurements, looked at the cheesemaker's two friends one last time and left just as she had come.

The conjectures were of an entirely different nature. No one really liked Armand, he was known as an ugly customer and no one missed him. But that didn't make anybody swallow whole the explanation of death by accident. The very next day, when people in the village talked about the wife and son, some of them said to each other:

"But what's going to happen to them now? Picking the fellow up on the road with his head fractured in two places, not calling anyone, not telling the neighbors — there's going to be an investigation. And things are going to come out!"

Everyone thought the death was suspicious, but nothing came of it. The doctor had certified the death as accidental, he'd signed the burial permit, there was nothing more to do. The cheesemaker was buried, and the two accomplices thought Félicie was a witch, for her prediction had come true word for word: one of the three thieves had died before the year was out.

Such incidents were not infrequent, I mean that kind of petty theft; fortunately not all of them ended so tragically. Even so, village relationships were often marked by that ancient primitivism. We spoke of the days before the First War as a bygone age. The older generation was aging, young people were breaking free, and technological progress was imperceptibly raising the standard of living. But the change was hard to notice in the course of everyday life. Habits and customs acquired over the centuries were as strong as the old hemp shirts we used to make, they withstood the wear and tear of time.

For example, the story of the mayor, the business of hanged man and son of hanged man — it was true but, still, it's preposterous, I mean you really had to be retrograde to mention it to him. Nonetheless, the mayor was very careful. When he decided to marry, he searched the whole region for a woman who had hanged men in her family too, and he did find her. Where, I don't remember anymore, but he did marry a woman whose father and grandfather had also been hanged. He went to all that trouble so that neither of them could ever taunt the other about his forebears. And it was like that for everything, for harvest, money, illness.

There was a peasant here dying of uremia. When I say dying, I mean he was on his feet until the day he died, but the doctors had given him up. The man had built up urea, six grams worth, and he thought he'd make it. He came to see me and said:

"Émilie, you'll come to the doctor with me. They say I'm an alcoholic, but have you ever seen me drunk?"

What answer could I give him? I said:

"No, I've never seen you drunk, but I have seen you take some healthy swigs."

"Émilie, they say I'm alcoholic, you have to come and tell them you never saw me drunk."

Indeed, I never had seen him tottering on his feet, but he drank his four liters of wine every day, supposedly because he did hard labor. He drank a liter with breakfast, another at lunch, another at four o'clock, and the last one in the evening. In his opinion, he was never drunk and he did not allow you to scold him for it, still less did he let you say it made him sick. For him that was inconceivable.

With six grams of urea he could not make it. The doctors said they had never seen a case like that, it was a record, but he didn't see it that way, he wanted to live. To get rid of what he called bad blood, the best thing he came up with was to have all his teeth pulled. It was as if he were crazy, he did not want to die and he said to himself: They'll pull out my teeth and it'll bleed; it'll bleed so much that I'll get rid of all my bad blood. I don't drink anymore, so my blood'll be like new and I'll stay alive.

It was no use saying a century had gone by between the beginning of the war and after, there were a good many things left to change, and that was precisely what concerned me at the time: the role I was to play with the children in regions like ours. It was hard to develop precise ideas, but I thought it was essential to try. Above all, I had to open their eyes, topple all those old customs to teach them to lead a different kind of life, release them from alcoholism, and alert them to the lies and foolishness of church and state.

Ever since I was a little girl, I'd wanted so much to be a schoolteacher that I had time to become aware of the importance of my mission. In my view, teachers are responsible for the whole of society. They are the ones who open youngsters' minds, who show them what is right and what is wrong. That responsibility was mine now, and I had to take on its consequences. I felt sufficiently brave and patient to achieve these goals because, when you have children around, it is not enough to teach them to read, write, and count; you must also teach them to read between the lines, that is, to reflect, to think for themselves, and that is not always easy. The main thing is for a child in a class, no matter who he is, to feel loved and respected, to feel that his teacher — man or woman — does not take him for a number or a clown, and that everything asked of him is for his own good. Given these conditions, a great deal can happen, but you need love to make it work. Without love, you are better off not teaching, you are better off in some other line of work. For me, it was a vocation.

And besides, there weren't only the children, there were the parents, too, and the grandparents. They were the ones who held up progress and kept the new ideas from taking hold. At the time, I already thought: "When you have the children, you have the parents," and it's true. It is the children who bring different ideas into the family; even if the ideas are not accepted immediately, they make their way, and gradually the children take the lead.

There were still so many things to do, so many old ideas and habits to air out. The patriarchy, primogeniture, the submissiveness of women, debasement by overwork, alcoholism, beliefs, superstitions, and many other things. It was up to me to teach them all that, and I was determined to fight if need be. I already knew that I would never have them sing "Wave little flag" or even "The Marseillaise," that battle hymn; I knew I would never tell any cock and bull stories about splendid battles, heroism, and saintliness. There was just one thing for me to do: open their minds, so that they might transform their lives and enjoy greater well-being, so they might emerge from their isolation and their alienation. That is what I wanted to teach them; I told myself that this, and this alone, was the influence I sought to exercise in the region.

That is how I spent the summer that year: living in the village, working like a peasant, and reflecting on my teacher's craft. In June, Marie-Rose gave birth to a little girl we named Marie. And so Marie-Rose was an unwed mother. My father endured it like Christ bearing His Cross. It was yet another ordeal for him. My sister fooled her family, and me first of all. At the very time we thought she'd calmed down, she went on seeing her Jacques Mercier in secret. She gave us to understand that she'd broken with him once and for all, but at night when we were in bed she would rise and go meet him. When I realized what was happening, there were tears and gnashing of teeth. At such times, Marie-Rose would promise the sun, moon, and stars, but then she'd do exactly as she pleased. As they say, she was going her own way, and no one, not even my father or I, could make her deviate one whit.

Chapter 14 ⟨⟨⟨⟩

One
of Their
Own

In 1924, I was assigned to Puy-Saint-Vincent on a provisional basis. When I went back not so long ago, I was shocked. People had told me there'd been changes, of course, but in my wildest imagination, I would not have guessed to what degree. The little mountain village I had known did not exist any longer. Like La Monta, it had been struck off the map, but not for the same reasons or by the same people. Ski lifts disfigured the landscape now; it was invaded by chalets and apartment houses, all of them ugly. A disaster. Vainly I searched that soulless decor for a few traces of the village I had known, and where I had come to teach fifty years before. There were scant vestiges of the past. All the old houses had been remodeled, the walls had been given a fresh coat of paint, the doors and windows made over with cement angles added, and the communal oven torn down. Looking very carefully, I just about managed to recognize a few old doors, or a few stone walls preserved by some miracle. The Puy-Saint-Vincent of my youth had disappeared, only to be replaced by what tourist brochures describe as "An Ultra-Modern Winter Resort."

Not only the village had changed. The people had changed too. In 1924, the peasants of Puy-Saint-Vincent were indeed poor. They had very little arable land, and they worked that little "like a garden," that is, with extraordinary care. They called it their truffle beds; for example, with potatoes, they planted the seed tubers very close together, and cared for them as if they were flowers. Every square centimeter counted. When I came back, all that was forgotten, it was not peasants I met but merchants and shopkeepers.

Meadows, pastures, fields — sold to promoters. All those people who had never seen more money than the strict minimum for survival had become nouveaux riches, solely interested in setting up displays and running restaurants and hotels.

What a change! It takes a leap in time to talk about Puy-Saint-Vincent the way I knew it. I think the poorer people are, the more generous they are; in any case, such was my experience the year I lived in that village.

Their mentality was completely different from what you met among the peasants of the Queyras, and even more from what you found in Val-des-Prés. I am convinced it was related to the extremely humble circumstances of their lives, for — I repeat — the poorer people are the better they are.

Their kindness and generosity were innate. What better illustration could I find than my memory of the pies they'd make up, and the king-size portions they'd bring me. They had a communal oven, and in contrast to our practice in Val-des-Prés, they kept it going the year round. Every day someone baked bread, and immense pies, too, as big as tables: cabbage pies, apple pies, potato pies. Each time, they brought me a wedge carved out of that huge mass; it was hot, it was fresh, and I had it for lunch. Obviously, I told myself, you don't have a right, you shouldn't take unless you give in return; it wasn't the thing in itself or how much it was worth, it was the gesture. So I did what I could: boxes of crackers, packages of figs, chocolate bars, anything I could lay my hands on. It was the children who came most of the time. They were so happy to present me with their gift! I'd say: "Here, since you brought me that, take some madeleines for snack time," and the youngster would go away delighted. Eventually, people without children came by too. Not sure how to go about it, they'd say awkwardly: "Oh, by the way, we know you like this, they say everybody brings you some, so we thought we would too." It was beautiful, and every time it brought tears to my eyes.

The peasants of Puy-Saint-Vincent had adopted me as one of their own. I must say that my arrival in the village had something to do with it. Puy-Saint-Vincent is located about thirty kilometers from Val-des-Prés, on the other side of Briançon. To reach my new post, I chose the cheapest form of transportation: mule and wagon. On the appointed day, I got up with the sun and loaded my two-wheel cart by myself. A mattress, a spring, a stove, a table, two chairs and my personal belongings comprised my whole fortune — enough for a person living alone. So I set out, helping the "miaule" pull uphill, and when I reached Puy-Saint-Vincent and knocked on the mayor's door, I had made an impression, as they say. A man opened the door, and looked at me without quite understanding what was going on.

"You are the mayor?" I said.

"Well, yes," the old fellow replied, and he couldn't stop looking in amazement from me to the wagon and back.

"I'm the new schoolteacher, and I'm moving in," and since he just stood there speechless with astonishment, I added: "I have my appointment letter with me if you'd like to see it."

"Oh, it's not that," he told me. "It's not that I don't believe you. But it's the first time I've ever seen a teacher arrive with all her things, her mule, and a whip in her hand just like a man."

"Well, I'm a peasant, you know, I've been doing it since I was little."

The mayor kept on staring at me. His look had changed and there was a hint of admiration in his eyes.

"A peasant!" he said as if the idea were inconceivable. "So where are you from, then?"

"I come from Val-des-Prés, in the Clarée Valley."

"For goodness sake! And you left when?"

"This morning. I left this morning and now I have to plan on getting back, I have to take care of the 'miaule' and unload my things."

"Oh no you're not, you're going to come in and have a bite with us, and I'll take care of the rest. I'll have your mule looked after and your wagon unloaded."

From then on, I was adopted. The mayor took me around, showing me the school, and telling me about the village, and he was so insistent that I agreed to have lunch with him and his family before starting back.

Those people were flabbergasted and they were proud. For the first time the schoolteacher was one of their own. I was a peasant like them, I knew how to work the soil, and I was familiar with their problems. Up till then, the teacher had been a creature from another world to those poor and humble people, often the daughter of a civil servant who was welcomed with respect but treated with distant politeness. For the first time a young woman from their world would teach their children. I remember telling the mayor that I wouldn't have starved to death if I hadn't been a teacher, I knew how to grow lettuce, dig up potatoes, and plow the mountainside. They were proud of that, I think, they gloried in it right away. They gave me their friendship straight off. That is how my year at Puy-Saint-Vincent began.

Chapter 15 ~~~

Fatback
and Wine-Soaked
Bread

What shall I tell you about the year I spent in Puy-Saint-Vincent? I had a class of about twenty pupils divided into five levels. All of them worked hard. Peasant children usually study hard, but you must not push them, and you must make them understand that they are learning to read and write for their own good. There too, I think, the fact that I was a child of the mountain, a peasant's daughter, led me to find the right words. I'd met enough distrust and lack of understanding with respect to school, I'd fought my brothers and sisters, even my father, for the right to go on studying, so it was natural for me to speak to these children about potatoes, so that I could get them to take history and math seriously. I'd tell them education was not intended to bore them, but to give them a minimum of knowledge, simple things their parents hadn't had the chance to learn. Those youngsters didn't know any more of the world than the end of the road in front of their houses and the shape of a goat's udder, but when they understood what I meant, they showed exceptional qualities.

At the back of the class, way off to the side, was a little girl all the others rejected because she was so covered with lice and nits. I had to do something about her. The child was an orphan living with her grandmother, a woman over eighty and practically blind. I set out to find her and talk about Valérie. My idea was to ask her to do something to get rid of the little girl's lice, but in the face of such misery, I offered my own services.

"You know Valérie is covered with lice, she can't go on that way. Would you like me to see about it?"

"Oh, I really would," the old woman said. "You see the condition I'm in, without my eyes and no one to help — it's hard enough to raise her, so yes, I would."

I began with what we'd always done in those circumstances. I bought some Marie-Rose lotion and twice a day, every day, I rubbed it into Valérie's hair and wrapped her head. But there were so many and they were so tough that the Marie-Rose lotion was useless. Still more radical methods were in order. I said to Valérie:

"Valérie, you'll be very brave. We've tried this lotion for several days now, but it's useless; it's time for extreme measures. I'm going to cut off your hair, it's nothing at all, you'll see, and it grows back very fast."

The little girl began to whimper.

"Don't!" I said. "Come on now, let me get on with it, and as soon as your hair starts growing back, I'll set it for you; you'll see, I'll tie ribbons on, you'll be very pretty; you won't have those bugs on you and you'll get your friends back."

I sheared her bald. Of course she had to put up with her classmates' teasing and jeers when she came to class without her hair. But that didn't last long, people get tired of everything, and Valérie's hair began to grow back. She became a normal little girl again, she got her friends back, returned to her seat among the other children, and since she had a pleasing personality, many of them sought her out.

Shortly after I settled down in Puy-Saint-Vincent, while I was still getting to know the ways of the community, a terrible fire broke out right near the school during the night, and within minutes the house was reduced to a blazing mass. It belonged to a widower with three children. The whole village rushed over, everyone trying to limit the scope of the disaster, and I went along to lend a hand. But what could we do without equipment and firemen, with only a bucket brigade from the fountain to the house? By the early hours of the morning, there was nothing left of the farm but charred ruins.

I was dead-tired and soaked to the skin when I got home, and there was barely time to change my clothes before I opened the school. The whole village was upset, not even the children had slept much, and there were those three orphans without a home or anything else.

The inspector's visit was scheduled for precisely that day, and I decided to change the normal lesson plan. No dictation, no math, just practical tasks. All the pupils set to work: boys and girls turned out shirts and pants for the three youngsters who had lost everything in the fire. When the inspector arrived, the class looked like a beehive in full swing. I said:

"As you see, Inspector, I set the program aside this morning, first of all because I'm worn out from carting buckets of water during the night and I didn't have time to prepare classes; besides, it seemed to me that even if you were coming, my first duty was to meet the immediate needs of those farm children."

"Fine, fine," the inspector said, "I see you know how to take advantage of a situation to develop a sense of solidarity in these children. It is a very good example for the community, but still, Mademoiselle Allais, do a little bit of your lesson for me so I can get some idea of the level of these children."

It wasn't hard to improvise a lesson, I was used to it. The youngsters answered my questions: they may not have slept enough, but they had lively minds, and the unexpected lesson at tables cluttered with bits of material, spools of thread, and boxes of buttons and scissors was fun for them, so they outdid themselves and won the inspector over.

Winter went by the way it did everywhere in the mountain villages, with long evening veillées. Outside of my classes, I looked after this one and that one, the sick or the old, as my own way of paying back their kindness and thanking them for their consideration. They often came to ask me for advice, and in return, they invited me into their families.

The hardest part was being so far from home. I was thirty kilometers from Val-des-Prés, and my father was pretty much alone after Marie-Rose got married. The moment I had time, I was off on my bicycle. The road I took was uphill for kilometers on end — sixty kilometers between Saturday and Sunday, that's something to reckon with. I did it for him; he needed me more and more, he was like a child counting the days between him and Thursday and Saturday. I picked up my tools again in Val-des-Prés, to help out in the fields, and for a rest, I looked after his clothes and did the cooking.

In March I reached the decision to bring Marie-Rose's baby to live with me. My sister was pregnant again and the home she'd set up with Jacques Mercier limped along on three hooves, as they say. The little one was nine months old, and what with the spring season and the farm work, it suited everybody for me to keep her until vacation. It didn't take me long to make up my mind, and I didn't give it a lot of thought either; I said: "All right, I'll take her," and I left for Puy-Saint-Vincent with the baby in my arms.

The first person I met on the train was the principal of my old school, a friend I saw from time to time. When she saw me with the cherub, she upbraided me bitterly:

"You've got to be crazy, Émilie! Don't you see what you're doing, taking your niece up there?"

"Why do you say that?"

"Émilie, you do everything backward: most of your colleagues manage to get rid of their baby if they have one; their mother takes it in, or their parents-in-law, so they're free to work. With you it's the exact opposite; you take your sister's child, that is a burden and you don't even realize it."

"Yes, I do! At Puy-Saint-Vincent there's my neighbor who looks after children; she already has two from Public Assistance, that's what she lives on, I'll let her have this one too."

"Émilie, if that were the only thing, but . . ."

"But what?"

"Well, that way you will never get married. What do you expect people in Puy to think and say? You can give them any story you like, tell them she is your niece — they will not believe you, to them you will be an unwed mother. They will all say you are making up any old story but it is *your* child all the same."

"They're nice people, you know."

"Nice or not, it makes no difference; you will find out whether I am wrong."

As it turned out, she was not wrong; good or not, that's the way people are, they can't help themselves, they insist on seeing evil even when it's not there. The peasants of Puy-Saint-Vincent were no different from the rest of humanity. I grant it was hard to understand how a young teacher like me would undertake to raise a child, and that's what they said among themselves:

"She's a good teacher, can't fault her on that, the best we've ever had around here — only she wants us to swallow the story she's raising her sister's daughter. It doesn't hang together, the little girl's hers — if not, why would she take her?"

That's what they said about me. It wasn't especially mean, I couldn't have cared less about the gossip, and most of all I was not afraid of losing a fiancé or a good match, that was the last of my worries — still, the principal had foreseen it all.

So I organized my life. During the day my neighbor watched the baby. Her house abutted the schoolyard, and I went to see them at recess. What a sight met my eyes one day, among the most extraordinary ever: she had two youngsters stretched out on a double bed, each holding a piece of fatback in one hand, and a crust of wine-soaked bread in the other. Both of them were sucking with all their might, a pull on the fatback, a pull on the wine-flavored crust. Fatback makes you thirsty and wine puts you to sleep, everybody knows that; but never, with my own eyes, had I seen parents put that strange remedy into practice. The two youngsters seemed to like it, but they weren't the only ones; they were covered with flies, not just their hands, but their faces and all around them — a terrifying sight. I called old Madame Robin over:

"Don't you realize the condition these children are in with fatback and the wine on their bread? It'll make them stupid and dull, not to mention the flies and disease."

She lifted her hands, taking heaven as her witness:

"My dear young lady, just think about it, I've got my work to do, there's the garden, the soup, the laundry, and if I don't get them quiet, I won't ever have time to do my work in peace. You have to get them to sleep somehow."

"And the flies?"

"Don't worry, the youngsters are healthy."

There was nothing to be done. It was a primitive measure, but my neighbor thought it worked, and that was the only thing that mattered.

Chapter
16 ❦

The Story
of
Marie-Rose

Summer 1925. The world goes on breaking out of its old skin. Not a day goes by that doesn't add to the evidence that the old world is nothing more than a memory. These are the "Mad Years," the Roaring Twenties. Everything is changing: styles, customs, technical knowledge. Electricity turns up in thatched cottages, the radio brings us news from all over the world, cars and trucks begin to streak along the roads. Telephones, aviation, medication — technology is taking giant steps in almost every domain. In the service of war, human ingenuity had invented a thousand and one ways to kill efficiently; but with incendiary bombs, tracer or explosive bullets, mines, tanks, shrapnel, poison gases, and other such things useless now, progress was graciously consenting to turn its attention to peacetime.

The "madness" peculiar to Val-des-Prés, however, remained unchanged. For three months of the year, our peasants fought time and the elements. Plowing, sowing, weeding, harrowing, hoeing, reaping, garnering were tasks from time immemorial, endlessly repeated, with not a moment's respite for anyone. For peasants, progress was still far in the distance.

Once again I swapped the red pencil for the spade and the house took on a semblance of life again for the space of a summer. But there was no use trying to fool myself, things were going from bad to worse since Marie-Rose went to live with Jacques Mercier. Each passing day bore out the fears I had expressed. Clearly, Marie-Rose was setting herself up for an impossible life. In the course of the months and years to come, all of us suffered the consequences of the drama she would live. That is why it is hard to talk about myself without telling the story of Marie-Rose.

Ever since she was small, she'd been rather like quicksilver, a good little thing, but her head was in the clouds and money ran through her fingers like water through a sieve. Maybe that explains how she came under the spell of Jacques Mercier. His reputation was already established. He was young, but it was no secret that he drank and was a threat to his parents. Rotten clear through — and *he* was the man she had to take up with!

They slept together, she got pregnant, and right away Marie-Rose insisted on getting married. It didn't much matter that she was marrying an irresponsible loafer, that he was far from the ideal man — the son-in-law my father needed to take the fortunes of house and farm in hand again. Marie-Rose couldn't have cared less, she was too thoughtless to worry about what would or would not hurt my father and she did not let up until she got what she wanted.

To hear her, our suspicions of her so-called "fiancé" were inappropriate. She displayed astonishing strength and ideas in the arguments she relentlessly devised to persuade us. According to her, Jacques Mercier was every bit as good as other men. She was convinced that he would change, that his parents were to blame if he was as easily aroused and violent as people said, and that *she* could turn him into a peasant, keep him from drink, and make him gentle as a lamb.

Meanwhile, Jacques Mercier was going around the countryside, telling anyone who would listen that Old Man Allais had better pay up if he wanted him to marry his daughter. Acting on the advice of one of those pillars of the bistro who whispered in his ear: "You can tell that Joseph Allais you'll only take his daughter if he gives you a dowry of 50,000 francs; believe me, he'll have to come through to save the family honor," he had the nerve — and the stupidity — to come to the "château" with his father and make his request.

"I'm willing to marry Marie-Rose, but it will take a dowry of 50,000."

My father didn't have a cent, so he refused, but the guy had the gall to ask, and that didn't bode well either. But what could we do? Marie-Rose could be underhanded and stubborn. That's the way she was, she never took advice, from either my father or me. Besides, she was in love with that man and behaved like an animal following its instincts; when I tried to reason with her, she'd answer that "*it* hadn't been made to measure oats with and that tools, if you had them, were there to be used."

So they were married. A backstreet marriage, as they say. They didn't even let me know.

They moved into the family house with my father, and violent, unpredictable quarrels erupted immediately. Gradually life became impossible, not just for them but also for my father who could not stand their lethargy and their dissension. When Marie-Rose gave birth for the second time, the situation went from bad to worse. The child was born — a little girl; they sent for the midwife the way people always do, and without a moment's hesitation, she said: "This little one won't do." That meant: She won't survive. The baby was in fact purplish-blue, with ice-cold legs and arms, and it hardly moved. The local midwife added: "The child's circulation isn't working, better baptize her right away."

They went looking for someone to give her holy water — I don't know who, because even then there wasn't a priest in Val-des-Prés any longer — and they baptized her with the name Jeanne. That night, the little girl's condition did not improve so Marie-Rose took her into bed to warm her, and when she woke up the next morning, the infant was dead.

When the priest came at last, the only thing he could think of to tell my sister was: "You smothered her in your sleep." How can a person say such things? Especially a priest. Marie-Rose was a believer and she could not have been more upset.

My expectations were borne out. Jacques Mercier really was impossible, a malicious man who took pleasure in doing evil for the merest trifle. Besides, he said the first thing that came into his head, spreading false rumors like the one about his elder daughter not being his, or that he'd been had by the Allais family; he took every opportunity to sow discord. For her part, my sister was not equal to influencing him for the better; on the contrary, she was increasingly subject to his threats and influence. If the war between them had at least been total, perhaps they might have broken up, but when they weren't having a row, they led a rip-roaring life together, and then they were thick as thieves at a fair. My father suffered terribly from the way things were. The "château" did not belong to him any more. Every morning, he'd call them to work with him but they didn't answer; they stayed in bed making merry and sleeping off their hangovers. One day he went into their room, furious, and said: "Come on now, you have to get up!" It was the first time he'd taken the liberty of entering their room. On the floor around the bed were bottles of wine. He realized — he who never wanted to think ill of people — that Jacques Mercier had moved in with him to drink his wine and loot his house at leisure, using my sister as security and nothing more. My father was desperate.

"Émilie," he said, "I can't get them to do anything and I don't know what to do."

"Papa," I told him, "don't worry, they don't have to stay here. All we have to do is move them to La Draille where they can live the way they want."

La Draille was at the far end of the village, the house where my father was born — farm, sheepfold, and house all in one — and it had been empty for years. They moved in, and lived somehow or other. They didn't have the minimum necessities and they had nothing of their own. My father paid for a mule, he bought the few indispensable tools for working the soil, and since he did not have one sou left in his purse, I bought the strict minimum required for the youngsters. Rather than give them money, I would bring sugar, chocolate, dried figs, all of them nourishing. Jacques Mercier was furious: "We don't need the stuff she brings, she can keep it," he'd say. "We're big enough to know what we need, and if she wants to help, all she has to do is give us money."

Money, indeed! The little they had went for wine or the bistro. The situation was increasingly beyond my sister. He beat her and threatened her to the point that she often left home with her daughter and took refuge with us.

They were separated for a while, and then they had a third child, a boy, and started living together again. Once more they settled into their rip-roaring life, wine, sleeping late in the morning, and work, nothing that made sense. The situation deteriorated so badly that my sister fell sick. The life he led her into was too chaotic to endure. Marie-Rose drooped, and more and more often erupted into fits of violence. Reacting against her own persecution, she would act out, saying: He did it to me, now it's my turn, I'll show I can take care of myself. In a sense, she was asserting her own existence and it was a way of saying no. She was young, barely twenty-three, and she wasn't short on strength.

The first time she was committed, I wasn't around; Jacques Mercier took her to the psychiatric hospital. That left the children: Marie, aged three, and Auguste, an infant just a few months old. *He* was incapable of looking after them, that's why we took over, my father and I.

Marie came to live with us and Auguste was put out for foster care with the in-laws. That was a long, sordid story too. Jacques Mercier's mother wanted to be paid for taking care of her own grandson. She went and told the mayor: "I'm willing enough to take on the little one, providing the young ladies of the 'château' pay me by the month." The mayor asked how much she wanted, she told him and we agreed, my older sister Rose and I.

My father looked after Marie during that period. I came as often as possible, but it was hard in the winter months, with the snow. I'd be away for a week, sometimes two, and my father managed alone with the little girl as best he could. In cold weather, she wore a wool dress — heavy wool, rough to the touch and scratchy as a rasp — and he absolutely would not undress or dress her. He left her as she was, without changing her for weeks: same dress, same undershirt, same underpants, and when I came back my father would say:

"I can't do it, I take off her shoes, I can't do any more than that."

It was a matter of sexual modesty; he was from the old school, and for him a girl was forbidden territory, even if she was his own three-year-old granddaughter. Nakedness must have frightened him. He belonged to the generation of the hemp longjohns you never took off, not even alone with your spouse, not even when you made love. An opening — "the top hole" — at the level of the lower abdomen, allowed for the necessary functions without ever revealing the body. I think that not once in his life did my father ever see a woman undressed and, clearly, Marie's body frightened him as much as any other.

If I'd Been a Washerwoman Beside a Stream . . .

I had just been assigned to Le Lauzet. My permanent appointment had come through at Puy-Saint-Vincent, and I took advantage of it to ask for the transfer since I wanted to get as close to Val-des-Prés as possible. Le Lauzet was not my ideal. Located just off the road between Grenoble and Briançon, it was still far from the "château," but even so, that road made it easier to travel and I could go look after the farm, the house, and my father more frequently. I took up my duties in September 1925 and I would stay there for three years.

Fifty years have gone by. Today this village too has changed for it is virtually empty: the peasants have abandoned it to work in the city, often in civil service. They left for Lyons, Grenoble, Gap, or Briançon, but they've kept their homes and come back for the summer months and vacations.

In 1925, life was rough in Le Lauzet, with harsh winters that lasted longer than ours, but the place was alive and the people welcoming.

From the very beginning, those living close to the school looked after me. Setting up house in a single room isn't always easy, even when you're used to a simple life. The peasants came to make sure I was comfortably settled, had all I needed, and wanted for nothing. There is always a degree of curiosity in that kind of situation, but it's perfectly natural: everybody wants to see and know the person who will be in charge of their children. Just as in Puy-Saint-Vincent, they insisted I eat with them:

"Now Mademoiselle, you're not going to eat all alone, come have your lunch with us; later on you'll see, you have lots of time to be all by yourself."

That was the truth; in the evening they all wanted me to join them for the veillée and it was hard to refuse. In any case, how could you do without veillées? Nightfall comes early, and you had to fill those long evenings, so I'd go tell my stories and sing along with everyone else. Afterwards I would go back to the room I'd fitted out, often bringing along a little girl from my class to keep me company. My place was isolated from the other houses in the village and there were a number of rascals in those parts with reputations as Don Juans who stopped at nothing. That's one of the reasons I kept one of my pupils with me, it gave me company. Besides, in that cold, being two, we kept each other warm; we'd bring home a boiling hot brick and sleep in the same bed. I felt more secure.

The room allotted to me was set in a tumbledown cottage that hadn't been kept up, and the roof leaked at every seam. It was a single room similar to the one I had at Puy-Saint-Vincent, without running water or other conveniences. What difference did it make if I filled my buckets at the fountain? I was used to that. What bothered me were the leaks in the ceiling; when you move in somewhere, there is nothing more demoralizing than to find the place is decrepit and neglected. Normally, lodgings were provided by the administration and the commune was responsible for maintenance. When there were problems, you had to write, complain, lodge formal complaints — I hated all that, but I was forced to go through with it. There were five or six cracks in the ceiling, and I navigated through the dripping water every time it rained. All my pots and pans were put to use, a soup pot there, a pan here, a stew pot way over there — my room wasn't a room any more. So I became angry, I complained to the inspector, and the mayor had the roof fixed. That's how my stay in Le Lauzet began, on the one hand friendly, and on the other aggravating.

Most families still lived in stables with their animals. But the cleanliness of those people was exemplary. When you walked into a house, you had an immediate sense of comfort, and you weren't at all uneasy about eating and living with them. Some places are cleaner than others — I don't know why. At Puy-Saint-Vincent, for example, people had more money, but you didn't get the same sense of cleanliness as at Le Lauzet. I think it has to do with upbringing, with habit; if people start out clean, they set an example, and as a result young couples follow suit. Cleanliness was second nature in Le Lauzet.

Recently, one of my friends came to see me. She had stopped by Le Lauzet to visit a family I had praised for its merits and cleanliness. The tale of what she heard and saw was not a complete surprise.

"Émilie, if you went back, you wouldn't recognize the house we used to visit. Remember the kitchen and the stable? There's just one door now for animals and people. The hens rule the roost: they're all over, on the table, on the furniture, they defecate wherever they please and it's never cleaned up. Nothing is clean anymore, neither kitchen nor stable. It's exactly the opposite of the way it was when you were teaching there. And Félicie's — where you took me! Well, she's still alive, but she can barely manage to make a little soup, the rest she doesn't bother about anymore. And the other two are there also — do you realize how old they are by now? To think we thought they'd never live past their thirties! They're still there, on their chairs, gone to flab. They never said a word while I was there, just stared at me — you can't imagine what they look like!"

Imagine? No, I cannot imagine what those two retarded children from my class might look like. Yet it was a model family, a family without problems that welcomed me when I settled in Le Lauzet. The mother, Félicie, introduced me to her husband, her father-in-law — an old man of eighty still playing the patriarch, and last of all, the two children who were to be my pupils. I remember my shock when that happened. In a stern voice, the father said:

"You'll have to bring them to heel for me, Mademoiselle. They're thick-headed, stubborn, and lazy, and I'm counting on you to make them into something."

What could I tell this man? He refused to recognize the obvious. After one look I had no doubts: the two youngsters were idiots. Rough treatment, and most certainly beatings, had made them even more fearful; both of them looked at me with their empty eyes, understanding nothing whatever. The girl was about eight and her younger brother maybe five. I stood there in wordless dismay. When the little girl came to school, I could barely get her to open her mouth, and besides, she stuttered. Still, I managed to teach her to read and write and to me it was a miracle. But I never could get anything out of her brother Auguste, who sat on his bench at the back of the class, never saying a word. When I insisted on making him talk, he'd start yelling:

"You can go to hell, you're a bad lot, if you keep it up I'll get my scissors and cut off your tongue."

The way he barked that sentence, it was hard to control yourself, and the whole class burst out laughing every time he did it. One day his grandmother told me: "Well, that's no surprise, when he comes here and doesn't listen to me, I always call him 'a bad lot,' and if he gets too rude, I add: 'I'll get the scissors and cut off your tongue.'" That's how I found out he was only an idiot when it suited him; he could very well learn and repeat, but with me, nothing doing, neither reading nor writing; he would never to do anything at all.

If I hadn't been a teacher, I would have been a washerwoman. Washing and especially rinsing have always seemed wonderful to me. When you rinse things in the mountain stream with a paddle and the flowing water, and see all the soap, all the impurities carried off, you have the feeling that besides the wash being clean, you too have been purified. I've always loved that; you're proud of the clothes you've washed, rinsed, and spread out. They smell so good from the sun, they're very white; sometimes you add a bit of lavender for perfume or tint them with bluing. You think to yourself: "These are my husband's things, those are my children's, and here are my shirts." There's pride in it . . . I don't know — all you have to do is look at a woman washing with her own hands, beating her linens in the brook . . . I remember, when I used to do the rinsing in the Clarée, I'd be drunk with ice-cold water, the splashing, beating with my paddle, my ears ringing, and my head spinning. When I came back up from the stream, my hands were frozen, numb with cold, but I was happy. For years I did the household wash.

In Le Lauzet, every family washed and rinsed in the brook, and there was one woman — the mother of a pupil of mine — who couldn't rinse. She was allergic to cold water, and every week it was a problem for her to find a way of getting the chore done. It weighed on her to ask other people around there to do it for her, so I offered:

"You know, I ask nothing better, I'm not making it up, I think if I hadn't been a schoolteacher, I'd have taken in wash, so it will be a real pleasure to help you out."

Since we were on friendly terms, she accepted. Our arrangement was that she would do her wash on Thursday and I'd rinse it out at the stream on Friday when school was over. What a meal that woman made me on those days! Local specialties, dishes I've never seen anywhere but Le Lauzet, and I've never tried to make any of them, why, I don't know. There were the *bugnes*° for example. You took flour and yeast — not ordinary yeast, but the kind bakers use, and there was always some around, people passed it from house to house when they needed it. Then you mixed the flour with mashed potatoes, using equal quantities of flour and potatoes, added eggs, butter and milk, let it sit for three, four hours, and then, once it rose enough, you took a spoonful of the dough and threw it into hot oil; it cooked in a few seconds, and when it came out it wasn't a fritter, or mashed potatoes — I don't really know what it was. With salt, it had an extraordinary taste. So that woman made me bugnes. She prepared codfish for me too, and aïoli; she always contrived to find out what I liked, and when I returned from the brook, she served me wonderful meals.

There are a hundred and one ways to help peasants out, especially in the spring when they run around like crazy. With two months less than we had in Val-des-Prés, nothing mattered but work in the fields once the weather turned nice. They left at three or four in the morning and didn't stop till dark, around nine or ten o'clock at night. They set everything else aside, house, children, the old and the sick.

I had made a friend in one family — a young woman named Berthe; she was about my age and we shared the same tastes, even though she was newly married. We both liked music, and since she had a record player and records, I often went over to listen to our records. In the spring, they all went off to work in the fields, leaving the grandmother by herself. Her bone structure showed a peculiar deformity: her spinal column had collapsed and taken the shape of a bishop's cross, pulling her head forward at chest height. With that infirmity, she couldn't do a thing but stay in bed and wait until someone would kindly take care of her. You have to understand that for those people, illness or infirmity stood outside of life. For them, life was plowing, sowing, and harvesting. Whether it was potatoes, rye, barley, or grass for the animals, working the soil was their life. Nothing else existed. I didn't stand on ceremony, I told them:

"If you like, I'll get Maman up, I can come over around eleven, sit her in a chair and take care of her."

They accepted too. They'd never have accepted it from someone in the village, besides, it wouldn't have occurred to anyone to offer anything at all, but coming from me it was different. To me, they said:

"That's very nice of you, because we don't have the time."

Around eleven o'clock I'd leave class, go up to my room and start my lunch. A few potatoes in water, because it was the simplest thing, and while the spuds were cooking, I went to my friend Berthe's house to take care of the grandmother. I got her up, sat her in her armchair, aired her bed, and then I washed her up a bit, doing her hair and tidying her a little. When she was settled, I went back to eat my potatoes, preparing them with oil and vinegar the way we do it around here. When I had a steak, I cooked that, or else I cut myself a few slices of sausage or took a piece of cheese. It was fast — most of the time I ate standing up. That's typical of schoolteachers, their meals are quick snacks, you don't have time, and besides, when you're alone . . . Afterwards, I went back to the farm, put the grandmother back to bed and stayed with her for a while, I'd tell her stories — I did my best to entertain her before I went back to teach my class.

Mère Olivine was Le Lauzet's leading woman. They sent for her when a woman was about to give birth, or when there was a stubborn illness and the doctor might have to be called in. Mère Olivine made the decision in those cases. Her abilities were recognized, her authority respected, her advice always heeded, and she was as important as the mayor or the priest. Mother, grandmother, widow who'd managed to raise her family and keep house, fervent Catholic, Mère Olivine was all of them, and everyone loved her; in every sense of the word, she was the *matrona*, the wise mature woman. Nevertheless, there was a case in Le Lauzet that almost got the better of her.

There was a woman who had just lost her husband. His grave was still warm when she took a lover. Obviously, she didn't want anyone to know; so for good measure, she went to the cemetery every day, at high noon, right when people went out to sit in the sun. In our mountain country, we're thirsty for the noonday sun; the nights are so long, the weather so cold, and the sun is so good in the middle of the day that you could even go bare-chested. Everybody goes outside in the sun, and that is precisely the time she chose for visiting the cemetery. My window faced that direction, and every day I would see her walk through the village. I am sensitive to this sort of thing, so I sensed she was putting on an act and her grief wasn't real and, to me, it was sordid and heartbreaking. What made it all the more striking was another woman who went to the cemetery at dusk. She'd lost her twenty-year-old daughter, and my heart bled for her every time I saw her walk by. I'd think to myself: Good heavens! She's going again. But why? What good does it do? I was unhappy for her. And what a contrast: so much sorrow and sincerity on the one hand, so much hypocrisy on the other. It was unbearable.

Sanctimonious and devious though she was, the widow still got pregnant, but she managed to fool us all to the very end, including her seventeen-year-old son and Mère Olivine. She came within a hair's breadth of carrying off her plan: give birth without anyone being the wiser and perhaps get rid of the newborn. Unfortunately for her, the day she went into labor, she took to her bed and could not hide the pain. Her son, of course, went for the midwife. What with all her experience and the births she'd attended, Mère Olivine understood quickly when she saw what was going on. She was not gentle, she just yanked off the covers, shouting:

"Come on, Noémie! Come on! The spirit is willing, the flesh is weak."

The infant, with its little dark head, was already there between her thighs, very much alive. The woman had nothing ready in the house, no linens, not a drop of water, not a single cloth. But it made no difference; once Mère Olivine took over, you could be sure nothing would stop her.

The most extraordinary part of the story is that no one in the village had noticed a thing. I myself was completely taken in and yet I got my milk from her every day; we'd always chat a bit and, well, even in the last months, her act fooled me. She was a woman in her fifties, on the heavy side, and she made a big fuss over her ailments. With her age as an excuse, she was always complaining, said the change of life was a torture and nothing helped. Enthroned on her kitchen mantelpiece, a whole colony of bottles and vials was prominently displayed — I especially remember Abbé Soury's Youth Elixir. She'd tell all comers:

"Just look at what I have to take, it's to build up my blood because I'm not feeling well at all; but things must be pretty bad since the more I take the worse I feel."

There were scratches on her hands and arms that wouldn't heal. She gladly showed them off, and told anyone who would listen:

"Look what I've got. It's no use taking care and dosing myself with my Youth Elixir. It's awful. I just swell up — it's my blood."

Later on we found out she scraped herself with a knife to keep them raw. It was not a pretty sight, but it was effective: people were impressed and believed her. In any case, on the memorable day she couldn't help screaming for the pain, the infant was born. What would have become of him without her screams and Mère Olivine? In those days, houses were equipped with large peat-burning stoves. You shaped the peat with water, and every night you filled the fire hole up to the top. You could assume the worst. The infant might easily have been stuffed in. I was upset, I could not understand how a person might reach that point. When I went to see her after she gave birth — I served as the village social worker — Noémie greeted me with her wailing:

"Oh, Mademoiselle, look what the Holy Spirit sent me!"

Her voice shook with sobs and her hands were folded piously. I had to fight to keep from exploding at her, and I really thought: What a waste of a few good kicks in the ass! I couldn't get over duplicity like that.

But the underlying logic was clear; her behavior was perfectly normal in a village where everyone was devout, especially the women. The sexuality of a woman just past middle age was incompatible with religion. Noémie herself was devout — at least she made a show of piety, by going to church — and of course she refused to be pregnant in the eyes of the community. She was stymied, and took it into her head to do anything she could to save face.

A few months later, Noémie tried to set things right. The man responsible for her troubles was one of those village Don Juans, an itinerant blacksmith known for his excellent work and, among women, for his gift of gab and impressive looks. Noémie was not the only village woman he'd seduced, but she took it into her head to make him recognize the child and marry her. The problem was to follow his trail and lay her hands on him. He was a local man, but he plied his trade all over the département, and finding him was quite some job. Noémie wrote letters, waited for answers and, one fine day, packed her bags and left with the youngster in her arms.

The blacksmith was in Briançon. She knew where he worked, and she knew his schedule. One day during the week, she took her stand right in the center of town, and waited for him to come out of the factory. It was lunch time, just when the streets are the liveliest. When he came into sight, she swooped down on him, grabbing his arm so he couldn't slip away.

"So," she yelled, "when are you going to recognize the little one: he's yours, yours!"

He could hardly avoid her, the people around slowed their pace or made no bones about stopping to watch.

"So when will you make up your mind to recognize him? You've got to give him an allowance . . ."

All the blacksmith could think of to get out of his predicament was to act astonished. Shrugging his shoulders as he looked at Noémie, he said casually:

"What are you talking about, lady? I don't know what you mean, and I don't know you!"

His sheer gall drove Noémie wild. She moved back a step and in front of all the assembled idlers, concentrated all her might and delivered two masterful slaps on his face. Very loudly, she said:

"And *that*, you know what *that* means?"

She then turned away without waiting for an answer.

"Joseph, You're a Thief!"

"Good day, Mademoiselle."

I was loathe to stop; I was on my bike, riding back to Le Lauzet from Val-des-Prés. The man who had just called to me was standing beside the road, his massive silhouette outlined against the russet-ocher of the fall sunrise. I knew that fellow only too well. Since I did not reply, he went on:

"You're certainly polite for a schoolteacher!"

It was too much; that second utterance was a challenge. I got off my bike, went over to him and, my voice trembling with indignation, I said:

"Look here, I'll be nice when you're honest. Why should I be polite to the man who insulted my father? You called him a thief, you insulted him in public, and when his innocence was proven, neither you nor your partners made one gesture, said one word of apology."

The man smiled at me condescendingly, attempting to maintain the superior air he had adopted from the start of our encounter. He said:

"Excuse me, excuse me. You don't know what you're saying, you don't know what you're talking about, you were much too young at the time."

"True, I was seven, but I remember as if it were yesterday. If you think I've forgotten your entering our house like a raging beast, you're mistaken. I remember it all, your insults, your black scowl, my father turning pale. You know as well as I do he could have cleared himself if he'd resorted to methods unworthy of an honest man, the way you did, but . . ."

"But, Mademoiselle, please . . ."

"But Mademoiselle nothing. My father kept quiet because he has a sense of dignity. My brother Joseph, when he came home on leave, had a little toy with him, and he was ready to put it to your head and march you straight through the village to the mayor to make a public apology. It's too bad Joseph died and didn't come back to put his plan into action. You think I'm going to forget that? So long as I live, you'll get nothing but contempt from me. Never, do you hear, never will I react to greetings from you any other way. My father was innocent, you insulted him, and you were too much a coward to apologize, ever. Worse still, you never told your children what the hate between us was all about; you were incapable of shouldering your responsibility."

"But, Mademoiselle Allais . . ."

"No, let me do the talking. This is my way of acknowledging your greeting. Except for his sense of honor and integrity, my father would have brought you to law. He had a right to demand redress, to clear himself of your unjustified accusations. But he was too good. In his place, *I* wouldn't have made you any gift, because you, if by some misfortune my father had been the guilty party, you would have had no pity, either for him or for us. My father remained silent because he is scrupulous and he was concerned for the children, yours and the other man's too—the one who was really guilty. Just you remember, you're lucky I'm not a man."

I stopped talking. I could not go on. I was at the height of my indignation. The fellow standing there in front of me didn't dare say another word. His eyes lowered, he walked away.

It's true, I was only seven when that deplorable business exploded; every detail has remained engraved on my memory, and the eighteen years that had flowed by since then could not erase the shame of those days.

We were sitting at the table, it was lunch time, the six of us were there with my father presiding as usual. All at once, that man came in without knocking, opening the door with a furious push. His face twisted with rage and hate, he strode over to my father and yelled:

"Vouɫeu, Vouɫeu! Jusè, vous sè un vouɫeu! [Thief, thief! Joseph, you're a thief!]."

My father went white but he did not flinch, he was like marble, answering with perfect calm:

"You are wrong. I am not a thief."

"Yes, you are," the fellow replied at the same pitch of fury. "We can prove it, we're sure, my partners and me at the sawmill. You made a trail carting your manure, and during the night you stole the finest log in our cut."

My father rose, calm as ever.

"No," he repeated, "it wasn't me."

"It's going to cost you dear. They'll sell the house you're so proud of, and your kids can take their bundles and go begging."

"I repeat, I did not take anything of yours."

"Justice will follow its course, they'll search the premises, and then we'll see. You can expect them to go through this house with a fine-toothed comb from attic to basement."

He left just as he'd come. Through the whole exchange, we were rooted to the spot with fear. My father said: "Finish eating," and not another word was uttered until the end of the meal.

Sometime that same afternoon, the real thief came to the house. It was only then that my father realized that this was the man who'd gone up to the cut by night to take the log. He came to have his cow covered by our bull. When the cow was serviced, that peasant had the gall to say:

"I hear they're searching your house."

"Yes, it's a sorry business," my father said. "What makes the stain on my honor even more unbearable is that I know the man who is really guilty."

My father looked the fellow straight in the eye, adding: "I even know what happened to that log; I saw it on a sleigh by moonlight, and I clearly recognized the person pulling it along."

The man changed color. All at once, his face turned white, and mumbling a few incoherent words, he beat a retreat with his cow.

My brothers and sisters were present during the scene and they understood. Indirectly my father had made things clear, and at the same time we all knew why he hadn't said a word to the man from the sawmill and why he never would. He detested stool pigeons so much that he would have remained silent even with his head on the block. To him, there was nothing worse than informing, and besides, he had the thief's family in mind, saying: "Poor Lydie, she has it hard enough as it is, she has four youngsters, and I don't have the right to burden her even more." The fact is, my father believed in justice and his conscience was clear.

I remember, we were all in the stable; Joseph and Catherine were shocked.

"Papa," said the elder son, "that's the man who stole the log; he knows you saw him and you'd better watch out. Now he'll be afraid you'll inform on him and he's liable to hurt you."

My father said nothing. He got ready to return to the woods with his sleigh. My two brothers did not want him to go alone, but my father was intransigent:

"Don't worry," he said. "You're exaggerating and you've got better things to do than waste your time coming along with me."

What happened next is hard to believe. My father left, but François and Joseph, convinced of the risk he was running, could not accept his going alone and they followed him at a distance. They had indeed scented danger, for in the middle of the woods, at a turn in the path, they saw the fellow coming out of a thicket where an axe was hidden. My father — staring at all three of them, my two brothers and the other man — could not get over it.

"I came for a bundle of kindling, but these bushes aren't the right kind," said the man by way of explanation. But none of the three was fooled; they'd seen the axe underneath the kindling, and there was no doubt that if my father had been alone, he would have been hacked to pieces.

"You see why we wanted to be with you?" said Joseph.

"Yes," my father answered, "he'd hardly have thought twice about killing me; he'd have gone home, making sure nobody saw him, the way he did with the log yesterday."

"Father, why let them go ahead with their legal action, when you could testify and clear yourself?"

"I am innocent. When they search the house and don't find anything, they'll have to admit they were wrong."

"But, Papa, there will always be a doubt."

"What's the difference? I won't be a stool pigeon. I have my conscience, and I don't want to drag anyone through the mud; if he were alone, had no family, maybe it would be different."

The search took place the next day. You have to understand the life and mentality of a village like ours to understand what that could mean. Being searched was the equivalent of being guilty. And that's not including a deployment of searchers far more numerous than for a murderer. There was the mayor with his sash, the municipal councillors, the bailiffs, the gendarmes, and all the others. It was an unprecedented event in the village; anyone who was envious, jealous, or had a grudge against the "château" was in seventh heaven. They scoured everywhere, even up under the roof, they didn't miss a thing. It was so humiliating for my father and for every one of us. They moved the heavy furniture, examined the floors, sunk hooks into the hay; through it all, my father accompanied them, upright, dignified, and silent. They were obliged to yield to the evidence in the end; there wasn't any log in the house, and the police inspector went off with his whole retinue, empty-handed and grumbling. And the others, the men from the sawmill, were equally sorry! Expressionless brutes, incapable of saying anything, not even a word of apology. After what had just happened, and in public, that was the least they could have done. But they didn't. They simply went away, leaving an aura of doubt over the house. That is where my father erred, he should have insisted on an apology. Since that time, nothing has budged; the matter has remained unresolved except for a search proving only that the log was not in our house. The other man played it smart in this story, using my father every step of the way. Otherwise, how could a log of that size disappear without leaving a trace? Only my father could have provided the explanation, but he never said a word. I think nobody ever knew the truth, either the family, the thief's children, or the men at the sawmill. Even today, something of the incident remains alive for us all.

A
Second
Family

I made true friends at Le Lauzet. Friendship that endures without growing old is a marvel. When I left Le Lauzet, they remained faithful over the years, speaking of me as someone they would never forget. Many years later, when I was married, they came to visit me in Val-des-Prés. They couldn't contain their feelings when they saw me, and they wept. Real tears of love and friendship. I remember, they came by taxi, and their joy was mixed with gentle scolding.

"Yes, you left Le Lauzet and you never came to see us, though your husband has a car; if you only knew how happy you'd make us!"

I was moved to tears as well. I had lived with them for three years like their own daughter. Each time I arrived up there, after my long bicycle ride, the wife was waiting for me; she had already set kerchiefs to heat in front of the fire; and as soon as I came through the door, she sat me down and rubbed my back with them. She prepared me coffee, and if I was late for class, she said:

"It doesn't matter, you'll keep them ten minutes longer in the evening or at noon."

I was coddled in that house like their own child, everything there was in perfect harmony for me. Those friends were unbelievably considerate. They were afraid I'd catch cold or fall sick; the minute I was tired, they couldn't do enough to take care of me.

"Émilie take this, Émilie take that, cover your back with this, you're not going to leave like that." It was extraordinary to have people take me in the way they did. We were neighbors with our front doors facing, almost touching, the street was so narrow. And so our friendship was born naturally, out of proximity. I was always with them for veillées and holidays, and they are the ones I meant when I spoke of cleanliness, they only had a stable but it was a jewel. The floor, the windows, everything was thoroughly scoured. Every day the table and stools were washed with sand and soap; the wood of the furniture was so silky that it looked as if it had just come from the cabinetmaker, and everything was like that. They were my second family; they loved me and I felt as comfortable with them as I did at home.

Then there was Laetitia. We weren't precisely friends, but I was the only person in the village to have a somewhat normal relationship with her. They called her the witch in Le Lauzet. Why? I never could find out, and aside from her looks, she acted like everyone else. She was old and as ugly as can be, with her hooked nose and undershot jaw almost touching, so every time I saw her, she reminded me of *la fée Carabosse*, the Wicked Witch.

The peasants of Le Lauzet avoided her like the plague and blamed her for all disasters and whatever went wrong. When out of sheer fatigue, she sat on a windowsill or leaned against a door, they anticipated a calamity. If an animal was sick in the course of the year, it was the witch's fault, they were convinced. The same for the harvest: when Laetitia sat down on a slope and someone noticed her, the news spread rapidly around the village and, in season, they avoided mowing the grass in that spot. When a field of grass was yellow, they said: "The witch came by." None of it held water, and whenever I could, I tried to make them see things more rationally. I would say:

"But that's all nonsense, there's no such thing as evil spells; look at me, I certainly talk to Laetitia, and nothing bad happens to me."

"Ah, but with you, it's different," they answered. "She only has it in for the local people."

They were convinced, and I really think they were afraid of her.

Last of all, I must sketch the portrait of my friend Jaunard. I knew him from Val-des-Prés. He was related to one of my teachers, and when I was ten, twelve years old, I'd see him every time I brought milk to the school. I met him again at Le Lauzet, and right away he was one of the people who welcomed me as a friend. Jaunard was middle-aged, around fifty; he was a widower, living alone but set on finding a second wife. While he waited for the lucky woman, he lived a bachelor's life, organizing his life around his garden, his goats, his cheeses, and his cooking. He was a very good cook; he'd worked as a valet, then as a head waiter, so he had experience and was very handy.

We saw a lot of each other during those three years. Given that we had friends and memories in common, and that both of us lived alone, it was natural for us to help each other out. Often he'd say: "Émilie, you'll come eat with me at the house," and I went every time he invited me. Besides being a good cook, he was an excellent cheesemaker. He had a herd of goats, and made a great deal of cheese with the milk. You were sure to find something to your liking all year round: fresh out of the mold, medium hard, and very hard. The cheeses were delicious. In return, I did a bit of housework and mending for him. That simple exchange was enough to make people talk — anyway, those people who see evil wherever they look. "There's got to be something going on, or she wouldn't be eating up there, mending his clothes, and helping out in his fields." They said that in spite of the wide difference in our ages. You just had to ignore them, shrug your shoulders and go on as if nothing had happened. So I helped him with the planting. Jaunard farmed his land like a garden. He had extraordinary taste and patience, and I learned a lot from him.

The only thing between us was confiding in each other. His one thought was to get married again; he gave me the letters from his correspondents to read, and asked for my advice. He was hesitating between two. I thought one of them was distinctly nicer and more human, but she was poor. My friend's wisdom and experience had their limits. Her poverty worried him, especially since the other woman showed a more realistic turn of mind, talking about money and giving him to understand that she too owned property. To me, there was no choice. I said: "You know, if you get married again, take Jeanne. She doesn't have money, but she sounds so nice, I think she likes you and you'll be happy." He listened with half an ear; I think he'd already made up his mind.

I used to read him my letters too. On one of my trips to Marseilles to visit Marie-Rose in the hospital, I met someone in the train. He was a workingman named Jean Carles and he was eleven years older than I. We had talked about this and that, and when it came time to leave, we exchanged addresses so we could write to each other. It didn't mean much; in fact it didn't mean a thing. There was everything to keep us apart. Nevertheless, that man wrote me letters eight to ten pages long, veritable treatises on subjects of his choosing. His letters would begin with something like "Mademoiselle, if you don't mind, I shall speak to you of the human heart today," followed by a long development of all the ideas that came to his mind on the subject. The style was simple and vigorous, the handwriting elegant, the images poetic. The treatise was studded with quotations from writers. They were exceptional letters, often beyond me, but I recognized my own way of seeing and understanding the world.

Jaunard would tell me: "Émilie, that man is somebody. Maybe he's only a workingman, but, don't let him get away, now. You see what I mean? Don't let him get away, because, from a man's point of view, he's an extraordinary catch."

And I'd answer: "That's a good one: don't let him get away! All the same I'd have to know what *he* wants to do, and he doesn't tell me anything about that."

Those letters did me a world of good, they opened my mind and my heart; however, from the moment I began talking to the man in the train bringing me home from Marseilles, not once did I imagine we might do anything more than write each other letters, not once did I see him as a possible friend, still less as my future companion for life. And yet that is exactly what happened . . . but that is another story.

Part Two

Chapter 20

You Have a Right
to a Life
of Your Own

"Mademoiselle . . ."

"You're going to Lyons, Mademoiselle?"

I looked at the man sitting opposite, and doing his best to start a conversation. He wasn't young, probably around forty, perhaps a little less, dressed like a gentleman, on the elegant side but without ostentation or bad taste. I noticed his brown hair, graying slightly at the temples, and a little sparkle in the corner of his eyes that I took for devilment. At the time, I thought to myself: Another lady-killer out for what he can get.

In all honesty, I was in a sad state of mind. I was on my way back from the psychiatric hospital and still in shock from my experience. You're different when you come out of a place like that. The atmosphere was appalling. I was shaken by the screams — there were every kind, none of them sounded human and yet all of them were. The inmates were all together, whether they suffered from paranoia or hallucinations, whether they were depressed or manic, and they each had their own way of uttering screams. When I left, I wondered if I was still normal and I had a feeling it wouldn't take much for me to be like them.

For my sister, things were far from bright. She was in a day room with other inmates, and when I arrived she hardly knew me. The few sweets I had brought in my bag left her totally unmoved when I unpacked them and spread them out in front of her; when she did speak later on, her speech was disjointed, and she looked straight ahead as if I weren't there. None of my attempts to bring her back to her right mind worked even slightly. She wasn't interested in the news of her children and our father that I'd brought from Val-des-Prés. She had no sense of reality.

However, the doctor taking care of her had given me a favorable report:

"You came at a bad time, Mademoiselle, because she's usually much better, she's calmer and more rational. Above all, you must not go by what you saw today; your sister can be salvaged, and with the treatment we're giving her, she'll recover as fast as possible."

Was he telling me the truth? I have no idea; in any case, what he said was not enough to reassure me.

"Mademoiselle?"

The fellow opposite me in the compartment was waiting for some kind of answer. Without stopping to think, I collected my baggage and changed seats.

I was barely settled in my new compartment when the man appeared, smiling and self-confident, prepared to charm. I was furious. My kind of woman does not hold her tongue and put up with a situation like that. I replied in the tone it called for:

"You have one hell of a nerve, Monsieur. How dare you come in here! You see that you're bothering me; you know perfectly well that if I wanted to strike up an acquaintance, I'd have stayed in the other compartment. The reason I left was to be alone and quiet."

"Oh dear," he said, his voice warm, and his way of speaking uncombative. "Oh dear, what's the matter? Do you have problems or are you just bad-tempered?"

Once more I tried to cut the conversation short: "Oh, look here!"

But he did not give me the chance to go on:

"Maybe you left your sweetheart in Marseilles?"

A sweetheart! He could not have been further from the mark, and I gave a nervous laugh:

"A sweetheart in Marseilles? If you knew where I've just been, you certainly wouldn't be in a mood for jokes."

He sat down facing me and looked at me. His eyes were kind. He asked:

"Then tell me where you've been, Mademoiselle."

"I'm coming from the hospital, if you must know; I've just seen my sister. You can't imagine how sad it is, and she's not even twenty-four. There aren't any words to describe that place, and my sister said anything that came into her head . . ."

I broke off. It was partly emotion, partly the fact that there I was in a train telling my life story to a stranger. So what, I said to myself and went on:

"It's awful. She has two little children I have to look after, then there's my father who's seventy-five, and I have to look after him, too."

"And you do it all alone."

"Of course. I teach in Le Lauzet and I come home every chance I get, it's about thirty kilometers. My father waits for me to come — that's the only thing he's got, and I can't leave him all alone with the little girl. If you only knew what the house used to be like, it was so alive, and now my father and his granddaughter, all alone . . . I'm the only one they can count on . . ."

"And the others?"

"What others?"

"Well, you must have had brothers and sisters?"

"Oh, of course, but . . ."

Once I got started, I couldn't stop, I told him the story of my life, and he — a man I didn't even know — sat there listening to me, he inspired trust. I needed to speak so badly, to confide in someone, it was marvelous to get it all out, thinking all the while: Anyway, this man will take my stories with him and that'll be that.

When at last I finished the picture of my family life, he said:

"What! You think your life is over because you have a sister in the hospital under treatment, because you're responsible for two children and an aging father? You say you have no right to anything anymore? But that's inconceivable! If I understand correctly, your father is seventy-five, but he's alive and healthy. Would you like it better if he were dead or infirm? But, Mademoiselle, it's wonderful to have your father with you, and a younger sister who's going to recover, and two children who ask only to live. I do not agree that you should be resigned. Have you ever really looked at yourself? You're young, you're pretty, you glow with life, and what you say does not correspond to the strength you radiate. You pass sentence on yourself. I say you have the right to a life of your own."

For a few seconds, he stopped speaking; I felt my heart beating faster. His words were right; they reawakened in me a strength that was manifest, a life force I had been trying to stifle for years. He added:

"At your age, it would be a crime to sacrifice yourself for your family, and you don't do anyone a favor when you slight yourself. Imagine giving your father the poisoned gift of telling him at the last: 'I sacrificed my life to you.' That would be so sad. No, you should help others, but you have to think of yourself too — otherwise, it's no good. You will be better armed, you will have more strength to do what you have to do."

That man restored my courage with his words, his concern, his tact, with the aptness of his remarks. For months and years, I had lived curled up tight inside myself; concerned only with Marie-Rose and my father, keeping myself in the background. I had become the "good sister" in both meanings of the word — sibling and nun — and I had forgotten to think about myself. Often I would tell myself: Émilie, you have never been young, there was the war, the deaths, the others went away, and the only things you've known are trouble and work.

It was only a step to the conclusion that my life was over, and I had taken it blithely. Suddenly, between Marseilles and Briançon, with a few sentences, a stranger in a compartment on a train had rekindled in me a light I thought forever extinguished; and as he went on talking to me, I tried to guess who he was, what he did, his ideas, and his tastes. I should have asked, but I was reluctant to seem indiscreet and did not dare question him. I told myself: He is certainly not just anybody. He is cultivated and sensitive.

That was when he began talking about himself. He told me his name, Jean Carles; he was a workingman, a house painter, and at the time I refused to believe it. He didn't look or act like a workingman and, more than anything else, it was clear from the way he spoke that he possessed an understanding of life and culture that was deep and beyond the average.

At Veynes, we had to part: he was going on to Lyons to see his mother, and I was returning home by way of Briançon where my niece and nephew, my father, and work were waiting for me. Before we said goodbye, we exchanged addresses and agreed to write.

"You'll send me cards from the mountains; I'm not acquainted with them, and they'll give me some idea of the place where you live."

And that is how it happened. In the local train taking me back home, I thought over everything that man had said to me. It was increasingly clear to me that his comments were sound, but there was something else: he had surged up in my life, lighting up the darkness like a beacon.

Chapter 21

Paris
Is Well
Worth a Mass

And so we corresponded, learning to know each other better, discovering with each new letter that our thoughts on life were in close concert. It was true from every point of view. As we revealed our ideas, our tastes, what we read, the natural harmony between us was confirmed. Close concert and harmony, these are what is essential between men and women. To my mind, it could only have happened through a chance encounter, an almost miraculous piece of luck, a gift from heaven.

I was twenty-seven and life had not exactly pampered me. In villages, there is always some boy to make advances to a girl, you have friends, and there are young fellows who offer to do little favors, cut wood, knock off some chore or other, and end up proposing. With me, things never went very far. By the time I was fourteen or fifteen, I'd seen so many young people caught in bad marriages that I instinctively distrusted marriage and everything that goes with it. I wasn't good at flirting and keeping company. I remember one time at the village festival — I must have been about fourteen — I left the dance and a boy came after me for a kiss. Right away I called my brother Joseph.

"Say Joseph, Louis wants to kiss me, he won't take no for an answer, and I don't like that."

"Keep your paws off my sister, y'hear, 'cause if you keep it up, you'll get a face full of fist."

That's the way I had always been, very suspicious. Particularly with Louis who wanted to marry me, and later on, at Puy-Saint-Vincent, with a local young man who courted me.

It was another matter entirely with Jean Carles. What I mean is that even those first letters made it clear that he was a totally exceptional being, and I thought everything he said was right. He was a man who wanted to live, he radiated life and found extraordinary words and images to describe it:

"Émilie, just look at a rose, look at a bird, listen to it sing, look around you, the countryside, the river flowing along — nothing is higher than that life."

For me, living like a recluse, these words acted like leavening. I had forgotten what was most important, and he opened my eyes to the beauty of the world.

He was a man who had done a lot of living, knocking around all over the place; he was experienced and kept a curious, open mind that made him the opposite of the pig-headed men I had known until then. He had read a great deal, far more than I, and he had ideas about the world and men. Nonviolent, a pacifist, he was head over heels in love with liberty. Compared to him I was no more than a child; he gave me the benefit of his knowledge and right away I came under his influence. For in spite of my education, I was the one to gain by the exchange and I was deeply and sincerely grateful to him.

In the spring, I received a letter suggesting that we meet:

We've been writing to each other for some time now; I believe we think well of each other, but some words must be said aloud. Since you are going to Paris for Easter, we can meet at Veynes. The train stops there. I will take time off from work and you will leave on the next train, and so we can have a whole day together.

It was an extraordinary day. We met at the station and went into a restaurant; when we ordered steak, the bistro owner looked at us as if we'd landed from the moon.

"But it's Good Friday!"

That was the least of our worries.

"We know, but it doesn't matter, we'd like two orders of steak."

"All right, we'll see if the butcher has any."

And that is how our day started. We spent the rest talking. We were ravenous for speech, ravenous for friendship and affection, and we chattered for hours, tackling every possible subject imaginable. We agreed on everything. But there was feeling along with words, and it only grew with the passing time. I was fascinated by that man eleven years my senior, I was

attracted, but I couldn't imagine what it would all come to. We had exchanged ideas in our letters, brought our opinions and our feelings face to
face, without ever bringing up the question of living together or getting married. He hadn't kept his views on marriage a secret, he believed in free love,
and all through those hours we spent together I wondered: Is he going to say
something or not? And what am I going to do? How will I answer? I was
well aware that all our words and letters were heading that way; the attraction between us had to lead somewhere.

The time was coming for us to part. We had strolled through the town
and soon it would be time for my train. Suddenly Jean Carles said:

"Émilie, will you marry me?"

I stared at him, astounded. Still, I'd expected the question. I even think
I laughed, and he got the idea I was making fun of him, but he didn't get
angry, he just said:

"I know, you think I'm too old."

"No, it isn't that," I said, "but there are so many things standing between us. You talk about freedom in your letters, about wanting to live a free
life, and with me it's different. I've got my father, I live with him, and he has
old-fashioned ideas from the nineteenth century. Even if I don't agree, I'm
bound to respect his ways and I do not want to hurt him. He'll never tolerate
my living with a man unless I'm officially married in the town hall and the
church.° He's suffered enough already, I could never do that to him, he'd die
of shame and grief. So I guess that makes it hard for us."

"Oh, if that's all there is to it," Jean Carles replied, "Henri IV said
'Paris is worth a mass,'° and I think you're well worth two, one in church,
one at the town hall."

The thought was so comical, so much to the point, that I burst out
laughing.

"Really? You really mean that? You're sure you want to get married?"

"Yes, I do, I'm ready for it; I've given it careful consideration, but," he
added, "do you think there's anything else that might stand in our way?"

"No, that's all, I think we can get married."

"Fine," he said. "Then I shall have to come see your father."

The moment of parting had come. We set a date for his visit to Val-des-
Prés and reluctantly said goodbye.

Grandfather Allais and his wife, seated. Standing on the left: Émilie Carles's parents.

Val-des-Prés and the Clarée Valley, around 1910.

Family photo, around 1906.

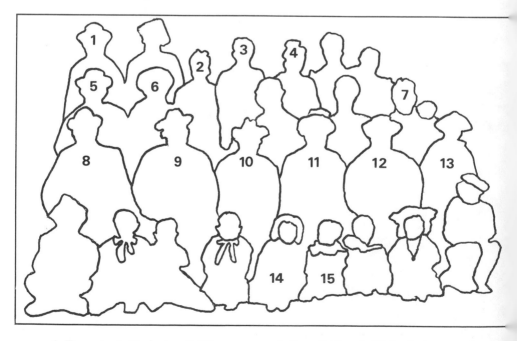

1. François, 2. Catherine, 3. The wet nurse, 4. Rose, 5. Joseph Allais, 6. Auguste, the pig-sticker, 7. Aunt Colombe, 8. The Guillestre uncle, 9. Uncle Alfred, 10. Grandfather Vallier, 11. Uncle Alexandre, 12. Uncle Jules, 13. Joseph, 14. Émilie, 15. Marie-Rose

Émilie Carles with her class in Nogent, 1923.

Émilie Carles in Paris.

Jean Carles as a young man.

Émilie Carles's family in 1911. In front, left to right: Marie-Rose, Joseph Allais, Émilie. Rear, left to right: Joseph, Rose, Catherine, and François.

The terrace at
Les Arcades.

Georges and Nini.

*Émilie and
Jean Carles.*

Émilie and Jean Carles (left), Joanes Cuat (center).

The table d'hôte at Les Arcades.

Jean Carles fishing with his son, Georges.

Émilie Carles at the demonstration in Briançon, August 13, 1975.

Val-des-Prés in 1977.

Chapter 22

Against
All
Comers

Jean Carles took advantage of the July 14 holiday to visit my father and ask for my hand in marriage. We were in the meadow at Fourches that day, turning the hay. I saw a young man coming toward us on a bicycle, wearing a straw hat and white trousers. I didn't recognize him, from a distance you'd have thought it was Maurice Chevalier, he really looked wonderful. I watched him stop to ask each group where to find me, and people point to our meadow. It was right in the middle of the haying season. Peasants run around like crazy when the hay is ripe, never pausing until it's all reaped and stored. That is exactly what we were doing, not losing a moment because although the day was beautiful, possible storms are always a worry.

My mother had been struck by lightning twenty-four years earlier in the very field we were working.

I said: "Look, he's here."

My father immediately stopped turning the hay to watch him approach. He knew I was seeing Jean Carles and I'd mentioned his visit, but I couldn't help feeling a little apprehensive. I had often thought about the two men meeting, and of course I wanted things to go as smoothly as possible, that's to be expected. They were so different I had reason to fear the worst. But everything went well. Jean greeted my father, introduced himself, and seeing we were in the middle of work, pulled off his jacket, rolled up his sleeves and set to work, turning hay right along with us.

That evening when we were back at the house, he asked permission to take a hand at the cooking. I said: "Go right ahead." I had no idea he knew how to cook, and he started off with his characteristic good humor.

"Fine. I'm going to make you tomatoes provençale." He talked as he worked, telling us about his life, his travels, what he'd seen. My father couldn't get over it, and neither could I. Things went so well that it was agreed Jean Carles would spend three days with us.

The next day he asked if he could do the kitchen over. It hadn't been painted in fourteen years and was sadly in need of a new coat. He didn't only scrape, scour, and whitewash the walls, he decorated them as well. He fashioned a stencil simulating ceramic tiles and with that he drew a colored fresco all around. With white walls the kitchen was transformed beyond recognition. Instantly the gray, dark kitchen I'd seen for years welcomed light with the sunbeams bouncing off the wall. I think my father couldn't get over the way Jean transformed the kitchen in such a short space of time.

But that was not the main point. When Jean asked for my hand, my father did not give a straight answer. He certainly didn't say no, he merely assumed a somewhat distant patriarchal manner, and said:

"I will let you know."

Still, "I will let you know" was closer to yes than no. Let's say that on principle, my father wanted to be coaxed. I did not have the slightest doubt that we would marry. I was twenty-eight and I was determined to take full responsibility for myself, but for many reasons my father's consent was important to me.

And so Jean left with an "almost yes," and in the days that followed I was sure I had successfully convinced my father. I was happy. But shortly afterward, things began to go wrong; my father wanted me to reconsider my choice: he explained that on thinking it over, he did not approve of the marriage. It bothered him that Jean Carles was a workingman with no property under the sun. In his eyes it was unthinkable for me to marry a man who didn't own anything, and he asked me to think it over too.

Coming from him, from my father, and on that subject, it was virtually an order. In a word, the suitor didn't amount to much; he had to be sent packing because he was nothing but a tramp. I saw the old antagonism between peasants and workers rising up once more. They all work like dogs, they all sweat blood and water to survive, to eat, to clothe and lodge themselves, but they despise each other nonetheless. My father was one of those people who cannot imagine a convergence of two worlds, his own and the other unknown world he scorned without knowing why.

I fought right back, no one would tell me what to do; father or not, I would not go along.

"I don't know what you want," I told him. "When you're a workingman you've got your fortune in your two hands. *You* saw what he did, how he cleaned up the kitchen in no time at all; besides, he's nice — there isn't any reason for me to change my mind."

I defended myself with all the passion I could summon, I was ready to do anything except give in: my happiness and my life were at stake. The idea of anyone else making my decisions for me was revolting, and I was not at a loss for arguments.

"Maybe you want an incompetent, alcoholic son-in-law like the one at Draille; well, I don't. There aren't any men around here, all we've got are louts. You won't ever make me back down; I'll never find such a fine man again; therefore, the answer is *yes* and if you don't like it, you can do what you please."

"All right," he said, "If there's nothing to be done, you do what you like."

Things would have been easier if my father had been alone. But there was the family; my father wasn't the worst of the lot because he loved me; I think he truly wanted me to be happy, and he sensed that what I wanted was not wrong. But one of my uncles stepped in as well, a tough man who had no reason to put on kid gloves with me. It all came down to family property; that was the fundamental question, but no one dared talk about it openly. I remember a conversation with my uncle. He said bluntly:

"You are not to marry that harem-chaser!"

In his haste to discredit Jean Carles at any cost, he had unconsciously mixed up "harem-scarum" and "skirt-chaser."

"And why not? What do you know about him?" I said.

"You're letting your feelings run away with you; the man's a good-for-nothing. We've had inquiries made, and if you are unable to keep a level head, with all your education, we will do it for you."

I was beside myself at such maneuvers and I got tough.

"What?" I said, "You have negative information? If you do, you must show it to me."

"We have no information to give you, all we have is advice, and it's advice that you are going to follow."

The more he added, the more transparent the scheme became. They didn't have any information; if they'd had the slightest knowledge, they surely would have used it. It was unworthy of my father; in a sense, he too had allowed his brother to use him. I stood fast, and once more I said no.

Jean did not have the same family problems, but he did have a mother who was a phenomenon in her own way.

Jean Carles invited me to visit him in Tarascon where he was painting a moviehouse. His mother was with him. It was an opportunity to meet her, so I went. They were both waiting for me when I reached the station. From the start, Jean's mother was as unpleasant as she could be. She was a very tall woman, much taller than I, and she wanted to impress me with her manners. The first thing she said was:

"So this is *it!*" looking at me as if I were a worm. Those words hurt, and I remembered them for a long time.

Jean did everything he could to smooth things over, but his mother had set the tone. Every time we were alone, she did not miss a chance to humiliate me:

"When I think of the beautiful girls who were after him; there was a schoolteacher too, but not like you — she was elegant and rich. What's gotten into Jean? What's the matter with him?"

It was unbearable. I think Jean did not realize what his mother was putting me through with her sarcasm. Of course, he told me to overlook all that, grit my teeth, and wait till we were married, but that was hardly satisfactory. Nevertheless, we loved each other enough for me to accept a great many things, and I did even more: at his request, I took his mother with me when I went home to Val-des-Prés.

"You'll take my mother up to Val-des-Prés; it'll be good for her, and I'll join you when I finish my job here."

I agreed. I don't know why I agreed, but I did it in full knowledge of the risks implied for us. She too longed to see our marriage plans quashed; that was so in line with my own family's plans that during her visit in Val-des-Prés, she managed to strike up a friendship with one of her own kind, my bitch of an aunt, and they both tried to break our engagement.

When Jean arrived, I went to meet him. His mother had put me through hell with her slander, and I was determined to put an end to all that. I blurted out:

"If you want to do me a favor, pack your bag — not tonight, it's too late, but first thing in the morning — take your mother and go, don't let me see your face again!"

"But what's going on? What is so terrible?"

"Look here, it's been unbearable, I've spent every night biting my pillow in bed so they wouldn't hear me crying. Your mother is impossible."

"Are you marrying me or my mother?"

"You, of course, but . . ."

"But what? What have *I* done to you?"

"Nothing, but . . ."

"So?"

"Look Jean, this past week I've heard the same sentences all day long; your mother can't stand me and she talks about it to anyone who'll listen, even when I'm right there: 'Jean could have done better; if he were a minor, I'd prevent such foolishness; there's still time, and I'll try to change his mind about marrying Émilie.' I've had it. I've been hearing that for ten days and it's enough already. Besides, she and my aunt, they've been saying the most awful things about me; my aunt said I go off on my bicycle for rendezvous in the woods; I've already been called a whore, but at least by a drunken woman who's not from around here, while those two . . . ! To say that about me when you know very well what I use that bike for, I ride to Le Lauzet."

It's true. At that point, I was seething with exasperation and resolved for the worst, including breaking off. Fortunately Jean took matters in hand, starting with his mother. He had it out with her, apparently crossing the t's and dotting the i's because tongues stopped wagging and everything was back in order. There was not perfect harmony, but it was bearable. Up to the wedding. That day Jean's mother launched a new attack; following Jean around, she'd poke him in the back and say:

"Come on, don't be in such a hurry to say yes."

That day my sister Rose who'd come from Lyons for the wedding chipped in her two cents. She ran after me to say: "There's still time," and after Jean with: "You should have married me. Émilie's too young for you, you'll never get much good out of her, while I'm an experienced woman."

All the same, we were married. It wasn't a big wedding, everything was limited to a strict minimum with the customary family, witnesses, and mayor in attendance.

We ate at home, and Jean catered the lunch himself as we had decided so that we could save money. Jean didn't have a cent coming in, in fact he had debts, and that was one of the reasons that had led him to postpone the wedding. "I have debts, I have debts," he'd say. It wasn't really bad; they were not even his debts but his brother's, and I told him: "At our age, it's time to live together, we'll work off the debts together just as we'll work out the rest."

My father didn't know. If he had, I think it would have been a dreadful blow for him. Furthermore, Jean and I were married without a contract, and that, I am convinced, made it a red letter day as that had never been done in those parts. By custom contracts were drawn up for every marriage, absurd documents, listing what each party brought to the union. I was against it for loads of reasons, and it took a quarrel with my father and my uncle to get my point of view across. I told them:

"It's not worth it, neither Jean nor I want one; if there are children, everything will go to them by law, and if there aren't, we'll see later on."

I wouldn't hear of it. In my eyes, a contract humiliates the person who has nothing. You go to the notary and you draw up the list. We would have written: "Mlle Allais: one house, situated at such and such a place, with so many rooms, and so many outbuildings, covering such and such an area, land worth so much, furniture, linens, livestock, and all the rest," whereas Jean would have listed what? Nothing. I knew that if our positions had been reversed, Jean would have acted the same way, but the others did not understand, all they thought about was material interests. We could not come to an understanding. They talked to me about property and full coffers, and I spoke to them about another kind of wealth. To me, the coffers are empty if the owner has neither love nor human warmth; however, a person with nothing can fulfill a kindred soul — but how could I have made them understand?

Jean was authentic wealth, the only kind I had always wanted and never had. A head full of dreams, a smile laden with promises, a heart heavy with all the goodness on earth, such was the wealth offered and given me. Material wealth cannot compare. That is why I was opposed to marriage contracts. When you love someone, you share everything, and if you part, the contract will not cure the pain. It is nothing but a matter of sous, and for me there is not a shadow of doubt that money soils whatever it touches.

My new life was totally different from the one I had led up to then. I'd been resigned to my life, telling myself I would never know anything but work and devotion to my family. It was not despair, but rather acceptance of my lot, and at twenty-six, twenty-seven, I told myself it was all over and I'd stay an old maid. Yet it occurred to me from time to time that I could have a child. It was the time when a number of women were seeking emancipation, it was the postwar Roaring Twenties with their bachelor girls and the reemergence of suffragette ideas. I would have liked to have had a child, but it wasn't easy. In public education, for example, an unwed mother was automatically dismissed and that's not all, there were other problems, too, like the difficulty of raising a child without a father. By chance, I came across a book on the subject, the story of a young postal worker who decided to have a baby without getting married; it was called *Madame 60 bis*. The subject was indeed the suffering of her fatherless child; she told how there was always some imbecile to call him "bastard" or "love child" at school or anywhere he went. The story gave me food for thought.

Meeting Jean Carles changed all that. Henceforth I could be a maman just as I longed to be. Jean and I agreed on that. My only fear was a bad pregnancy like my sister Catherine's, so I went to see a doctor to find out where things stood.

"No," the fellow told me, "you're completely normal; there is nothing to worry about and you can have as many children as you want."

"Once bitten twice shy," they say, but it doesn't help to watch out or take every precaution; when calamity is on the way, nothing can stop it. My first child was a boy, but he did not survive his difficult delivery. The infant presented so badly that forceps were necessary; the doctor made a false move, injuring the head with his instruments, and the baby was already dead when the doctor pulled him out. I did not even see him; I was so worn out that I was conscious of nothing but pain and tears. But the ultimate absurdity was that while I thrashed about in torment and Jean was like a madman, incapable of tending to anything, the mayor had the infant's body buried in the far end of the cemetery, in the common grave reserved for people who've been drowned or hanged. That is what happened. I know we could have demanded compensation, but neither Jean nor I had the heart to take the necessary steps; we both thought it was better not to look back, and so life went on, life was stronger than all the rest. One year later I gave birth to my son Jojo, and two years after that I had a little girl we named Janny. Jean and I were fulfilled.

Those were happy years. Jean was an extraordinarily considerate and attentive companion, always seeking to please me, and from him I received all of earth's gifts. I always had the privilege of the first violets he had gathered under the dry leaves, the first strawberries from the garden, the first cherries. For my bedside table, he brought the first roses, and to my plate the first March trout. And so, the man who owned nothing under the sun shone on the people around him. Through the warmth he radiated, the gifts he lavished on everyone, Jean Carles dealt out happiness.

He was head over heels in love with liberty. For him there was nothing higher. He stood up for his ideas and was well informed. I had never seen anyone read so much. Right after work, he'd settle down in a corner to read. He subscribed to all the progressive periodicals of the day: *Le Canard en-chaîné,*° *The Human Homeland,*° *On the Outside,*° and contemporary literature. It was through him that I discovered Panaït Istrati,° Céline,° Albert Londres, and many others, as well as Henri Poulaille's *New Age in Literature.*°

Jean was an idealist, authentic, uncompromising; he was like my father in that respect, he too lived his ideas and would never have tolerated the slightest gap between what he said and what he did. That was not easy, because it's all very well to preach generosity and fraternity, but then you need the wherewithal. It didn't matter. Jean was also a dreamer and a poet; he loathed bureaucratic pettiness, and he couldn't count — or he didn't want to. I am the one who kept our accounts and he called me "the ant,"* telling the children:

"Your mother is unique in this world, there's not another like her."

He might well say that because I don't know how he would have managed without me. Money slipped through his fingers like water; he gave away what he had without counting, and when there was nothing left and his purse was empty, he'd say: "But that's impossible!" and I would reply: "Of course it is, there's nothing left." He counted on the ant so much that the ant had to save up. It was a matter of temperament. At times, I would fly into a rage, and then Jean would put his arms around me and recite one of those poems he had a knack for composing:

> Oh the sweet joy of the lips of a friend,
> To light each day's life with fond words of love,
> And on your lip lighting for yearning caress
> Pour into your soul, that trinity fine
> Of Love and Goodness and Madness divine.

Thus sang Jean Carles, the man who owned nothing under the sun.

Chapter
23

Does
Your Teacher
Hit You?

I see I've forgotten one of Jean's fundamental quali-
ties in my portrait; from what I've said, you might think he was a gentle
dreamer and poet solely concerned with liberty and fraternity. But Jean was
also a workingman and not just any kind, he was good. He was in fact a
peerless workman with a lofty sense of his craft.

Before our marriage we raised the question of how to set up our lives. I
would say:

"Good heavens, where will they send me after Le Lauzet? I'll have a
job but you won't, you'll have to find work."

"What's the difference?" he would answer. "I only feel at home when
I'm with you, so wherever you go, I will go."

By some fluke, I received an appointment right here in Val-des-Prés. I
was lucky; I could look after the house, my father, and my two godchildren
at the same time. Jean moved in, went to Briançon to look for work and
found a job. It was not easy, for while Jean's idea of work was consonant
with his whole way of thinking, it was not in line with local practices among
workers or employers.

He called on the town's major firms, and one of the employers hired
him on the spot, saying:

"Fine, I can take you on; it's so much per week."

It wasn't much of a salary, and Jean had his own way of settling matters of that sort. He told his employer:

"Before you offer me that amount, you should wait and see what I can
do; we'll talk about money afterwards."

"Well, okay, if that's the way you want it," he said. Jean spent a week on a job and on Saturday when he went to see his employer, they gave him an envelope with the ridiculous sum of money Jean hadn't wanted in the first place. Jean refused to take it. He handed back the pay and told the employer:

"Keep it, I don't want it."

"Why?"

"Because I draw the line at earning less than my wife; I deserve to be paid what I ask; if you think I'm not productive enough, put me on a job by myself and you'll see."

That's where the difficulty really lay: here in Briançon, workers were badly paid, and since Jean had traveled and worked all over France, he could make comparisons.

"It's only natural, they're not paid well and they never will be because they're jokers, they fake it, and they don't even earn the little they make."

He must have said something like that to the employer, must have said that his concept of work was different but that would not be apparent unless he worked by himself. The employer agreed, saying:

"I have a job starting on Monday, it's for the most demanding woman in Briançon; her whole apartment needs redecorating and I'm putting you in charge."

Jean took the job, and did it alone as he'd asked. That way, he could organize his work as he proposed. He redid everything, laying paper everywhere, and at noon he put everything back in place before he went to lunch, so that everything was cleaned up as if there were no worker and no job in progress. When she paid her bill, the woman told the employer:

"I've never seen such a worker; I hardly knew I had one in the house, and my place is spotless."

The employer couldn't get over him either, and told Jean:

"Well, I don't know how you did it, but that old lady has a reputation for being more demanding than anyone else around, and she had nothing but good to say about you and your work. If you satisfied that one, you really must be special," and he gave him what he asked for.

But money isn't everything, and Jean suffered greatly from the climate. In winter, his ears froze when he traveled back and forth between Val-des-Prés and Briançon. It was hard on a person like him who'd been to warm places and spent the best part of his life in the Midi, in départements like the Vaucluse and the Var. We decided to shift our bearings. Jean went to work near Cavaillon where we had friends, and thanks to the Roustan Law,° I joined him as soon as I could. Life was dull there, with him working for a business concern and me taking care of the preschool. The only thing I re-member is putting up with a shrewish principal for a year and a half, and fighting with her and her husband during the strikes. I was the only one who honored them; it was in 1930–1934 just as the social struggle was picking up momentum and the Popular Front* was in the offing. That is why we came back here as fast as we could. Unfortunately my post at Val-des-Prés was gone and I had to take what the academy was willing to offer: the school in Alberts.

The most extraordinary story of my whole teaching career took place in Alberts. Two, in fact. I call the first "The Tale of the Inkwell." One day a youngster decided to throw his inkwell at my face and just as he was raising his arm, I turned around and saw him. Right away, I remembered Armand hitting Félicie with a stone. This boy too was one of the biggest in the class, he must have been around fourteen and he was obstinately disobedient. In situations like this, where there is a physical threat, you commit yourself by the way you react, and it is in your interest not to make a mistake. And it so happened that this boy already had a record. This kid had flown into a rage at home with his brothers; he'd picked up the pig-sticking knife and hurled it at one of them. A pig-sticking knife is a dangerous weapon, and he meant to do injury when he threw it. He intended to hit his brother in the head or chest, but the boy had turned around just in time and jumped so the knife caught him in the buttocks. Blood spurted out in such quantities from all over that they couldn't stem the flow and had to take him to the hospital in Briançon.

Matters hadn't gone any further; it was only a youngster reacting an-grily against his brothers. Some time later, however, talking about anger in a civics class, I decided to use his example to get across to my kids the foolish-ness of anger. I said:

"It is always idiotic to get angry. When it happens to me, I'm sorry; and I think everyone acts like me: you're sorry afterwards because you know you let yourself get carried away, you know you talked nonsense or did dangerous things, and you're sorry. You, there," I spoke to that boy, thinking of him throwing the knife, "you're in a good position to know," but he didn't see it in that light and said in front of the whole class:

"Me? I'm never sorry!"

"How can you say that?" I answered, "What about hitting your brother with a knife? Aren't you sorry?"

"Yes, there is one thing I'm sorry for: I missed him and he got up from the floor."

Well, that was the boy threatening me with his inkwell. Fortunately, I faced him down, otherwise I would have had it.

"So go ahead. Throw it," I told him, walking toward him all the while; he was totally disarmed by my self-possession. One thing is certain, if I had been afraid, above all if I had shown it, and if I had survived, I would never have been mistress of my class again and not one child would have obeyed me, not ever.

But that's nothing compared to the other story that happened to me in the same place. There was an air captain in Alberts who had settled in the region with his family. There were lots of rumors about him floating around; they said he beat his wife and terrorized his kids. He had two boys in my class, but I had no reason to get involved with him so long as I had no problems with his youngsters. However, one day I went to his home to talk to him about his two sons, little problems of no consequence concerning their studies, and during our conversation, I caught a glimpse of his wife. The little I saw enlightened me. Sure enough, she was covered with black and blue marks and though I didn't make much of it, I must have said something to the local people. It was enough to unleash the captain's rage.

A few days later, the fellow brought one of his sons to school just before starting time and sat him right down at his desk in the classroom. It was in the morning before I got there, and the children were playing in the yard. I arrive, the bell rings, and I start my class. After a few minutes, I notice the boy rigidly erect on his bench, looking very pale and biting his lips nervously. I ask him what's wrong: "Pierre, what's the matter? You're white as a ghost." The strain of getting his words out was patently visible:

"Nothing, Madame, my leg hurts a little."

I go on with my class and at recess, the child doesn't budge; he asks permission to stay at his desk because of his leg.

"But what's the matter with your leg?"

"I don't know, Madame, my father will take care of me later."

I don't know what to think, so I say: "All right, stay there."

When class is over, he doesn't budge and says: "My brother went for my father because I can't walk."

I was puzzled but far from suspecting the scheme that had been set up. In the meantime, the captain had notified the inspector of my academy that I beat the children and had broken his son's leg.

The fact is that he was the one who had broken his son's leg and hatched a plot to pin it on me. The child and his brother were too terrorized to say a thing, and while they put on their shabby act for me, he had gone to lodge a complaint for blows and injuries to children.

Very early the next day the inspector was there. I thought to myself: "What's going to happen now?" and he attempted to reassure me, saying:

"But Madame Carles, I am here to protect you, not to do you in; I know very well you didn't break that child's leg; however, since the man lodged a complaint, I am obliged to make my inquiry; I must question the children in the class and the rules require me to do it in your absence."

I went out, leaving the inspector with my youngsters. He gave them each a sheet of paper, and wrote on the board: "Does your teacher hit you?" telling them: "Write the answer." They all said "no."

"Has Madame Carles hit any of you?"

"Yes, her Jojo" — when I did chastize one of them, it was always my own and I occasionally slapped him when he went too far. They all said the same thing and Jojo wrote: "Yes, my mother smacked me."

"Did Madame Carles touch Pierre Gentil?"

"No."

"Did she hit any children besides her son?"

"No."

The inspector got the information he needed and the captain got nothing for his pains.

"You see," the inspector said, "I came to protect you; I knew you would win your case and all the children confirmed what you told me."

I was staggered at the idea that anyone might do such a thing. To break a child's leg just to accuse a teacher of beating her pupils . . . I'd never experienced anything so monstrous in my whole career. What's most astonishing is that I did not react when it happened, I was too happy that my youngsters exonerated me and I took no steps against the fellow. I think today I wouldn't let something of the sort go by; that character was an unmitigated bastard — there's no other word for him, and he deserved to be beaten to a pulp, but at the time I let it drop. Jean agreed, he said it wasn't worth wasting your time over such people. Then too, joyously immersed in our own happiness, my husband and I had better things to do than lower ourselves to that.

Chapter 24

My Four Wards

One day, Carles said to me: "Look, if we're going to stay here, in a house like this, we might as well try to do something with it. It's a big house, most of the space is unused, I know how to cook — we could turn it into a hotel."

I liked the idea. For one thing, Jean had had it with knocking around as a painter, working for other people, and even more important, there was nobody to keep up the farm. Together with my father, we talked it over and finally decided to go ahead. We had some money set aside but everything had to be done, and since we didn't have a cent coming in, hiring a contractor was out of the question. We did every bit of it ourselves, first of all fitting out rooms, installing running water and putting up partitions.

Jean had also said: "First we'll do the rooms and then we'll set up the hotel when we can"; it's true that we couldn't be in a hurry with our methods and our means, and it took us several years to create something more or less finished. The idea was not enough in itself; we needed money to buy bricks, cement, washstands, and pipes. Jean was our mason, and he asked his brother to come give us a hand. He also took care of the bedding, managing pretty well with the springs and mattresses, and my father combed out wool from his sheep that we used to stuff the mattresses and chairs, and we had our blankets made with it. This was indeed a family enterprise.

There wasn't much of a tourist business then, it was still in its infancy. We started out by placing classified ads in the papers we subscribed to, *The Human Homeland, On the Outside,* and the first year, we had five guests, then it went up to fifteen, and each year there were a few more. We started out serving meals family style, but eventually we had to give it up because family-style eating is very special. In the first place, you can't have too many people, then the guests who happen to be there have to like each other; if they don't, the slightest squabble will throw things off completely. All it takes is one uncomfortable person to do in the whole table.

Jean found a name for the hotel: Les Arcades. From the very beginning we threw ourselves into the business body and soul, and for me it was a major change. Besides plastering and painting, I looked after the hotel from the time it opened. After school, I did the rooms and washed the linens, waited table in the evening and cleaned the kitchen, not to mention the hours I spent keeping the books, making up orders, and paying bills. All that was unimportant to me, we had created the hotel together and it was our life. This is what I said to Jean:

"Instead of going away on vacation, we have our hotel."

His answer was: "Wait till you see our happy old age; for now we have to work our tails off, but one day we'll live like kings; we'll put money aside from your pension when you retire, and every year we'll take a trip."

We never did take a trip. We thought the hotel would be a good investment, but it never earned much profit. The seasons are too short here, and people did not usually take time off in the thirties before paid vacations were required by law.

No matter, we were happy. The house had recovered its past life and liveliness; besides Jean and me, there were our two children, my father and my mother-in-law who lived with us, and more and more often Marie-Rose's children coming to us for refuge.

For in the meantime Marie-Rose had come back from the psychiatric hospital. The doctor told us she was cured, but the fact is that her health depended on the kind of life she would lead, and the moment she came back, her husband started beating and harrassing her again. They were both crazy, in their own ways, and when they were together, they couldn't help falling back into their old wild life. Neither one of them was able to make decisions or assume responsibility; having children was the only thing they agreed on. Marie-Rose gave birth eight times while she lived with Jacques Mercier; only four children survived.

It was pitiful. When a more serious crisis erupted, they would all go their separate ways, my sister would hide somewhere or other without bothering about anything, and the youngsters managed as best they could. Marie would come to us for shelter with her brother and sisters. She was about ten at the time I'm talking about, as mature and serious as an adult. She was like all children forced to protect themselves: she made her own decisions. When her parents had a fight, she would flee from La Draille with the smallest child in her arms, pulling along the two others who were hanging onto her smock, one on each side. Marie had a sixth sense when she came, she would say to herself: I mustn't go to my godmother's house as long as there's a guest up, or they'll wonder what we're doing at our aunt's at this hour of night.

Meanwhile, she hid with the others in the shed across the road, waiting in the dark — and frequently the cold — until I was alone in the kitchen. I made it a practice to give the kitchen a thorough going over every day when the last guest left and I was by myself. I would clean the tables, benches, and floor with caustic soda and a scrubbing brush, and the girl always waited for that time to come in. You should have seen those four youngsters walk in. I'd say:

"So, you're back. Have you had anything to eat at least?"

"Yes, Aunt Émilie, we had a little soup before we left."

"And where's your mother?"

"I don't have any idea."

"And your father?"

"Oh, like always, he grabbed the axe and wanted to cut our mother with it, so we left because we were too scared."

It was happening more often than usual, and that Jacques Mercier gave us all kinds of trouble because he could not stand his kids coming to us at Les Arcades. He kept them away whenever he could, using threats to dissuade them. As a result, our relations were on the strained side. The man was eaten alive with hate; he was jealous and mean and he'd tell his kids:

"I forbid you to go to the moneybags's 'château,' I forbid you to take what they give you."

My sister had done everything possible to push him over the edge so she was to blame too; anyway I think she should have had the sense not to provoke him with her remarks. In their earliest quarrels, she had told him:

"What the hell are you doing here? You don't have a thing of your own; the house is mine, the land is mine, my father paid for the donkey and the cow, so what are you doing here?"

People should never speak that way. It is a shameful trick to use your possessions to reproach the person who has nothing, but my sister was not wise enough to understand; she made him feel the weight of her power and strength and as a result she made him ten times more malicious and violent. I wonder, if I'd done something like that with Jean, if I'd said: "Nothing here is yours." He would have left on the spot and I would never have seen him again. That's natural, a man has his dignity. Besides, with four youngsters there to hear every word, a man won't put up with harrassment like that. One day, Jacques Mercier told my sister: "What's the difference? Some day you won't have anything either, you'll lose it all and you won't have any more than me," and that is precisely what happened.

Thanks to Marie-Rose, that man with a grudge against the world from the start became ten times more vicious. The dissension between them was endemic, with scant respite, and unfortunately, the tragedy assumed increasingly frightful proportions with each passing day. They had a fifth child, a boy, Jean-Baptiste, who lived only three weeks. The infant virtually died of starvation; they had reached such a degree of penury and disorder that there was not enough milk, no money to buy any, and one out of two bottles was made with water. Who could have suspected the drama that was brewing? Jacques Mercier went around telling people everywhere that his fifth kid entitled him to the Cognac Prize. What a disgrace! To have children for the money! The Cognac law itself was disgraceful, a temptation designed for the poor. In those days, the state awarded a bonus of 25,000 francs to couples under thirty with five children, and 25,000 francs was a lot of money since you could buy a house for 2000 or 3000 francs; and little Jean-Baptiste was their Cognac Prize and nothing else. They weren't even capable of feeding him properly.

The night the child died, Jacques Mercier was drunk as usual; he'd taken refuge in some bistro or other in the commune, and my sister was so afraid of him that she went and hid too, which meant the baby was alone. It was already too late when Marie-Rose came for me at Les Arcades. She was fretting and fuming, repeating over and over: "Come, I can't go back there alone, we have to dress the little one." She had nothing to dress him decently, even to bury him in, and I had to look through my things to find something, and when we reached La Draille, Jacques Mercier was there with his mother. The first thing he said to us was: "Just look what she did to my Cognac Prize!" It was monstrous to make a remark like that with the body still warm; it was so monstrous that even his mother would not put up with it, and she said: "Shush, she's not the only one to blame, it's your fault too." Jacques Mercier stared at his mother. "What!" he told her. "You, lady, you get twigs ready for your straw fire, you strike the match, and then you don't want it to burn?" Decoded, that meant: "You've always talked against Marie-Rose and now you blame me." I heard it all, I was there trying to clean the little body and dress it for burial.

I wonder, what if the youngster had lived, what if they'd received those 25,000 francs? I cannot say whether things would have worked out. I don't think so; there might have been a respite, but once they ran through the money, it would have been the same old story. As it was, things didn't drag on; a few months later, Jacques Mercier set La Draille on fire, convinced when he did it that he was roasting them all alive. He lit three fires in three different places, one in the hay, one in the woodpile, and a third I don't remember where. Luckily, my sister had left with the kids — as if she had had a premonition — and they all fled to the communal baking oven to escape him. He went off to sit on a hilltop to watch the fire. Everything burned up; the firemen arrived too late and nothing was left but the walls and a few odds and ends of frame. Such was the accomplishment of Jacques Mercier. He was tried and served time in prison. But what was that in comparison with the damage he had done? The four children were traumatized by that night and Marie-Rose was not much better off; she sank back into her madness and we kept her at home with us. It was not long before she had an especially violent fit; I remember she came to Les Arcades and went straight up to my father's room. She began to scream and break everything, hurling everything that came to hand against the wall. She was like a fury; I had to call my husband to bring her under control. He managed to calm her down, but we could not keep her with us any longer and she went back to the psychiatric hospital.

When Jacques Mercier was released from prison, we asked him what he planned to do with the children while his wife was in the hospital.

"Come on," he said, "I can't take care of the four of them."

"But in your family, do they want one or two?"

"Of course not. Put them on Public Assistance."

My husband wouldn't hear of it, he insisted we take in Marie-Rose's children:

"We must not allow Public Assistance to take the children, they'll be scattered all over the département and they'll never know they're brother and sisters."

He was right, there's nothing worse for youngsters, but four more children — that was a burden and a responsibility of no small proportions, and I hesitated. I was willing to take one or two, I was willing to take on Marie, the eldest, since I had raised her from the time she was a baby, but the four of them together were too much.

Jean could be very persuasive when he wanted.

"Look here, Émilie, we don't have the right to let them go off like that; it's worse than sending them off to die. Here, we'll always find some way to work things out; we'll eat what's around, raw dandelions or cooked dandelions if we have to, but they won't go to Public Assistance."

He spoke so well that we were finally won over, my father and I, but it was no simple matter since the courts had to decide. The youngsters had already made their choice; they wouldn't hear of anything but Les Arcades, but the court had to rule.

My older brother François agreed to take the boy Auguste, but only because he was old enough to work and help him out. François exploited him the whole time they spent together in Briançon. He never sent him to school, he made him watch his flock with no thought for his education, and the schoolteacher came to see me at regular intervals:

"Madame Carles, you must tell your brother to send me the little boy. At the rate things are going, he's turning him into an illiterate, the youngster is going on ten and he doesn't know how to read or write."

I went to see François to put him on the right track. I told him: "You must send Auguste to school, or the gendarmes will take him away from you," and he sent him to school for a week and then it started all over again.

Things went on like that for several months. What was intolerable is that an alcoholic pyromaniac, Jacques Mercier, sentenced to prison for setting his own house on fire, was still his children's legal guardian. Even though he was far from being responsible in any sense of the word, the law held that to reach the point of forfeiting his paternal rights, he had to do something more. Jacques Mercier was always after money; when I say money, I mean a little change for the bistro, and he'd have done anything to obtain it. He was known in Briançon for playing the buffoon, and for a few francs, the local jokers would get him to do anything they wanted. With those sous, he'd go straight off to buy cigarettes and drink wine. During one of his drinking bouts, he dropped his trousers and showed everyone his wee-wee. It created a scandal and he was brought to trial for the second time for obscene acts on the public thoroughfare, and for that reason alone the court stripped him of his paternal rights. That is what they call justice! Here's a man who for years did not ever look after his children, who let one of them die of starvation, who tried to burn his whole brood alive along with his wife, and not for an instant did the judges even consider stripping him of his paternal rights. But the moment he exposed his backside in front of the post office in Briançon, he had it. Shoddy justice, taking offense at a harmless indecent act when they had no qualms about abandoning children to the authority of a criminal. After the award was made, the social worker came to see me to find out what we planned to do. I told her:

"What we plan to do? But that's obvious, we'll keep the little girls, besides they don't want to go anywhere else."

"But you must take the boy too," that woman replied. "If you don't, I will be obliged to remove the three girls."

"You think I don't have enough already?"

"Do as you please, but by law they must stay together, otherwise I have to turn them over to Public Assistance."

Jean and I decided to take him too. That made four wards to raise, plus our own two, plus my father, plus my mother-in-law. It was 1936. The hotel frequently brought in less than it cost, and all we had to live on was my monthly salary. At the time, I was earning 700 francs. It came by money order from the prefecture, and when the postman brought it, I signed it but never saw any money. Instead I filled out three pink forms: two 300-franc money orders covering foster care for Catherine, the youngest, and Louisette, and a third for Marie's board at the orphanage. It was a closed circle; there wasn't one cent of my pay left over.

One of my cousins said: "Now really, Émilie, that's crazy, you're not being fair to your children, you're giving away everything you have," because with my father's help, we'd kept a few animals, sheep, rabbits, a little live-stock, and we lived on them and on the little the restaurant brought in during the summer. Like many people, my cousin thought we were squandering these assets, and she could not refrain from telling me: "You're not being fair to your children."

I was beside myself: "What! I'm not being fair to my children? How can you say a thing like that? They have everything they need, they aren't naked, they've got shoes and clothes, they're not hungry and they're not cold, and I don't see how I'm being unfair to them. I couldn't bear — not ever — for my children to have everything and then leave the others to Public Assistance."

Jean was the one who had said: "We'll eat dandelions raw and dande-lions cooked, but they will not go on Assistance," and that is what we did: we kept them and raised them like our own children. It was hard, but what did that matter? Once Jean convinced me, I was the more tenacious of the two. I had to be, or I don't know how we would have managed. Whenever things got tight, the "ant" was there, and sometimes Jean felt bad about it:

"I was the one who forced your hand, and you're the one who has the most worries with those kids."

That was most certainly true; I had the hardest job, washing, mending, getting them registered in schools, applying for scholarships, and Jean was well aware of it. I'd say:

"When there are children, no matter what you do, it's always the woman who knocks herself out."

There are no two ways about it, when something went wrong, it all fell on me, up to and including borrowing money from neighbors when we didn't have any left. It was a hell of a struggle to raise those four kids, but we did it, and I have never been sorry.

Chapter
25

The
Golden
Age

One day, I went to see Bernard, our deputy in the département. I don't remember how the occasion arose, but I'd gone to talk to him about our peasants and their living conditions. Change was long in coming for the most part. Many families lived without any conveniences, still using the fireplace for all heating and cooking. In our family, we had a furnace and a stove that worked on butane gas, but we were exceptional. Imagine what life was like for women who had to manage with that primitive system, lighting the fire, putting up with the smoke. It was so impractical that at the height of the farm season, peasants didn't cook lunch, eating their food raw, not taking the time to light the fire or even heat anything. With household appliances, a gas stove, they could have done it. That is why I went to see the deputy, to tell him it was truly deplorable that peasants did not have those minimum conveniences, that they could not afford them and we needed a law making it possible for them to get the equipment they needed more easily. The deputy listened politely, but it was obvious that he didn't much understand all my fuss about peasants. When I finished, he said:

"Of course I understand, Madame Carles, but I can't do much, you know."

"Why not?" I said. "To get elected you promised all those people you'd do your utmost to improve their living conditions. What we need is a law that makes it possible for them to buy household appliances at a lower price. It is your job to talk about it in the Chamber of Deputies."

"I certainly do understand you, yes I do, but I don't carry much weight in the Chamber, I'm only one against 600."

"Oh, I see. You're only one against 600. Now I understand. Don't say another word. You promise the peasants whatever they want to get their votes, then you tell them afterwards you can't do anything for them. It's obvious that the 599 others act exactly like you, and the voters pay the piper."

That is what comes of democratic elections. It wasn't a complete surprise for me; I had always known elections were sweet talk and window dressing and here was more evidence. Ever since my school days, I had instinctively distrusted what textbooks call universal suffrage. That celebrated suffrage, pride of the republic, what is it anyway? *I* don't see what makes it so universal, given that a half plus one is just the thing if you're trying to get elected, but if you get half minus one, you're swindled. It's like any other kind of injustice, legal and accepted, but injustice all the same. Not to mention that in small places like ours, elections are a matter of influence.

As election time neared, you'd see a Rothschild or a Petch come around. Overnight, those bankers from Paris, rich as Croesus, would land in our villages to visit our voters and win them over. I remember, I saw it with my own eyes, the future deputy would stroll around arm in arm with the mayor, and the two of them would visit all the houses, distributing fifty and one hundred franc bills to the peasants. The mayor would point out the people worth consideration and the amount:

"You'll give this one a hundred francs; fifty'll be enough for that one."

It was all very simple; they were buying votes. Afterwards they worked things out between themselves. The mayor got his payoff too and he received favors. That's the way things happened. And that is why I would tell my youngsters that universal suffrage was a fraud and they should be wary of it like the plague. I tried to open the peasants' eyes as well, telling them:

"How can poor, hardworking people like us vote for millionaires? They cannot protect the interests of working people."

They would answer:

"Oh, but you never know what might happen. We might need those people."

Even my father did not understand me when I tried to explain the stupidity of those votes; if I asked him to explain why he voted that way, he answered:

"Well, the mayor votes that way and you don't know what you may need."

The mayor didn't have to grease his palm; he came to see him and gave him a ballot, saying: "This is the ballot you'll hand in," and that's what my father did. I think he didn't even look at what was written on it, he simply put it in the ballot box. Everything worked that way. That is how conservatives operated. There was virtually no opposition, or so little it hardly counted.

My husband's ideas were totally different, and he did not hide the fact. For a long time he was the only man in the region who voted Communist; later on there were a few others, but they were never more than a drop in the bucket. I remember, in '32 or '33, he locked horns with the mayor over the municipal elections. It happened when Jean's brother was working with us at Les Arcades. Jules was fonder of the bistro than his brother, and the afternoon or evening of the elections, he said to my husband:

"Come Jean, let's go on out, we'll walk over to the café and see what they're saying about the election."

It was pure curiosity, we already knew who had just been elected mayor of Val-des-Prés. So they went, and the mayor was buying drinks to toast his victory. He was the very man who brought the ballots around to his constituents after marking them with a pin. He made little tiny holes on the upper left, on the right, on the bottom, in the middle, a single hole or two side by side, and he recorded the marks in his notebook beside the name of the person receiving the ballot. Since he was the one who counted the votes, he knew who voted for him and who did not. It was rather primitive, but on the scale of the commune, it worked.

When Jean and his brother reached the bistro, the party was on and the mayor came right over to them:

"Monsieur Carles, have a drink on me."

They accepted, they drank to him, they had another drink, and then one more. When they had sufficiently toasted his victory the mayor said:

"Do you know you betrayed me, Monsieur Carles?"

My husband said: "*I* betrayed you?"

"Yes, you did!"

The previous night, or the night before that, the mayor had come by the house, asked Jean and my father to vote for him, and also left a ballot for each of them. To me the choice was obvious — women didn't have the vote yet — I did not want them to vote for that clod. Once again, Jean proved magnanimous:

"We can certainly trust him for one term; then we'll see, we'll have plenty of time to work out something else if need be."

Jean didn't know the fellow or all the complications trailing in his wake; and my father told me in patois:

"I promised; I'm obligated."

So both of them had voted for him, but they made changes in the slate of town councillors.

"You betrayed me, Carles, and so did old man Allais; you voted for me, that's a fact, but you didn't vote for my slate."

He'd surprised my husband and his brother, and lost no time in taking advantage of it to add:

"Just you wait, I can tell you one or two things more: the names were crossed out, and your wife wrote in the names on your ballot and your father-in-law's."

That's true. I had struck all the names on the mayor's slate of councillors, and I put in other names, decent local people for the most part. I couldn't help playing that trick on him.

"Well, you do know a thing or two," Jean said.

"But tell me, Monsieur Mayor," said Jules when it came his turn to speak — he was more direct and acerbic than my husband — "how do you know?"

"Okay, I brought the ballots over here, they went and got letters from your sister-in-law to her uncle when she was in Paris; it was the same handwriting, so we know perfectly well who wrote the names on those ballots."

Then and there, Jules exlaimed: "Good God, do you know what that'll do for you? The fact is you can fucking throw your election in the garbage can. All it'll take to void it is a phone call to the subprefect because you have no right to take ballots home with you, still less to go get personal letters to see who wrote on the ballots."

"But . . . , but . . ." said the mayor, not knowing which way to turn.

"There are no buts that'll hold up. What you did is totally illegal and we can get your election voided."

The more my brother-in-law threatened, the more the mayor deflated.

"Monsieur Carles, I beg you, tell your brother not to do anything like that, it would create a scandal."

That's the kind of mayor we had, the kind of elections that fell to our lot. The only time I saw a candidate come forward honestly was in Briançon, a little guy who was up for deputy on the Communist ticket. You can say what you like about Communists, their dogmatism, the blinders they wear, but the only righteous candidate I've seen in my whole life was a Communist. He was a young worker from Briançon, poor as Job and dressed almost like a tramp — I remember his clothes were awful when he came to Val-des-Prés for his campaign meeting, he didn't even have shoelaces and he was in rags. There had never been a Communist candidate in Briançon; it was such a backward region that whenever you talked about a Communist, people would look at you as if you had cholera or the plague. Still, this child of poverty wanted to run on the party ticket and that is what he did. He toured the election district, asking to stay the night with the few sympathizers to be found. It still brings tears to my eyes. You meet a person like that once in a lifetime; he had courage, he was transparent as a diamond, and he was a true believer. When he came to our valley, we had to fight to get him to dress properly. We bought him a pair of shoes, and to make him wear them, we said:

"Just imagine if you came out of this a deputy: you couldn't appear in Paris looking like that, you have to have a suit and shoes with laces."

That evening after the meeting in the town hall, we made him stay for dinner at Les Arcades, and my husband served him a few trout he had pulled out of the Clarée. That kid was paralyzed when he saw the trout on his plate, his eyes were as big as saucers; he'd never seen anything on his plate besides potatoes and fatback, and when he said: "When I tell my mother I ate trout, she'll fall over backwards," it was so spontaneous, so naïve that I couldn't help crying. He was simon-pure, a Communist, but simon-pure, a man who wanted to protect working people. He didn't have a chance, we all knew that, he better than anyone, but no matter. He said himself: "You have to start somewhere, you have to make your voice heard; I don't know how many votes I'll get, what's important is to do something."

I don't know how many votes he got, maybe a hundred putting together all the pals, the sympathizers, and people on the fringes. For Jean and his friends, voting was a matter of principle, whether they were anarchists or libertarians. In their judgment, if you abstained you played into the hands of the Right.

It was '36. At the beginning of the season, Jean said:

"Émilie, we have to make our statement; we have to do something for the Popular Front. For the first time, workers have a right to vacations with pay; we're going to lower our prices to ten francs a day, everything included; that way, the comrades can come breathe our mountain air."

At the end of September, we were showing a deficit, we'd run through all the money in sight. But how can you regret such impulses and such moments? '36 and '37: those years were the Golden Age of Les Arcades.

All the friends who came to spend their vacations with us were pacifists or pacificist sympathizers. We subscribed to journals that were on the side of nonviolence and conscientious objection, and to make sure that we'd attract some guests, Jean had sent them classified ads: "Room and board in a rustic setting, moderate prices. At Les Arcades, you will be among comrades in a congenial family atmosphere." The ad appeared in *The Human Homeland* and *On the Outside,* and the people who came to us were from that milieu.

For years Les Arcades was marked by that intimacy. As they say, "it was a family affair." That's what Jean wanted, and so did I. By nature, I was very sociable and I liked things that way. For the summer we took on a few in help, but it didn't make much of a difference; we all ate together, we lived together, and when there were guests, we all did the chores together if necessary. We had special ties, and when we met in the kitchen at night, we would open a few bottles of clairette,° do the dishes and clean up, singing and joking as we went along. The atmosphere was wonderful.

We never had enough rooms at the height of the season, so Jean, the children, and I would give ours up for the guests and sleep in the hayloft. Everybody called it the bosses' room; there was straw for the whole family and we hung *bourras*[1] from the rafters for partitions.

Once or twice a week when there was a car available or even when there wasn't, we all trooped off for a picnic. We would go up as far as L'Aile-Froide or well above Névache with our baskets. In the evening, before bed-time, drunk with pure air and exhaustion, we'd gather around the table and eat up whatever was left in the pantry.

In '36, with room and board at ten francs a day, we had so many guests we didn't know which way to turn anymore. People would come and Jean took such good care of them, fed them so much, that nobody wanted to go back home. We didn't know what to do or where to put them, there were beds in every corner. It was an extraordinary summer in terms of atmosphere, but aside from that, I had to take money out of my salary in advance to make up our losses. You might say we paid the freight for the Popular Front! Those first vacations with pay for working people spelled the end of my own. From dawn to dusk, I was on the firing line, working for the glory of it.

What's the difference? There wasn't enough money, but what wealth we had! Endless discussions with all those friends, all those comrades. In the evening, we'd exchange ideas, airing our opinions on political events, on writers. It was like a crucible at full boil and everything went in. Most of the men and women coming to us were rabid individualists; to them nothing counted but liberty, the conquest of liberty, the defense of liberty. The

---

[1]*Bourras:* a large piece of cloth made out of old sheets and used to transport hay. — AU.

Sacco-Vanzetti case was still hot; the murder of the two Italian anarchists still weighed painfully on the hearts of all humanists, and we signed petitions to have their trial reviewed and them exonerated. The Popular Front had rekindled hope, that was something; it was new and good, we'd say, but it was just the first step. We'd have to fight, for the goal was the Social State, the real one. We were already looking to Spain — anarchists were numerous there, and every one of us dreamed of a libertarian Europe, free of bosses, army, and church.

We often had impassioned arguments as you'd expect when you're playing with ideas; with men of that stamp there are always spurts of enthusiasm and verbal exaggeration. Jean was among the most acrimonious; he charged straight ahead, whereas I was always aware of the limitations of anarchism. At such times, I would say:

"Your ideas are beautiful, but they're not constructive; so tell me when we'll see a libertarian society that works? *You* think simply taking power means utopia. 'Neither God nor master,' that's all you have to say."

"Émilie, Émilie, are you for the priests? Are you for the military, the bankers, the unscrupulous businessmen?"

"No, of course not, but they're the ones at the controls; it's not enough to be an individualist and an outsider and read *The Human Homeland*. Look at how the workers are divided on politics. They each live in their own camp, there are communists, there are socialists, there are anarchists; they all want the same thing, but they're all wearing blinders, and they're so shortsighted that sweat and exhaustion are the only things they seem to have in common. Me, I'm against cliques."

"Precisely."

Reading brought us back together. I have already said that Jean was a voracious reader. *The New Age in Literature* kept us up to date on the latest publications, and every month we bought the most interesting novels: Panaït Istrati, Albert Londres, Henri Bérault,° Céline. We had every single Panaït Istrati in the house, twelve, and we lent them around. There were fascinating things in those books. And Henri Bérault? He was marvelous too; he wrote *The Wood of the Hanging Templar*. I think of all the things I've read, it was among those that made the strongest impression on me. It was about the persecution of the Knights Templar in the Middle Ages. Bérault knew how to write. It was valuable, it carried weight, there was something fantastic about his book. I cried when they killed him: imagine killing men like that!

Pacifism has built-in contradictions; what I mean is that you're caught in a web of contradictions when you're faced with a given reality. You don't want anyone going to war, you don't want any more soldiers and warmongers, and at the same time reality forces you to make choices. For example, at the time of the Maquis° and the Liberation, it was hard for a pacifist to say: "I'm not for either side," because you knew the Germans were the spirit of evil, the concentration camps, the murder of the Jewish people. Facing them were men and women in revolt against all that, who RESISTED all that because they did not want the New Order. And there was Céline. The only reason they didn't kill him, they didn't MURDER him is that he escaped, he fled; otherwise, if he hadn't left Paris, they would have shot him like the others. Even if he was wrong, even if he made unfortunate statements during the war, Céline remains a monument as a man and as a writer. *Journey to the End of the Night* is a literary masterpiece, it's fantastic. That man touches on everything. He foresaw the Second World War when he was writing *Trifles for a Massacre*. We read all his books together, Jean and I, but the one that struck me hardest was *Journey*, because it includes everything and, above all, because you identify with it. The first pages were a revelation for me, what he said about the war corresponded so exactly to what I had lived and felt, it was so real — the reality of Catherine and her husband, of Joseph — that once I read those pages I could not ever go back to them. Everybody ought to read them and learn them by heart; then I really think no one would agree to fight in the name of anything. I quote:

> But the fact is, we're all seated on a great galley ship, we all take our turn at the oars, you can't tell me any different, and what do we get for it? Nothing! Nothing but beatings, bullying, and baloney, then more filthy tricks. . . . We're working, they say, that's more stinking than all the rest — work, they say . . . we're down below in the hold, panting, reeking, oozing sweat, but look who's up on deck, in the fresh air, the guys running the show who don't give a damn, with beautiful peaches-and-cream women on their knees, swollen in all the right places. They bring us up on deck, they put on their fine top hats and they yap in our mugs like this: "Gang of swine, it's war, that's what they're up to; we're going to ram the bastards on Homeland No. 2, we're going to blow them to bits, move along now! Move it! Everything you need is on board; all together now, let's hear you holler till the timbers shake "Hoorah Homeland No. 1," let 'em hear you way out there, and for the man who bawls loudest, there's the medal and those good little sugarcoated almonds like you get for christenings and first communion. . . .
>
> . . . Then we marched and we marched, street after street after

street, civilians and their wives all along the way, shoving hoorahs at us, throwing flowers at us from sidewalk cafés, from railroad stations, from loaded churches. . . . Oh! was there ever such a mob of patriots . . . and then there weren't so many patriots, the rain came down, and then there were fewer and fewer, and then no more hoorahs at all, not a single person along the road. . . . Oh! so now we were alone together, one behind the other, the music stopped. "So that's what's up," I said to myself when I saw what was going on, "it's no fun anymore, I'll have to start over." . . . I was going to clear out . . . hey! too late! they'd quietly closed the door behind us civilians, we'd been trapped like rats. . . .

. . . Way off down the road, as far as the eye could see, were two dark dots in the middle, like us, only they were two Germans, very busy shooting for a good fifteen minutes. . . . Maybe our colonel knew why those two people were shooting, maybe the Germans knew too, but me, I really didn't have the foggiest idea. . . . I guess war was everything you didn't understand. . . . It could not go on, so something extraordinary must have happened in those people's heads that *I* did not feel at all . . . still I kind of wanted to try and understand their brutality, but even more I had an immense, compelling urge to clear out of there! since all of a sudden it looked so much like the result of some fantastic mistake. "When you're in a bind like that," I told myself, "there's nothing you can do, so you just have to get the hell out." . . . Buzzing along above our heads, one after the other, two millimeters, maybe one, from our foreheads, those long alluring threads traced by bullets aiming to kill you in the hot summer air. . . . Never had I felt so useless as among all those bullets and that sunlight, an immense and universal sneer. I was only twenty years old at the time.

A savage wind had risen on all sides, poplars blended their bursts of gusting leaves with the small sharp sounds coming to-wards us from down there. . . . Those unknown soldiers kept on missing us, but all the while they wound a thousand dead men round us so it was like we were dressed in them, I didn't dare budge. So that colonel was a monster! I was sure by now; but he was worse than a recruit, it didn't occur to him that he too could depart this life. At the same time, I grasped that there must be lots like him in our army — all brave men, and no doubt just as many in the opposing army, who knew how many? One, two, maybe several million in all? So my jitters turned into panic: with creatures like that, this hellish idiocy could go on indefinitely, why would they stop? Never had I sensed such implacability in the sentence passed on men and things. . . . There's virginity for horror as there is for sex, and I, how could I have guessed at that horror when I left Place Clichy? Before you got inside the war, how could you have foreseen what went into the filthy human soul, the heroic sluggard soul? Now I was caught in that mass flight toward mass murder, toward the raging fire: it all came up out of the depths and now it was here.

That is the sort of text we ought to teach our youngsters; they would learn the French language, and once and for all they would have done with war, not one more person would agree to go off and be killed.

There's another page in Céline that struck me, it's when he goes to see a girl who is pregnant by her boss and has attempted an abortion. She did it badly, she's losing blood, and the hemorrhage must be stopped. Céline treats her and tells her that to get well she must have good wine and good meat, and then he has to collect his fee. Céline writes: "If I take the money I'm shit because I know she doesn't have any money, I see it and I sense it, but tomorrow morning my rent is due, if I don't pay up, the landlord will throw me out, so if I'm shit, he's a dung heap, he's a pile of shit because he has more money than I do." I thought that was so human that I never forgot it. There are a great many things of that sort in Céline. But what's so terrible is that people around here never read anything.

The father I adored was of that race; he had never read a book in his life or even a newspaper. I remember at the time of my marriage, that was one of the things he didn't like about Jean, and he said in all sincerity, as the ultimate proof that Jean was not for me: "He reads too much," thus revealing the source of his fear and distrust. How could they think for themselves? They're neither for a writer nor against, nor are they for an idea nor against. In the long run, that deficiency teaches them only one thing: to remain silent and to live in a silent world, just like stagnant water. The slightest breath, the slightest word out of the ordinary sends them packing. That's what our peasants were like here; and to all practical purposes, nothing is different, for there have only been material changes; other than that they are still the same: conversation, participation, simply being against something and speaking out, that they do not know how to do. You might call the church responsible for this frame of mind; it had a tremendous grip on people and marked them. Later on the patriarchy took over; the father was the undisputed head of the family which was at his beck and call, and he in turn bowed to the laws of church and state. It is true that schoolteachers are all at fault for what goes on in class; they are the ones who have a chance to change the young-sters' mentality, open their horizons, teach in such a way that the world will change. I did what I could; I never had them sing the "Marseillaise," the words are so bellicose, so chauvinistic that for me it was out of the question to make them learn and recite it. On the contrary, I tried to get them to drop their distrust of other people, I had them learn by heart passages against racism, texts like "The Death of the Jew"°:

"He's a Jew," they said, "come out of who knows where;
Enemy to the God we worship in our land,
He'd attack our God again if He returned to earth,
Polluting with his body any holy Christian corpse,
So let's drag the dog and drop him on the rocks."
The Jew's sad wife and trembling little ones
Implored the leaders' pity all in vain.
Holding tight the feet of the dead man in his shroud
They fought the crowd's revulsion for his corpse.
When I came upon the scene as witness to their plight
I shamed those so-called Christians with the hardness of their hearts,
And blushing bright for them, to make them bury him, said:
"Come on and take the boards right off my bed."
My few words were enough to work a change of heart,
And they argued who would shelter those bereft.

Jean was on the side of liberty; with respect to the kids he'd say: "You have to let them live free; children are not property, so people do not have the right to decide for them," and he tried to live in accordance with that princi-ple. I was in complete agreement, and I can say that on the whole we left our children completely free. I know that this is not the way most parents think even today, but I believe they are making a mistake. They are wrong to impose their point of view, especially since most of the time what they are really doing is carrying out through their youngsters what they were incapa-ble of doing themselves. It's crazy when you see how virtuous people can feel through their children! It's like a mirror, but when you look close up, you see that frequently the only dialogue between parents and children consists of: "Do what I tell you, but don't do what I do." Nothing worthwhile can come of that; on the contrary, trusting in our own lives, we have every reason to let our children live as they choose. That is what my husband and I always did.

One day, I met a school principal in Briançon, and she asked: "What are you doing these days?" I sketched my life briefly for her saying:

"Now I'm in Val-des-Prés permanently, we have Les Arcades, my husband is in charge there; I have my teaching and I help him out too."

"What about your children? What are they doing?"

"Oh, they've decided what they want," I told her. "I think they'll both be ski instructors."

"And what does your husband have to say about that?"

"My husband is all for letting them do what they want. They love sun and snow, and so . . ."

Looking at me for a moment, the principal said: "Émilie, your husband is a wise man."

I understood that she was making her mea culpa. She had compelled her two daughters to become pharmacists, forcing them to stay in school until they earned their diplomas, and then she'd gone on managing their lives and kept them from marrying any of the men who came around under the pretext that they were not good enough for her girls. Gradually, she had ruined their lives, with the older one marrying some elderly fellow and the second remaining an old maid. The principal had become aware of her own responsibility for the mess she'd made of their lives, and that is why she repeated: "Your husband is a wise man."

Some time later, she visited Les Arcades, saw all that we had done together, Jean and I, the rooms, the decorating, the furniture, and she said:

"Why it's amazing the way you and your husband complement each other! You've got a fortune right there! With his two crafts, painting and cooking, and your help, and then you teaching right next door: it's extraordinary."

Chapter 26

Like a Bird Fallen from the Nest

Who could have foreseen the tragedy? When you're happy, it's absurd to think of tragedy. If someone predicts it or simply talks about it, you call him a bird of ill omen, and you turn away. In 1938, after those few years of happiness, clouds began to gather over our heads. The Popular Front was fluttering its wings like a wounded bird, civil war was raging in Spain and we were helping the refugees as best we could. We collected old clothes for the Loyalist children already flocking to southern France. The war craze had overtaken all Europe; in Germany Hitler and his triumphant Nazis became more threatening with each passing day, and in Italy the Fascist order knew no limits. For pacifists like us, it was hard.

They talked about nothing but war all around us, and the most pessimistic had the feeling that it was inevitable and imminent. But what kind of war? I could not help thinking back to the dreadful years after 1914. I told myself that if they started in again, with modern weapons and technology, the slaughter would be universal. In those circumstances, it is easy to become selfish, and I reassured myself with the thought that Jean was too old to go off and fight and my children were too young to be hurt. My son Jojo was eight, my daughter Nini was six. On that score, I felt secure. How ridiculous! It was directly through the family that tragedy lashed us right in the face.

For years, the soldiers in Briançon had been nothing more than nice young fellows doing their military service, but now they were on the move. Every day they were more in evidence, assuming the importance of people everything depends on. They crisscrossed the countryside in whole convoys.

The Italian border is not far, a few kilometers as the crow flies, and the commotion turned into a nightmare at the time of the Munich business. They went by in strings of trucks, traversing villages without slowing down, supposedly transporting war materiel to the Echelle Pass. I wonder what they could possibly try to defend up there, as if the Italians would attack in a spot like that. . . . But there was nothing to be done, the army was in full steam, nothing could stand in its path.

The absurd thing is that at the age I fell from a height of two stories onto the threshing floor, my little girl fell under the wheels of those trucks. Nini was six, she was riding her little bicycle, she loved it. We had bought her one so that she could come to school with me in Alberts. Every day — morning, evening, and for lunch at noon — we'd travel together. Usually, she rode ahead of me. I often saw her slow down as if she planned to stop. I'd say:

"What's the matter, Nini, that you're slowing down?"

"Maman, didn't you see the little bird? I didn't want to scare him, so I waited till he flew away by himself without me scaring him."

Poor little girl, she was the one who died. She used to play in the road on her bike while I did the rooms of Les Arcades. When the trucks came along, Nini got out of the way, standing beside the road to let them pass. They were carrying enormous posts, projecting several meters over the back of the trucks, and when one of them swerved, the posts teetered and we never knew why. My little girl was caught and blown away like a butterfly. My husband rushed over, he knew as soon as he picked her up that nothing could be done; she was still breathing but her brains were leaking out through her nose. He came back with her in his arms, but he didn't say anything; he acted as if we might still save her. He laid her on the bed while I phoned all the doctors in Briançon. They all said:

"Bring her in right away, we'll give her a transfusion with her father's blood."

Jean agreed to go. He took the car and left with the little one. I stayed home, I did not have the heart to go with them. When he returned two or three hours later, my little girl was dead. Her life ended on the way home. Of course they had not tried anything: the moment they examined her, the doctors saw that her little skull was empty, it was all out there on the road. They did not even try a transfusion, it would have been pointless.

I almost went out of my mind. I think there are no words to describe what I went through at that time. Losing a child, it's . . . How can I put it? I became another person. Nothing was real to me anymore; there was only pain and the terrible longing to disappear, myself. For days on end I did not emerge from that state of combined prostration and aggression. I was like a tigress; I could not tolerate anyone and no one could come near me, not even my husband or my son. I was like an animal broken loose, unable to endure the sight of life. Everything hurt, their voices, their gestures. And my nieces . . . it wasn't just that I could not bear to see them or hear them, worse still I wished I'd never see them again, all I could think of was my little Nini playing with them. I became nastier by the day, I didn't like anyone anymore, or anything. My husband hovered over me like a soul in torment; he had always been a fatalist, and often tried to make me see life the same way. But now, when he tried to reason with me, I could not listen to him.

"I beg you, Émilie," he repeated, "accept the fate meted out to us. That child is like a bird fallen from the nest. On the day of her birth, the day of her death was already written, there was nothing we could do, not you, not me, not anyone."

And my father . . . he was unbearable. For all the love I owe him, I still maintain he was atrocious at the time. He refused to understand why I would weep and be sick because my little girl had died, or else he simply could not bear it. He said:

"Now, you stop crying, it's getting ridiculous. Nobody needs that little girl."

Words like that were unbearable, and I did not understand how my father could say such things.

Guilt followed on pain. I told myself that if my little girl was dead, it was because I hadn't looked after her properly. I found every reason to make myself responsible for her death. It was because of the hotel, because of my nieces, because I worked too hard. All day long, I turned those ideas over and over in my poor head. It was wrong, as wrong as can be, and it served no useful purpose. In the country like here, it's not the same as in the city, no one ever keeps an eye on children, they come and go freely; but the feeling was too strong for me, I blamed myself, I tortured myself, I suffered, and I was destroying myself as time went on.

Her death was so unjust. All the deaths I had seen were unjust — my mother's, Catherine's, Joseph's — but this one was far beyond what I could bear. Once and for all, I lost my faith and I broke with the church. It was impossible for me to accept the idea of such an unjust God. If I had abandoned my nieces to Public Assistance, Nini's death might have been a kind of punishment from heaven. Imagining a God of vengeance is harsh; but even so my case was the opposite, I'd kept all four with me, raising them like my own and there was never any question of reward or duty, and when I saw my little girl dead, right away I said: But there is no God of goodness, and if there is, where is He? What is He doing? It's not true, it can't be true, that God is a monster.

From 1918 on, I had kept my distance from the church, but now I broke completely and I never went back.

I was in such bad shape that something had to be done. One day I asked a doctor friend if I was going crazy.

"I'm not alive anymore, I don't let the people around me live either; she's the only thing that matters, the rest doesn't exist for me. Do you think I'll end up like that?"

"No," he said. "Your reactions are human, they are the reactions of a mother who has just lost her child; the passage of time will take care of it. My only advice for you is not to stay here; get away from this place where everything reminds you of your child. You'll see, leaving for a while will do you good."

Jean and I decided to take his advice. We closed the hotel, buckled on our knapsacks and left on foot, straight south. I remember we walked like animals, without saying a word, climbing up and down across the mountains until we couldn't go on, exhausted, breathless, our heads intoxicated with air and altitude. To eat and sleep, we stopped wherever we were, sometimes a climbers' hut, sometimes an inn, mostly out in the open. That hike was like a purification. I don't remember anymore how far we went; we set out for the sea, but we didn't get that far.

Fatalist or not, Jean was right: that death had to be accepted. The passing of my little girl was one more injustice in a family positively singled out by fate. It began with my mother, killed by lightning at the age of thirty-six; next it was Catherine's turn, dying in childbirth at twenty-two, followed to the tomb by her husband the cheesemaker a few months later; then Joseph, also twenty-two, dead of starvation on the day the armistice was signed. My other brothers and sisters were to meet quick dramatic deaths. Marie-Rose and Rose-Marie both died on the operating table, and as for François, he had the most absurd death of all.

François was one of the "Living Dead" Panaït Istrati describes in *Kyra Kyralina*, people who are dead inside and prevent others from living. He never had any individuality to speak of, he had followed after his priests and they made him a sexton. He was so crafty and unctuous that the job fit him like a glove. Relations between the two of us were never more than cool. From the time we were children, he exasperated every one of us with the constant assertion of his rights as our senior; he was insufferable. When I married, the gap only widened. He never accepted the fact that I married a man who was not from around here and a worker to boot, and he never accepted our being atheists. From that time on, he never spoke to us, neither to Jean, the children, nor me. When I happened to meet him in Briançon, it turned my stomach to see him cross the street to avoid me; and when he came upon my children, he would tell people:

"Just look at those little pagans; my own sister had them with her anarchist."

He died a nonsensical death one night during a local fair. It was late afternoon when he realized that one of his lambs was missing, and since he had probably drunk a little more than usual as happens at fairs, and since he insisted on getting his lamb back right away, he set off to look for it. He did try to find a few fellows to keep him company, asking everyone he met:

"Will you help me look for my lamb?"

But no one agreed so he left by himself. He went up to the Fort des Têtes, one of the isolated forts above Briançon, and in the process of looking for his lamb, he leaned a little too far over a well and fell in. They spent two or three days searching for him until they found his swollen body at the bottom of the well.

On my mother's side too, almost all of them died in accidents. One of my aunts was killed by her mule; an uncle, who was an orderly to an army officer in Nice, fell down an elevator shaft — he'd just taken off his shoes and socks, and thought he was going into his room. My mother had two other brothers, and they both cut their throats with a razor.

You could say that every region has its own traditions for suicide. In one spot, they all jump into wells; in another, they drown themselves in the river; somewhere else they use buckshot. Every region has its customs, and you could say their suicides show a family ressemblance. In our valley, most men who wanted to end it all would hang themselves in the hayloft, while a few others would drown themselves in the Clarée's icy waters. So it's no surprise that when my uncle killed himself with a razor, people had the impression he was eccentric. Why did he choose that way to die? We never knew. He was a customs man, rather good-looking, and he married well. He had every reason to be happy. Unfortunately, he was the devil's own for gambling; he played like a man possessed, and the more he played the more money he lost. His debts piled up so high that he didn't know which saint to turn to, and gradually he reached the point where extreme measures seemed the only alternative.

He'd married a woman with money and property, but she was impossible to live with. She was an orphan whose guardians did not bring her up properly, She had grown up with the idea that money and property were the be-all and end-all. Her wealth had gone to her head and she had an inflated sense of her own worth. My uncle was miserable with her, beset with complexes over his problems with money. When they married, he gave his solemn promise that he would keep his hands off her dowry and her property. Why had he made such a stupid promise? I think it was pride; in any case, it cost him his life, because instead of talking over his gambling problems with his wife, and working out a solution with her, he chose to keep silent and find his own solution. One evening at suppertime, he said he was going to the cellar for wine, and he did not come back up. When she went down to see what was the matter, she found him stretched out in a pool of blood; he had slit his throat with a thrust of his razor.

They buried him in the potter's field as custom decreed in such cases, and my aunt couldn't think of anything better to do with the razor than give it to her husband's young brother. A rather ghoulish gift, but the boob accepted it and carried it around. That uncle was singled out by fate as well. As a handsome youth of fifteen, he contracted a bad case of scarlet fever that left him deaf and dumb for the rest of his life. He didn't completely lose his voice, but what was left wasn't worth much; he could just about say sentences like "me wit yuh," which in plain language meant "I want to go with you." His disability brought him suffering. Besides, he was a sentimental and supersensitive man, reacting to the misfortunes of his loved ones as if they were his own. In '14, during four years of war, he saw all his friends and close relatives die while his disability kept him home in the village. One after the other, his nephews disappeared in the trenches; he watched his sister waste away bit by bit as each of them was reported missing. She was my Aunt Colombe. When her last son died at Cassino in Italy, she said to me:

"Your mother, well, she's lucky she died."

I was sixteen at the time; it was hard to hear a sentence like that from the mouth of my mother's own sister. I thought to myself: What kind of reasoning is that? and to her I said:

"I don't understand you, Aunt Colombe."

"What do you mean, you don't understand? Émilie, I know what I'm talking about; she didn't see her children die and I have seen every one of my little ones die."

My uncle suffered more than anyone else from those recurring tragedies. He could not bear his nephews dying or his sister's anguish, and he went around saying:

"I can't take it anymore, I'm going to do like Alfred, I'm going to use that thing of his."

He meant the razor that idiot widow gave him to remember his brother.

But nobody believed him when he talked like that; instead they made fun of him, and his pals would say: "You talk about it too much to do it," and he would answer: "I'm telling you I will, just like Alfred."

Every time we met, he'd say:

"Jules is dead, Clément is dead, Alfred is dead, my sister Colombe is going to die too."

He looked so sad and desperate that I did not know what to say or do to lift his spirits.

"No indeed," I'd say, "Colombe is not going to die," and I would try to make him see that as it was, enough people were dying from the war already.

One morning they found him dead. He had slit his throat with the razor. They say that it's hard to escape the special attraction those objects hold. In any case, he finally used it. When he was buried the mayor — still the same one — could not think of anything better to tell the gravediggers than:

"Better bury him with the razor."

I don't know, he could have gotten rid of it, thrown it away somewhere or other, but not there, not in the grave. Still, that is what he did, he even threw it in himself.

Seeing my family so markedly singled out led me to reflect, and I came to understand how right my husband was when he talked about fate. "It's not that you should be resigned," he'd say, "but when death comes, you have to accept it; that does not mean that man must accept everything; on the contrary, he must fight all forms of human inequality, he must revolt against exploitation, poverty, and drudgery." That is what he called being alive, and he would add: "The dead must not prevent those who are alive from living." That is how he put me back on track, and when we returned to Val-des-Prés, I was fit to take my place once more in the bosom of the family. We kept what was best of our little girl, the memory of a sweet, innocent child who had not known either evil or sorrow.

We took up our normal activities again, a little on the farm, a little in the hotel, and the rest of the time for family life. It was a period when I had time to take care of the house, for the inspector refused to let me return to my class in Alberts:

"Not right away; you couldn't bear teaching in full view of your daughter's empty desk."

And since I was expecting another child, he granted me a leave, adding:

"You'll resume your teaching later on, and you will come back to your school in Val-des-Prés. That I promise you."

Chapter
27

The
Phony
War

War was declared on September 2, 1939. This decla-
ration of war was very different from the one I experienced in 1914. This
time no one was surprised, on the contrary. I think most people were waiting
for the storm to break. In Val-des-Prés, war was in the air, and not only
because of the increasing number of soldiers coming and going. For months
on end, we had the feeling that Europe was sneaking off and taking peace
along with her. Mussolini, Hitler, the invasion of Austria, the death of the
Spanish Republic, and the end of the Popular Front only confirmed the fact.
The invasion of Poland was the drop of water that made the cup spill over.
Jean and I did not approve of this war any more than we did the others.
Jean had his own ideas, and he held to them, not just as a pacifist but as a
Frenchman too. To his mind, it was clear that France was not materially or
morally ready to launch another war.

"This war will be a phony war," he'd say.

He said it well before the term became fashionable, but he repeated it
so often and so emphatically that it finally got us into trouble.

As I've already said, there were soldiers all over the countryside in
those months; they were of every rank and every sort: reservists, conscripts,
and, of course, officers with boots and riding whips. We, the very people
who couldn't stand them, were obliged to deal with them, since they were far
from put off by Les Arcades with its good food, pleasant location, and reasonable prices. We were literally invaded.

They were there in such numbers in the early days of the war that the
Germans or Italians ended up shooting their cannons at us. They were firing

from the Montgenèvre Pass and the shots fell at random, as always happens in such cases. They were aiming at Val-des-Prés, and specifically our corner of it with the hotel and the school. The Germans apparently thought the army's headquarters were located there. The prefect sent the mayor evacuation orders, and overnight, the whole population of the village was forced to leave.

It was May or early June of '40, the phony war was just about over. The mayor left for a village in the Ardèche with all the people from the commune. We stayed behind. My father refused to leave Les Arcades, and no argument could make him change his mind.

"I'm eighty years old," he said. "I don't want to leave this house. At my age, if I have to die, I'd rather do it at home."

We could neither compel him to go nor abandon him, so we stayed too.

It never occured to us that we were harming anyone when we refused to leave Val-des-Prés. The only danger was a shell falling on our heads but, as we told the mayor, that was our business, and besides the shooting grew less and less dangerous, with the shells falling short or too far. We hardly worried about the mortars. When the Germans got a little more excited than usual, we hid in the backwoods and waited for the mood to pass.

One day the soldiers — French soldiers — came back and *they* invaded the village. It was evening, around five, we were working in the vegetable garden when an officer came toward us. He was a haughty little fellow, quite "Vieille France,"* with a swagger stick in hand. He asked:

"What are you doing here? The village was evacuated."

"We couldn't leave," Jean said. "We have an old man here who doesn't want to move away."

"I don't want to hear about it. I'm giving you an hour to get out, otherwise I'll have you shot."

The time allotted was absurd, to say the least, but the officer and his men seemed to take themselves so seriously that they were fully capable of doing something idiotic. Nevertheless, Jean did not want to give up before he had it out with the man. He said to the officer:

"Shot? I hope you are weighing your words carefully. You've got a French family with six children here — one of them an infant a few months old, an elderly man, and my wife who is the village schoolteacher. We aren't spies."

"Precisely! No one is to stay here, this zone is off-limits to civilians. *You* say you're not spies, then why are you here? Maybe you send signals to the enemy when you hide in the woods at night. I give you two hours to leave."

It was outrageous, so outrageous that we had to take it seriously. Jean told us:

"I think we'd better not insist this time, Grandfather. We'll go to the other side of Briançon."

My father set out on foot with the sheep, the ewes, and my nieces. For Embrun. I think deep down he was delighted to follow that route with his flock again; it must have reminded him of his youth and his smuggling days. Jean and I loaded the car — in those days we had a Citroën B-12 — stuffing it as tight as we could. Luckily we had all the groceries for the summer season in the hotel: canned goods, coffee, sugar, oil, soap; we filled the car with them since we had no idea what would happen nor how long we'd be away.

When we reached Embrun, we moved in with my old teacher who had presented me as a candidate for my "Certificate of Studies" in 1912. We had been on good terms ever since, and she had room for us. But living together is a delicate matter. We had a few scenes over the baby's crying, or having an accident on the carpet, and we quickly had to find some other solution. Our groceries came in handy; oil, sugar, and coffee began to be in short supply, and for as long as we had them, we could barter for what we needed.

At last Jean somehow managed to find an ancient rabbit hutch big enough to hold us. A peasant offered it to us, but the place was awful. The structure had been abandoned for years, and it was dirty and dreary. Jean went off for whitewash and brushes, saying:

"We'll move in when it's clean; in the meantime we'll sleep in the car."

That is how we lived through our "exodus," with the B-12, our sleeping bags, our knapsacks, my father's goats, and my youngest, Michel, who wasn't yet ten months old. Our travels were not so much dramatic as ludicrous, and on the eleventh day, the subprefect sent word that we could go home. The invitation was in fact an order: we were to return to Val-des-Prés without delay to defend the village from looters. With the armistice newly signed and the soldiers gone, the abandoned village was vulnerable, and the subprefect was counting on us to watch over the grain until the residents of the commune came back from the Ardèche.

So we went back to Les Arcades and did what we could. In actual fact, people had already come through and helped themselves. Our village was the only one evacuated at the time, and for peasants there is no greater temptation than carrying off manure and hay when nobody is around, and they do it very fast under those circumstances. As soon as they found out Val-des-Prés was abandoned, they wasted no time; they came in their trucks from Granvillard, Pont-de-Cervières, and Saint-Chaffrey and took what they wanted.

What could we do, my husband and I? Not much. We were usually in our vegetable garden and as soon as we heard a truck or a motor, we rushed out on the road, running around and gesticulating rather like scarecrows; the kids came with us and they thought it was funny. But our efforts were largely ineffectual. It is hard to be honest and protect other people's property. We had agreed to do it, thinking of it as a good deed, but when the village people returned, we had to face disappointment. For twenty days, we had done our best to protect the village against looters, but as soon as they came back, peasants circulated the rumor that we had looked after their property only as a subterfuge to help ourselves.

I don't want to dwell on those times. Nevertheless, they reveal so much about people's mentality, and the consequences were so serious, that it's hard not to talk about them. First of all they returned empty-handed after a month away, and the first thing we did was help them as far as we were able. Since there was a fair supply of groceries left in the hotel, the moment I heard an old person or a baby was in need, I took them what we had, soap here, sugar there. I did it gladly and without any hidden motives — well, there turned out to be a good number of people who said:

"It's easy enough for her to give, since she robbed us in the first place."

No one ever said anything to my face, and I think that was for the best, since I wouldn't have stood on ceremony, I'd have grabbed him by the scruff of the neck and dragged him over to the subprefect so he could explain that what we did was done under orders from him. Jean and I tried hard to understand why people would go so low. Either it was jealousy pure and simple, or else they were incapable of imagining behavior different from their own if *they* had been alone in the village. What it comes down to is that they couldn't swallow the fact that we had refused to leave with the rest of the village and then managed better than they. In June, if you interrupt field work for a month, the harvest can be a disaster; ultimately, that was the crux of it, they were jealous that we had gotten ahead of them, even though we were protecting them from thieves. It should be added that in the climate of collaboration settling on a country where Pétainism would flourish more than might have been expected, Jean's ideas and the people we associated with could only contribute to the general distrust. In the course of the coming months, we would feel the weight of their surliness; friends were to become few and far between but, as was only right, they would be all the more precious and dear to us.

As the inspector had promised, I was named to teach in Val-des-Prés in September 1940. Jean and I were naïve; we thought that after the unpleasantness of June, the petty annoyances and backbiting were over once and for all, and that at last we could lead a relatively peaceful life. At the end of the first trimester, that is, in December, I received a letter from the academy in Gap, notifying me that I was subject to a disciplinary transfer to Le Casset, a small village in the Guisane Valley. In the teaching profession, a disciplinary transfer is a serious punishment. It was a rough blow. My husband and I tried to discover who was responsible, and we imagined all sorts of things. Was it the mayor after what happened in June? We were most certainly at odds with him for a host of reasons, but it was unlikely. Then, who? And why? Suddenly Jean thought of the colonel.

"What colonel?" I asked.

"You know, the one I had a row with in '39."

"Oh, yes! You think he's the one?"

I had to get to the bottom of it, it was my right and my duty, and in any case I could not accept that sort of bullying passively. My first step was a telephone call to my inspector, and right away I sensed his discomfort. He said:

"It's an order from the prefecture — doesn't fall within my province. I think you would do well to be very careful in handling this matter, and if there is one piece of advice I can offer, it is for you to come to the academy in person for an explanation of why you are being transferred."

In the meantime, he had made inquiries, phoning Gap to ask: "Why are you transfering Madame Carles? I have no reason to find fault with her."

They had invited him to hold his tongue and do nothing, and in substance, he told me that I was the only person who might find out what had happened.

I went to the academy in Gap. The fellow who met with me when I arrived was furious.

"It's insane to come see me about this matter; all I did was carry out orders from above, from the prefecture. You don't realize the position you're in, and it's in your best interest to not rock the boat."

"No, indeed. I want an explanation, I want to know why I've been disciplined."

"Madame Carles, you should be glad things have worked out this way. Your husband's gotten himself into a bad fix saying whatever comes into his head. He's lucky all his defeatist chatter came before war was declared, otherwise the penalty would be the concentration camp for him and not a transfer for you. You see it's not in your best interest to stir up a fuss. Accept your new appointment, otherwise you could pay a much higher price."

It was all clear now, I knew the source of the attack, it was indeed the colonel. Even so, what sickened me most was the fact that the officials of the academy were nothing more than toadies to the prefecture. I told the fellow:

"But still, six months later Pétain said exactly what my husband said, and besides it is absolutely unthinkable that I should be penalized for what he did."

"I beg you, Madame Carles, accept the appointment, that is the best advice I can offer."

I signed, I accepted; I didn't dare run any risks or impose them on my husband. Ultimately they had the upper hand and their blackmail worked. All that for a sharp exchange with a nonentity colonel who thought it incumbent upon him to make a scene in the restaurant of Les Arcades.

But the story was not recent, and my husband and I had long since forgotten it. It was a few weeks before war was declared, the end of summer in 1939. The colonel had come to Les Arcades, asked if he and his officers could take their meals with us and we had agreed. At the time, a group of reservists on a regular training stint were eating with us. It is well known that when reserve soldiers reach a certain age, they will not put up with the company mess, and that is why they came to us for their meals. Since there were a good many of them, we had two sittings, one at ten o'clock for them, another right afterwards for our regular guests. When the colonel appeared with his officers, their table was already set up. We had done what we always did for our guests, so it was quite nice, but obviously the restaurant was crowded. I had noticed the colonel wince, but I was far from suspecting the trick he would play on us. He was the dry fart type, and without an ounce of humor he said:

"Madame, couldn't you set us up in another room?"

"No, Monsieur, this is the only one we have."

"But you surely have another place to serve us, a bedroom, or even the terrace upstairs, anywhere you like, but certainly not here with the men."

Coming to the rescue, my husband told the colonel:

"No, Monsieur, your table is nicely set up in here; I do not have the personnel to serve you on the second floor, it's too far."

"I'll give you two men to help serve."

"No," said my husband, "I'm not used to having soldiers help out and I cannot serve you on the terrace, there are too many stairs."

"Then if I understand you correctly," the Colonel said, "you are throwing us out."

"Not at all, we're waiting on you, your table is ready."

"Do you think for one minute I am going to eat with the men?"

"And you, do you think I am going to make some thirty men leave to make room for you? To us, they're the same as our other guests."

"Well, if that's the case, I'm leaving. But you can be very sure that you have not heard the last of this."

My husband shrugged his shoulders and the colonel went away with his officers. As promised, he returned sometime later trying to make life hard for us. One afternoon, he appeared at Les Arcades, saluted, clicked his heels, and said:

"I must requisition your room" — he was still talking about the dining room. "The horses in my unit need a stable."

Jean walked over to him, he managed to stay calm in situations like that:

"Colonel, I believe you can requisition me in wartime, but the war hasn't started yet, we're still at peace, and I know that you must have an official requisition order. If you do, the room is yours, if not . . ."

"If not, what?"

"Look here, I don't have time to waste; if you don't have a requisition order, you can't do a thing and you know it perfectly well; when they declare war, come back if it makes you happy."

"But the declaration will come at any moment."

"You know that when it comes, this war will be a real farce," my husband said, beginning to lose patience, "it'll be ridiculous; we're bound to lose because we are unprepared; the English have a way of using other people to fight their wars, and they'll ask for an armistice before the year is out."

The colonel's reaction was immediate and violent:

"I see you talk like a defeatist!"

"Yes, after all I am a pacifist, and for me war and the men who wage it are not the best arguments; there are other answers."

"Talk like that is not to be tolerated; you are striking a blow at the nation's morale, and I shall see to it that the matter does not end here."

We didn't put much stock in his threats. In the meantime, the course of events had only confirmed my husband's words: there had been the collapse, Dunkerque, the government's flight, and Pétain's speech. But the colonel had wangled punishment for us from the prefecture. Because he could not find a way to take revenge on my husband.

When I returned to Val-des-Prés, I had a routine visit from a doctor in Briançon who was also a friend, and he had heard about my transfer to Le Casset.

"But how did you find out?" I asked. "We haven't told anyone."

"Ah, Madame Carles, these things get around fast; from what I can make out, they're giving you a dirty deal, they're playing a rotten political trick on you. It has to do with your husband's opinions and your way of thinking in general, and you have to protect yourself. To begin with, I'm going to authorize a month's sick leave; after that, we'll see."

At first I refused: "No, I don't want you to; if they ever check up, you could be in trouble, and that I certainly don't want."

"Not at all," my friend said. "Quite honestly, I owe you that leave; first of all, you have a child of fifteen months who is still nursing; besides, I made inquiries: out there you'll have a class of nineteen kids, boys and girls, and you don't realize how tired you are because you're as tough as a peasant. I'm taking this interruption of your work on myself. I'm giving you a month."

At the end of the month, I had to take up my new post. Jean and I decided not to fight the penalty; besides, how could we run the risk of even worse trouble? At the end of February, Jean came with me and the baby to Le Casset. We got off the bus at Monestier in a blizzard. Our trip was not over, we had to find some way to reach Le Casset and the school. Monestier was a big town, and I'd done my shopping there for the three years I taught in Le Lauzet. I counted on finding old friends when we got there during the ice storm. Alas! News of my disciplinary transfer had preceded me, hollowing a chasm between us. Everywhere we went, we met closed doors. Even the people I had been really close to — the postmistress, the mailman — shunned me and avoided speaking to me. I have never understood their reasoning. They must have imagined I'd been transfered for the worst sort of crime, and the spirit of collaboration weighed on people in those days. It was the reign of fear, distrust, and hypocrisy. At the time, we were more astonished than distressed. To think that people I'd known and lived with for three years refused to acknowledge me, and all because they were afraid of being compromised, was so outrageous that we chose to laugh about it.

After going around in circles in Monestier, we finally found peasants from Le Casset getting ready for their return trip. We fell on them completely by chance as they were setting out for home with their sledges and snowshoes. They had just delivered their milk to the cheesemaker, and explained that they had come without their team of horses because the snow was so deep that no horse could have gotten through. There were five or six of these men, looking us up and down, neither kindly nor unkindly. They knew who we were, but they agreed to let us go along with them. They put my suitcases on one of the sledges. Jean put our little Michou on his shoulders and we followed the men, carefully walking in their tracks. We trekked through the blizzard for two hours to cover the two kilometers to Le Casset. Every few steps, we ran the risk of breaking our necks and tumbling in the soft snow. Without those men, we would never have gotten through. At Le Casset, our welcome was as frigid as the weather. The first thing people did was look at me as if I were an animal exhibited at a fair; then when I went to ask for bread and milk, they were unwilling to help me on the excuse that they had nothing left. Here too, they had been warned against me. But I had no intention of letting them get away with it. I absolutely had to have milk for the baby's soup, and I was determined to get it somehow or other. It was shameful of mountain people to greet us like that. My lodgings in Le Casset were shabby: a single room without any conveniences, without a log for heat. Jean looked it over in dismay:

"I won't leave tonight; I won't leave you all alone here with Michou; these people are awful."

"You certainly will leave and I'll manage; just stay and take care of Michou while I go round the village. I'll be right back."

When I returned, I said to Jean:

"Well, they're so Pétainist they don't have any humanity left; but don't worry, I found a few odds and ends at the grocery and I have enough covers to hold out for the night, and tomorrow I'll work things out."

"But Émilie!"

"Don't say another word. Go take your bus to Briançon. I don't want you to leave my father alone with the little girls, and don't worry, we've seen worse."

When Jean left, I began to put my things away; I didn't have milk or bread, but as I told my husband, I'd seen worse and I could hold out till the next day.

The next day? I was uneasy over what it had in store for me. The worst of it was not lacking for everything, it was the hostility I met, as if I were an outcast. I knew that tomorrow, and the days after that, I would find it hard to ask people for what I needed. The people of Le Casset had more than enough reasons to have qualms about me. To begin with, I was not only suspected and condemned for what they must have imagined as the most monstrous offense possible, but more important, I had been sent to educate their children, and I am sure they found that very hard to accept.

There was a knock on my door. I opened it and saw the face of a woman I had met when I was teaching in Le Lauzet.

"Hélène, my God! It can't be. What are you doing here?"

"Good evening, Mademoiselle Allais. I heard you've just come with a baby, and I brought you a cradle with a straw mattress, for you to put your little one to bed, and I brought you enough wood to make a fire, because it gets very cold here, you know, and you mustn't be cold."

"Hélène, you, here? What a surprise! Just as I was giving up on humanity, here you come with all that, it's a real miracle, but . . ." I knew she was very poor: "Hélène, you mustn't deprive yourself for me."

"Don't worry, Mademoiselle, I'm very glad to do you a favor; you were so kind to me when you were in Le Lauzet, it's the least I can do for you."

Le Lauzet! It was so long ago that I'd almost forgotten. It seemed like another time, another life. In Le Lauzet, Hélène was doubly poor as a girl, first of all because she had no money, second because she had no family and had lived alone for a long time, and above all because she hadn't found a man who wanted to marry her. She lived a poor peasant's life; she was not pretty and nature had not been kind to her, she was given to stuttering, and there was only her married sister to come with her husband every once in a while and give her a hand with plowing and harvests. Solitude was the essence of Hélène's life, a desperate solitude with no end in sight. As a result, without looking too closely, she snatched the first opportunity that came along. The suitor was a shepherd from Le Casset, as poor and solitary a creature as she and who, like her, had been unable to find someone to marry. He drank too much, but what difference did that make? Hélène had seen the union as an unexpected piece of luck. Living alone in our mountains with only the land to farm and animals to care for was the worst kind of life. Communications were still primitive, there was neither radio nor television. For a woman, it was dreadful to live isolated from one end of the year to the other, with animals as her only company and her only warmth. That is why Hélène had agreed to live with her shepherd without a moment's hesitation.

"And besides," she added, "my husband and I will give you whatever you need, all you have to do is ask; we'll do everything we can to help you out. If we don't have what you want, we'll find a way to get it somewhere else."

A few minutes after she left, there was another knock on the door. It was a man this time, a middle-aged peasant with a lovely face. He said:

"Good evening, Madame, you don't know me, but that doesn't matter, I know you."

"You know me?"

"Yes, Madame, I've heard of you; the way I see it, once you're subject to a disciplinary transfer, it means you're on the index,° and as things are these days, I can guess what's going on, and I wanted to tell you that you can count on Toussaint as a friend."

He had brought a basket and he put it on the table; it was stuffed with leeks, potatoes, and lots of other things. He gave me a loaf of bread too, beautiful homemade bread that had not come from any bakery.

"I make my own bread," he told me, "and I'm bringing you a loaf because I know they wouldn't give you any, and they wouldn't give you milk either. But Toussaint has a goat, and he has milk, and as long as I'm around, you won't ever lack for anything. It's disgraceful what this community is doing."

The man was extraordinarily generous and open-minded; a person of that mettle was an exceptional find in such a place, and I didn't know how to thank him.

"Don't thank me; if they point the finger at you, it means you're somebody."

We became close friends and did each other favors according to our complementary abilities. I helped him make his bread, did a little housework, and he provided me with vegetables, milk, and cheese.

Toussaint was another farmer without much land; the goat was his only livestock, and richer peasants boarded their animals in his stable for the winter. But Toussaint managed; he was a man of experience, but above all, he stood out among all those cowards for his independence and nobility of mind. Off in the countryside, it is always astonishing to find men who do not think like everyone else, all the more so since being few in number, they are noticeable. Toussaint was one of them; although he had never been ouside of Le Casset, he was against power, against bankers. He'd never voted for a Rothschild in his life. Toussaint had innately felt that there was another side.

We talked together a great deal, but I never really found out how he had arrived at such radical and open ideas in so closed a region. Without him, without Hélène, I don't know how I could have stuck it out.

As time went on, though, the situation improved. One day I heard that the priest had delivered an angry sermon on Sunday, taking his flock to task for their attitude. It was especially remarkable and courageous, since he had the same information on me as his parishioners; he knew who I was, he knew I did not attend church, but he was a good and tolerant man, and he told them:

"Before you refused that woman bread and milk, before you pointed your finger at her, did you know who she was, did you know what she has done? You have failed your Christian duty in this affair; you have failed to show the most elementary Christian charity. If you had made inquiries, you would have found out who she is and what she did as a young girl. For three years she was the schoolteacher in Le Lauzet. Well, all you have to do is ask the people there who she is; they still speak of her with tears in their eyes; they would give their last shirt for her, while you people have acted like Philistines."

The priest's speech shook up minds in Le Casset a bit, and from that day on, people looked at me a little less suspiciously. And then, as usual, I had the children on my side, and when you have the youngsters, you have the parents. No one could do anything about that: I love children so much that they feel my affection very quickly and they return it. By slow degrees, families mellowed and my position became more bearable.

Still, I had no intention of spending my whole life in Le Casset. A few months after my transfer, Jean-Hérold Paqui, Pétain's minister, came to the region for a lecture tour. When he stopped at Monestier, we were all summoned to hear his speech. Teachers, priests, municipal councilors, civil servants, none could avoid the meeting whose theme was: "Are you satisfied with collaborationist government?"

Jean-Hérold Paqui gave his talk; roughly, he tried to justify the government's policy of collaboration, saying that Pétain had been the right man in the right place; that but for him, France would have been plunged into the abyss of war; and that in any case, Pétain had stood with his back to the wall at a time when France had no choice but to bow to German demands. As he spoke, I remembered that my husband had said exactly the same thing a few months back, and that because he spoke these obvious truths to an irascible colonel, both of us had been punished.

When he finished his speech, the minister made it clear that he was there to hear everyone, including those who were critical of the collaborationist regime, and he asked if anyone in the audience wanted to offer an opinion. No one in the audience uttered a peep; for several minutes there was dead silence, an uncomfortable silence for Jean-Hérold Paqui, standing there waiting at the podium. Then I stood up and asked to be recognized. Very politely he said:

"Please go ahead, Madame."

"Look here, Monsieur Minister, I have a request to make. Because my husband said exactly what Field Marshal Pétain said a few months later, he was almost prosecuted; but since they could not prosecute him legally, the administration subjected me to a disciplinary transfer. I appeal the punishment in particular because the conditions under which I am obliged to live prohibit my looking after my three wards. I am legally responsible for my wards, but my husband has to take care of them because I was transfered; however, the law is categorical: it forbids entrusting these three little girls to a man."

The fellow let me talk until I finished. I could picture the dismay on the faces of my colleagues and the mayor, but I could not have cared less what they thought; come what may, I had said my piece. When I finished, Jean-Hérold Paqui said to me:

"Very well, Madame, I shall take your request under consideration, and I will do what I can to help you."

As we left the lecture hall, the mayor came over to me, still flushed with emotion.

"Really, Madame Carles, I might say you always astonish me; you're the only one who can come out with things like that."

"Well, he did ask if we had anything to say. Why should I have kept still? None of the others opened their mouths."

"Look here, a person would think you're not afraid of anyone; I feel like a coward beside you."

The most extraordinary part of the story is that my nerve paid off. A few months after I spoke out in Monestier, the academy notified me that I would get an appointment in my valley. Jean-Hérold Paqui had intervened just as he promised.

Chapter 28

Nine Names for a Hostage List

After that, the years flowed by in relative calm. It was wartime, but the war was far away; the soldiers had disappeared from our horizon and the village had recovered its seasonal rhythm of winter and summer, giving priority to work in the fields and the material problems implied by the restrictions imposed on us. We experienced deprivation; like people everywhere, we had food and ration cards, but in a place like Val-des-Prés everyone managed to work things out. All the peasants had gardens, many killed animals on the sly, and some were in the black market.

The war years went by without anyone being really involved. No prisoners, nobody missing in action, the exact opposite of the other war. As far as ideas were concerned, they were doubly snuffed out; since the peasants did not have opinions about anything and had always followed the mayor like sheep, they did not depart from their own rule of caution. When a few Germans came by, they all but licked their boots. It was the reign of fear and silence.

We too were careful. The school, the land, and the kids were enough for us. After what we had just been through, it made sense to pass unnoticed. Jean stood aloof from political passions; he was against fascism but he wasn't a Gaullist either. To him, General de Gaulle was just another man ambitious for power. To be sure, he'd had the foresight to proclaim Free France, but afterwards, when the war was over, he would become the country's master. To what purpose?

"A general cannot govern from the left," Jean would say. "Perhaps he does have a sense of History, but when the time comes, he will have a sense of his own class."

What disgusted us most was that once again men were agreeing to kill and be killed in the names of their respective countries. In our eyes, nothing could justify that commitment. Of course, without any doubt there was a good side and a bad side. Franco's victory sickened us as much as the Nazi pogroms or reprisals, but we looked beyond that organized hell, we thought of all those workers and all those peasants going off to get themselves shot up while the people who tolerated and organized the war advanced their careers and amassed fortunes.

"Afterwards," Jean would say, "I bet you they'll ask the survivors to shake hands."

My husband suffered a great deal from our isolation. His was the only leftist voice in the village, that was well known, and he would have loved to play an active role on behalf of the workers, "but why lock yourself into a clan and bow to a party's rules? I am an individualist and that is what I'll stay until the end." However, I think he was aware of his limits; when we argued and I forced him to add up all his contradictions, he admitted them, but in the end he always came back to what he cherished most: nonviolence and liberty.

Even though he was cautious and intended to stay aloof, he did some-times quarrel with a local fellow. When that happened, he did not mince words in defense of his ideas, and he could even get carried away. Those arguments were infrequent, but they were enough to get him classified as a scapegoat, and the day the subprefect in Briançon needed to provide the Germans with a list of hostages, the mayor of Val-des-Prés didn't have to make a long search for someone to put on it. Thanks to him, Jean Carles was at the head of the list.

We have always wondered why there was a hostage list in the first place. Did the Germans demand it, or was the subprefect showing off his zeal? Because nothing had ever happened around Briançon during the years of the Occupation. There was only one incident where a German soldier was the victim, and that was more of an ordinary news item than anything to do with the Resistance. It was in '43 or '44, when the Germans were working on the Névache road, and had a maintenance crew from the Highway Depart-ment putting it in good condition. No one ever knew exactly what happened, whether one of the workers was too thin-skinned or whether, on the con-trary, the soldier supervising them was too arrogant. It's a mystery. In any case, there was a violent quarrel between them, and one of the fellows from the Highway Department pulled out a pistol and fired. The German was not killed on the spot, and before he died he admitted that what had happened was entirely his fault: he had provoked the Frenchmen, pushing them to the limit of endurance, and he claimed responsibility for the tragedy. The soldier had added: "I don't want anyone killed because of me," and the matter had ended there. The fellow who fired the shot vanished into thin air and nobody ever attempted to find out what had become of him. Except for this story, there had been no hint of violence in the whole Briançonnais. All the same, the subprefect had drawn up his list, obliging nine villages to hand over the name of one man each. All nine were fellows like my husband who had attracted attention for their nonconformist ideas.

In Briançon, everyone was talking about the hostage list, but no one had seen it. The subprefect was keeping it a secret, and to be sure that it wouldn't be stolen, he always kept it on his person. But the fellow was not only a systematic collaborator, he was a womanizer too; and one evening, over the telephone, he arranged for an intimate party with several prostitutes. At the time, all phone conversations were inevitably monitored so this one immediately became public knowledge. Several hours later, while the subprefect and his cronies were carousing with champagne in private dining rooms, some local youths managed to steal the list from his pants pocket. Without losing a second, they hurriedly copied the names and warned the nine hostages.

Jean was warned too. Once the initial surprise was past, we had to act swiftly. While Jean hesitated, I did not; I was the more resolute and told him:

"No way are you going to stay here one more minute! You must get going immediately. Just think, if there was any trouble with the Germans, the Gestapo would pick you up and shoot you as an example."

"But Émilie . . ."

"No way! I don't want you taking the slightest risk; it would be too dumb for you to get yourself caught here."

I made up his bundle with a few odds and ends, two shirts, two pairs of socks, a sweater — light enough not to attract attention, and he left on his bicycle with his fishing pole like a humble fisherman. It was almost midnight when I saw him disappear around the bend in the road; the village streets were empty, but in Briançon it was the eve of a fair and we hoped there would be enough hustle and bustle to cover his trip through town.

Two or three days later, I had the privilege of a visit from the gendarmes who asked about my husband's whereabouts.

I told them: "He left for his mother's in Lyons," and two days later I was summoned to the subprefecture. The subprefect greeted me in person, and led me into his office.

"Madame Carles, when you spoke to the gendarmes, you asserted that your husband went to Lyons to see his mother; I have had inquiries made and it's not true, he is not there!"

What could I answer? I had to say something, but what? In my excitement, like a fool I had told the truth, at least what I believed to be the truth. Jean had taken off straight for Lyons, where he was hoping it would be easier to hide, but they were as jittery over the Germans there as anywhere else. When my husband told his story to his mother and brother, they burst out immediately, exclaiming that they could not keep him:

"If you stay here and they come for you, we'll be trapped like rats."

So Jean had left, the subprefect was already informed, and thinking I knew his whereabouts wanted me to tell.

"Madame Carles, you must know where he is."

"But I tell you he's in Lyons."

"No! You're lying. You know perfectly well where he is."

"But that's what he told me . . ."

The subprefect interrupted savagely: "How dare you! Tell me where he is or else . . ."

"But I can't tell you anything; if he's not in Lyons, I don't know where he went. He surely won't be away for long."

At that moment, I was absolutely sincere: I no longer knew where my husband was, and I thought to myself that was for the best since I was far from sure of myself with this fellow who looked capable of doing who knows what. I thought to myself that he could just as easily have his men interrogate me or hand me over to the Gestapo; and even though I was dying of fright, I was happy that whatever they might do to me I could not tell them anything.

I had too much imagination. The matter was between the subprefect and me, nothing more, and for two hours he went on asking me questions.

One thing fascinated him and he kept on coming back to it.

"Who warned you that your husband was on a hostage list?"

Playing the idiot, I replied:

"My husband, a hostage? I didn't know that, you're the one who's telling me. How awful!"

"Of course you knew, it's all over the countryside, because your husband went off and so did the eight others. Are you aware of the gravity of the situation, Madame Carles? All nine were warned; don't bother making up any stories, your husband was warned too and you are an accomplice in his flight."

I sat and listened, thinking to myself: Carles is out of your reach and he's all right; he's not about to get caught by a bastard like you.

The subprefect finally got so excited that he said whatever came into his head:

"It's madness! You realize the risk we're running? The risk *I* am facing? Every last man on the list has disappeared, and if anything bad happens tomorrow, if a German gets killed, the Gestapo will come to me for the list, and when they go to get the hostages, they won't find a single one. What will the Gestapo think? What will they say to me? That I'm an accomplice, and I'm the one they'll take. I'm risking my neck in this business."

Then and there, my courage returned; I said to myself: Well, well, my friend, if you think your neck is more precious than Carles's and the eight others, you're mistaken! If all we need is a guy like you to take their place, why that's just fine! What difference could it make to me if the Germans arrested the subprefect and shot him? There would be one rotten bastard less in the world.

The mayor of Val-des-Prés also tried to worm something out of me. The man was a scoundrel; not only did he have the nerve to give Carles's name to the subprefect, he came by regularly to torment me, taking the opportunity to proposition me as well. He'd been hanging around me for a long time, and early in my marriage, the first time I settled in the school at Val-des-Prés, we'd had it out on the subject. At the time, he played one of his own special tricks on me. The school was in a sorry state, particularly the apartment that went with it, and I had asked the local administration for permission to have the walls whitewashed and to have my husband take charge of the work. It was his trade and this would give him the chance to refurbish the place the way he thought it should be. The town council agreed; but Jean, in his usual way, did far too much, not only whitewashing the walls, but also doing frescoes and painting the rooms, and when it came time to pay the bill, the council balked.

"It's all very well for your husband to paint the rooms," they said, "but all we owe for is the whitewash."

The mayor came by the following day to check what had been done:

"Before I pay the bill, I am obliged to check the quality of the work, therefore you must show me through the apartment."

I was alone that day and I agreed; I think in the ordinary course of things, I had no right to refuse. I showed him through all the rooms, the dining room, the kitchen, and when we reached the bedroom, before I had time to suspect what was happening, he rushed at me, tumbling me onto the bed. I did not let him get away with it, I put up a fight and unceremoniously threw him out of the house. The matter went no further; I didn't even mention it to Jean for fear he'd punch him in the face, and for years only the mayor and I knew what had happened in the bedroom. But from that time on, he had nursed an excessive malice and rancor where I was concerned, and he never missed an occasion to make me feel it.

That explains his surly cynicism when my husband fled to escape the subprefect. He really was a poor excuse for a man, and he came to me asking:

"So Émilie, any news from your husband?"

I allowed myself the pleasure of pulling his leg. I am not a hypocrite, but for once I had no reason to hold back. He too was in a mess with his hostage disappearing into thin air. I suppose the subprefect hadn't been gentle with him and I did not put on kid gloves when I answered:

"So you didn't know Carles was a skirt chaser?" was what I said. "He's always had mistresses, and this time he made no bones about it, just went off with a tart. What do you expect me to do about that?"

"But, but . . ." he was taken aback, "you're going to raise your kids all by yourself?"

"Of course. I don't need anyone, I'm big enough to take care of myself, I have my salary and everything I need."

He went away sheepishly, half-convinced, not knowing whether what I said was fish, fowl, or good red herring.

The gendarmes returned regularly too. After the subprefect interrogated me, they came back several times, asking the same questions repeatedly: "Have you heard from your husband? Do you know where he is at the present moment?" And every time, I'd answer: "No." They were the people I was afraid of most, because I imagined that the day would come when they would take me away and hand me over to God knows whom. When I caught sight of them on the road while I was teaching my class, I lost all my resourcefulness, thinking to myself: This time they're coming for you, Émilie!

When that happened, I was rattled; I'd get up, go to the blackboard, write whatever popped into my head: the number of a problem, the title of a lesson, and right away I would ask the youngsters:

"Doesn't anyone want to go to the lavatory?"

There were always one or two who jumped at the chance. When they came back, I asked:

"You didn't see anything?"

"Yes, Madame, the gendarmes are walking up the hill, they're going on towards Montgenèvre."

I would heave a sigh of relief: they'd gone on by, it wasn't for me this time.

My fear was absurd, I knew it; but I could not help thinking about torture, knowing I would not resist for long before I talked. Because in the meantime, I had heard from Jean and I knew where he was.

My father died at that time, in February 1945. He was eighty-six years old. We had known for a month that he was going to die, he was ravaged with diabetes and the doctors treating him left us no hope. He knew it too, and he would say to me:

"I have reached the end of my road."

That man had been everything to me; for years he had been both my mother and my father, and in a very real sense we had never been away from each other. We had gone forward in life side by side, with our own individual sets of ideas but always close to one another. He had been affectionate and harsh, his world was the opposite of ours — Jean's and mine — but how could I have held it against him? My father was a man of the old school who had never left the region where he was born. The farthest reaches of his experience were Briançon, the few villages where he'd gone to fairs, and the Italian villages where he had bought sheep in his years as a smuggler. He knew nothing of the world beyond.

He had never read either, not a book, not a newspaper. He was already seventy-five when he opened his very first book. Jean and I had succeeded in working this small miracle. I remember that it was a book by Émile Guillaumin, I don't remember which one, but for him it was a revelation. When he finished, he said he liked it because, he explained, it dealt with things he had experienced in his own life. It was one of the most touching moments in my whole life: to think that a man of almost eighty spoke about a book as enriching, he who had always mistrusted everything in print; and when he ended up asking me for another, I was so moved that I found it hard to hold back the tears.

The day he was buried, the whole village was there. My father was an elder; most of those present loved him, some revered him for his rectitude and moral rigor, and a few had taken advantage of his goodness to play abominable tricks on him. He was one of the last of his generation to go.

Jean's absence weighed heavier than usual that day, with anxiety outweighing grief to my surprise. I had been without news of my husband for over a month, and a month is a long time when you know a man is on the run, hunted by the gendarmes, obliged to hide in one house or another. In spite of myself, I could not help thinking of death or deportation to a camp. Just then, as people were offering condolences, a man I did not know slipped a letter into my hand. My heart began to pound: it could only be a letter from *him*. As soon as I could, I went off to the stable by myself and opened the envelope. Jean's news was good on the whole: he was in the Midi, getting along pretty well, and he'd had no serious problems up to then.

The rest of the funeral went by without my noticing. I was incapable of tears, I was too happy, and I am afraid the village people thought that I did not love my father. My anguish had evaporated in an instant, I felt as light as a bird and incapable of putting on an act.

Only the mayor dampened my joy, returning the next day to question me once again. He took my father's death as his pretext, noting his obligation to take back his food ration cards. I considered it monstrous for him to retrieve a dead man's bread coupons, but he didn't, and he could not have been more brazen, even cynical, and finally he said:

"So it's finished with your husband, it's all over since he didn't even come to the funeral."

"That's enough! Take your cards and leave me alone."

"Well, all right! Still, I would have thought he'd come."

"How do you think he could come when I don't even know where he is?"

I played the game to the end; I, who thought myself incapable of lying, did it quite naturally that day, and without the slightest remorse.

All the while, Carles was wandering over the countryside, roaming the Midi, going from one place to another, careful not to attract attention. Most of the time he slept in barns, asking shelter only when he could not avoid it.

I do not know whether he was saved by his vagabond roving, but in any case the gendarmes never could catch up with him. He finally took refuge with a cousin of mine in Tallard. He stayed there long enough for us to set up a regular correspondence. My cousin was a produce dealer, and since we had to take some basic precautions to write to each other — mail being monitored like everything else — we naïvely used the following cover: when I sent him news, sometimes by telegraph, to keep him informed on the situation in Briançon, I would write: "The fruit and vegetables arrived rotten." It was our code for: "The climate is still very bad for you, no point in returning." It wasn't much, but our lives depended on it.

Later on, Jean had to take to the road again. His situation in Tallard turned precarious, and rather than risk being picked up by the gendarmes, he chose to take refuge in the mountains above Curban. As luck would have it, he came upon a Maquis camp and they took him in.

Carles had no intention of ever picking up a gun to fight: it was against his principles, but he could be useful to a group of men as isolated as these and he told them:

"I am a pacifist, I am against the war, but since they put me on a hostage list, I left my village because I don't want to give my hide to the Germans."

The leader of the Maquis answered:

"That's your right, but if you stay with us, you have to help out. What can you do?"

"I'm a chef, I can do your cooking."

"Agreed," said the maquisard. "You can stay with us."

Things went well for a while, that is up to the day Jean couldn't bear for the kids — because they *were* kids, all between the ages of seventeen and twenty — to stand guard in his place. He asked the man in charge:

"Why don't I ever stand guard? That, I can do."

"But Carles, you're too old, and you told us you're a pacifist and you don't want to handle a gun."

"That's awful! I can't have anyone stand guard in my place; a young man's hide is worth as much as an old man's; if someone has to get it, it might as well be me, so I'd better be off."

"Carles, we're going to miss you," said the leader of the maquisards. "We'll be sorry you're gone because you make good soup, but we respect your ideas, and you may leave whenever you like."

That is how he left them, buckling on his knapsack, off to try his luck somewhere else. Two days later, the Germans cordoned off the forest where the Maquis were camped. Before attacking with their tanks and their machine guns, they set the trees on fire and killed all those who were not burned alive. Not one of them survived. Jean had escaped death by a hair's breadth.

Several weeks later, with the Liberation, Carles returned to Val-des-Prés. Strange liberation for the Clarée Valley! We saw no one. The American and Allied convoys went north toward Grenoble by way of Montgenèvre, Briançon, and Le Lautaret, instead of taking the Echelle Pass. We were too far off the beaten path to be of interest. As a result, we heard about the Liberation on the radio while we remained in the background. But once the Americans and their friends went through, the Germans and Italians recaptured the valley, the passes, and the villages. For four months, we lived under the yoke of the Nazi regime even as the rest of the Briançonnais was

liberated. We did not know what would become of us anymore. The F.F.I.°
were increasing their pressure on the remnants of the German army, and, as
we harvested, guns were shooting from every direction. Things moved from
bad to worse as the days went by and no one felt safe. The village people
with chalets in Granon took refuge up there with their cows and sheep, and
we decided to hide and wait for things to calm down. The Cave of the Fifty
Mules seemed the most suitable place to us.

This cave, located in the mountains between here and Plampinet, was
an ideal hiding place. It dated from the era when the Briançonnais was an
independent republic named Les Escartons Briançonnais, comprising Lom-
bardy, Piedmont, and the Briançonnais. In 1815, the Sards and the Austrians
invaded the region, looting and massacring everything and everybody falling
into their clutches, and the inhabitants had fled to escape requisitions, taking
refuge with their mules in the countryside, and particularly in this cave.

We stayed there for about ten days, living like nomads. There weren't
very many of us: Jean, the two boys and me, plus one other family from Val-
des-Prés. We had brought along our goats, our sacks stuffed with supplies,
and for sleeping, Jean fashioned bedding from grass and heather. For meals
we took pot luck; our cooking was as simple as possible, and we ran out of
bread and potatoes very fast. We tried to make rudimentary round loaves
over the fire: it wasn't great but it could still pass for bread. Potatoes were
different; those we had to dig up in the fields, a risky business. My eldest son
would set out with a knapsack. One day, as he was crossing the fields to
replenish our supplies, we heard shots. Right away, I imagined the worst.
My son was fifteen, a strapping young man, and with his knapsack the Germans could very well take him for a Resistance fighter. Fortunately it was
only a false alarm and he returned. As soon as he heard shooting, he hid in
the bushes and crawled back to the cave. From then on, we did without
potatoes rather than take any further risks. We still had milk from our goats
and the cheese we made, we had rennet and ate our cottage cheese with our
bread which resembled a blackened sponge.

One fine day, my husband went out to call the goats; when he came
back, he said:

"That's odd. I saw lots of soldiers running though the fields; they
weren't Germans or Americans, I really think they're maquisards."

We waited a while, long enough to be absolutely sure. When there
wasn't the slightest doubt that the Germans were gone, we left the Cave of
the Fifty Mules and returned to Val-des-Prés.

We were obliged to face facts when we got home: the Germans had
ransacked the place, looting and stealing whatever they could. The doors and

windows of Les Arcades were ripped out and smashed, not a sheet or blanket remained. We had been so proud of those blankets woven from the wool of our own sheep! A neighbor had seen the Germans use them as wrapping for bundles of loot that they threw out of the windows and loaded onto their trucks. The devastation in the kitchen was even worse. A few days earlier, Marie had come down from Granon with the blueberry jam she had just made. The Germans had opened every single jar, eating a spoonful or two from each before they hurled them against the wall. All the jars were smashed, and the walls were stained violet where the blueberry jam had run down. It was a disheartening sight.

What difference did it make? We were liberated, the war was over and people were all reckoning up their accounts. Strange way of reckoning accounts! Up to then a picture of Pétain with his little tricolor ribbon sat enthroned on the mantlepiece beside the post-office calendar. Overnight the General's picture replaced the Marshal's, only the ribbon was the same.° It happened quite naturally, with no one apparently suffering any pangs of conscience; it was rather as if they had all turned the page of a book to proceed from one chapter to the next.

Even so, it was not quite so easy for the mayor: during the Occupation he had played the subprefect's game, and when the leaders of Gap's Committee for the Resistance came around, they removed him from office. Jean was named to replace him.

At the time, during the first weeks following the end of the Occupation, the prefect's authority had been superseded by those notorious committees which had the backing of the Compagnies Républicaines de Sécurité,° the elite state police force. My husband had been classified as a member of the Resistance in Val-des-Prés; he was at the head of the hostage list and he had fled. For those reasons he was asked to assume leadership of the commune and he accepted. The day he took office, he went up to the former mayor's bistro. When he walked into the barroom along with his deputies, the fellow was on his knees, his head resting on a table. He said:

"I knew you'd come for revenge. Now you're going to pick up an axe and cut off my head. Go ahead, make yourself at home."

Schoolteacher in Val-des-Prés

"Get up, Monsieur Mayor," said my husband. "We're not here to settle scores or hurt you. Just admit that you backed the wrong horse, you were pro-German, you sold them potatoes and other things, not to mention what you did to me personally. Under those conditions, don't be surprised at what's happening to you. Today, I am the man replacing you, but don't worry, I won't keep the job for long; there will be elections and if the spirit moves you and you run again, I won't fight you for the spot."

Carles did not hold grudges; many people in his position would have taken advantage of the situation, but we were not like that. As mayor, my husband had one driving concern: to protect the interests of the village, and make sure that all those plundered through requisitions and damage to property received compensation. This is what he told me:

"The first thing we have to do is obtain credits to reimburse our peasants for what they lost from '40 to '45."

I pointed out that we were in that category too.

"That is certainly true," he said, "but as mayor I must go last."

He went to see the authorities in Marseilles and plead the cause of the peasants of Val-des-Prés. First priority was to make it possible for each of them to obtain at least a draft animal for plowing and working the land. Jean did so much and so well that he won his case, and when he returned he asked all the families to prepare their requests. From then on, it was a crooked "grab-fest," with the majority of peasants arranging to claim more than they had lost. They came to see Jean with their lists and their witnesses, and the witnesses were a sham. Each person had to have his declaration confirmed by two witnesses, so they all turned up at the town hall accompanied by neighbors and relatives, signed their names and then exchanged roles. It was easy to claim anything they wanted; for example, there were perhaps two electrical household appliances in all Val-des-Prés, but they all inscribed an appliance on the list, and so it went. It was a flagrant breach of trust; Jean saw it, it made him sick, but there was nothing he could do. He was the one who had set the wheels rolling and he was obliged to stand behind all those lies.

The most gluttonous reaped the rewards, receiving a tidy sum of money, and some of them made an impressive profit; as for the others, the honest people who handed in claims corresponding to reality, the awards were ridiculously low. Beyond the shadow of a doubt, the war had changed nothing; everything went along the same as before and justice was as lame as ever. Whenever I asked Jean to take care of our claim, he answered:

"Don't be impatient, our turn will come when the others have been taken care of; we have plenty of time."

When he judged it was our turn, he filed our documents. The response came almost immediately: it was too late, the credits were used up, and we got nothing but crumbs of the money we had hoped for. My husband understood then that he had played the fool; we were disappointed, but we had to accept the situation since he was the person who had set up the system. In any case, his job was done, and when the elections came around, he withdrew from the race; he did not want to run for mayor because, he said, he'd already seen enough. Carles emerged from the experience weary and aged; he knew that by stepping aside, he was leaving the field open to schemers and to businessmen who were after profit alone, but once again his individualist and libertarian nature came to the fore. When I pointed out all that a man like him could have accomplished, he replied: "Power gets you too dirty."

We crossed that period out of our lives; we had to start again from scratch. Given the state of Les Arcades, there was no way to reopen the hotel, so we decided to go back to tilling the soil and restocking the farm. Jean was a workingman, he knew very little about farming and raising livestock and he had never wielded a scythe, but he set to work. Together we got the soil back into condition, though it was not easy going. Time had passed since we had let the land lie fallow or rented it, and it was difficult to get our bearings. We began by consulting the commune's land register to map all the boundaries. We traced a sketch of the family holdings in a notebook we bought, since harvesting a neighbor's grass by mistake was unthinkable and would have caused endless complications.

I remember that the two of us would leave with our tools while Marie stayed home to look after the children. In the evening, to gain time, we would sleep on the spot in a tent. Jean reaped and I raked, and together we bundled the hay the way we did in the good old days. Lacking a mule or a team of horses, we were obliged to depend on the goodwill of people who did to bring down the hay. The price was high — one bundle for us, one for the owner of the horse. It made rough going but we had no choice, no other way to manage.

We raised rabbits at Les Arcades, along with hens and one or two pigs, and my father had left a few ewes and a cow. I made butter as well as cheese, and for the first year after the Liberation we lived almost entirely on what we produced. At every free moment, I would go tend the flock; it reminded me of my younger days. I took the goats just outside the village, or farther out into the commune's fields on the road to Plampinet. The grass was high there and the goats did well; as Daudet said: "They were in grass up to their bellies." I would settle down with my young son in some pristine meadow, he with his toys, I with a book or my knitting: it was paradise. Those days along the banks of the Clarée have left extraordinary memories. The goats always began by eating the corollas of the flowers; next they tackled the bushes, and when they were drunk with grass they would lie down and sleep. It was time for us to rest too. Michou and I would open our sack and eat lunch; the menu was simple: ham, a bit of sausage, a few hard-boiled eggs, cheese, and bread. Afterwards, there was time for us to nap just like the goats. Sometimes we had to run after them when we woke up, for goats are obdurate climbers. It was a marvelous summer, living simply, very close to nature. We felt happy and rich.

But for all that, we were unable to settle into the peasant economy. With all his goodwill, my husband was not a farmer. Neither was my elder son; he had always dreamed of snow; he wanted to be a ski instructor, and we were not about to oppose his vocation. But what were we to do? Les Arcades was in such poor condition that a good deal of work was needed to put it back into shape. Neither Jean nor I felt we could begin all over what we had done twelve years earlier. We decided to call in a contractor from Briançon for the heaviest work, and after that we would see. I had practically forgotten those times when a man came by to see me at Le Vivier a few days ago. With one sentence, he brought back the whole period for me.

That day I was sitting in the sun on my terrace when two strangers appeared. One was about sixty and the other was younger; the older man approached and introduced himself:

"Good day, Madame, I'm Monsieur Colle."

Monsieur Colle? The name didn't mean a thing to me; I racked my brains, but I could not figure out who he might be. I said: "Hello," and since I was so visibly waiting for something more, he said:

"You don't remember me?"

"Frankly, no." Still, as I went on staring at him, he began to look familiar, but I could not tell why.

"Madame Carles, I worked for you right after the war. Don't you remember? I was a mason with Forbras . . . Gaston."

The name did in fact ring a bell. Forbras was the contractor who had restored Les Arcades. The man went on:

"Well, he's dead, the company doesn't exist anymore and now that I'm retiring, I need a certificate from the people I worked for. If I don't manage to get declarations and signatures certifying that I worked for you during such and such a year, and for someone else for such and such a year, I could lose my pension. So I've come to ask if you'll be willing to write me a letter, . . . and the man with me here is my son-in-law."

He introduced us and I told him I was willing to sign the paper certifying on my honor that he had worked for us in 1946.

While I was writing his note, I sensed that he was preoccupied and curious, and indeed he added:

"Still, you should remember, particularly since you were the one who presented me for my Certificat d'études.

For a moment I could not get over it:

"*I* presented you for your certificate?"

"Yes, you did, Madame Carles; I was thirty-six years old. Don't you remember? We were all eating together around your kitchen table. You were teaching school, and when you came in we would all sit down to eat, and one day I told you my story; I said I wanted to be night watchman for a lycée in Briançon so I could build myself a little place during the day, and the only thing standing in the way was the headmaster. Because I needed a certificate to get the job, and I didn't have one. Your husband was listening and when I said that, he looked at you, and you . . ."

I recalled that moment instantly. I saw our kitchen at Les Arcades again, the big table with all the workmen seated around it, and my husband standing in front of his stoves and saucepans. I also recalled the man and what he told me. Jean and I did not need words: he looked at me, and right away I knew what he meant.

"All right, then," I had said. "We'll see, we'll give it a try."

"After that, every noontime while the others were smoking their ciga-rettes and taking their naps, you would say: 'Colle's school' and we would go off to work in the other room, and you looked at your watch because you had your class and I had my job."

We did indeed spend that hour after lunch getting him ready for the certificate. He was an attentive student, I did not need to repeat any gram-mar rule twice. He wanted his certificate so badly that he let nothing go by: agreements, spelling, math — it was all grist for his mill. For the rest, I had a notebook with a hundred exams, and I told him:

"If you read this and learn the questions on history, geography, and science, you'll know enough to get through the exam."

"Well, I got my certificate, you know."

"You did?"

"I got it at age thirty-six, thanks to you."

Tears came to his eyes as he said those words; I saw that he was trem-bling with emotion and I could not hold back my own tears either.

"Afterwards I got the job as night watchman and I did build my house, just like I wanted. When it was finished, I called it 'The Colle Hut.' It was my dream come true."

This is the most beautiful memory of my whole career as a teacher. That thirty years later, this man should come tell me that thanks to me he had obtained his certificate of study at age thirty-six, his job as watchman, and his house is the most beautiful reward I have ever received.

In 1945, I was finally appointed to teach in Val-des-Prés, and I stayed there until I retired in 1962. For me, teaching the children of my own village was the culmination of all that I had dreamed of since I was a little girl. I could not have wished for more.

Teaching younsters to read and write is one thing, it is important but not sufficient. I have always had a loftier notion of school — the role of the school and the teacher. In my view, children take stock of the world and society in the communal school; later on, whatever their trade, whatever direction their lives take, it is too late, the mold is already set. If it is good, so much the better, if not, nothing further can be done.

In a backward region like ours, considering the life I had led, what seemed indispensable to me was opening their minds to life, shattering the barriers that shut them in, making them understand that the earth is round, infinite, and varied, and that each individual, white, black, or yellow, has the right — and the duty — to think and decide for himself. I myself had learned as much through life as through study. That is why I could not judge my pupils solely on the basis of their schoolwork, and why I also took into account the way they behaved in their daily lives. For example, I never hid the fact that every last one of them would have to face social reality, and that when all was said and done, they would have to work for a living. But at the same time, I put them on their guard against abuses. I told them that a man must defend himself against exploitation and the stultifying effect of work. I also told them:

"The most important thing for a young person is to choose a trade he likes and enjoys, otherwise he will be a slave, unhappy and consumed with rage."

To conclude this line of argument, I always spoke to them about liberty, repeating that our famous Liberty should not simply be a word inscribed on pediments along with Equality and Fraternity — those basic Rights of Man, an abstract and illusory liberty — but rather that it should be a reality for each one of them.

"Beware of politicians, beware of silver-tongued orators, do your utmost to judge for yourselves, and, above all, take advantage of the beauty life offers."

Such was the message I tried to make them understand over seventeen years in the village where I was born and where I have lived.

I knew that the most powerful curbs were situated outside of school, within the family, and that in the final analysis change would have to come about right there. How could I make it happen? I tackled patriarchy, alcoholism, and chauvinism. They had wrought such great havoc. It was not to everyone's taste, but I could not have cared less. I knew that when they grew up, the children would take over the lead from their elders, and that they would retain something of what I had taught them. There were families stuck in the mire, of course, but I told myself that in the long run, the young people would take over and shake up the old ideas.

When you educate children between six and fourteen years old, when you have them with you every day, and you want them to hear you when you speak, you must not tell them nonsense or say: "Do what I say, don't do what I do." If they perceive that the teacher is lying, they will go on sitting at their desks because they must, but they will not believe another word you say. They are very exacting, they want what they are taught to be consistent with what they see and live every day.

That is why I always tried to put my lessons into practice. Whether it was hygiene or morals, I did my best to go beyond words and sentimental platitudes and to offer them direct contact with reality. When I talked to them about cleanliness and personal hygiene, I took them to Les Arcades. I showed them a bathroom, a lavatory, a washing machine or dishwasher and turned them on. I was lucky to have all that at hand, and I must say that once the youngsters saw one of those machines operate, they understood and there was no need to say another word on the subject.

It was the same for civics lessons. I remember one day I was doing a class on alcoholism, and to help them understand precisely what the degradation of an alcoholic means, I spoke to them about a concrete case the whole village knew. That was always my method, using an example not to moralize and say: "This is right, that is wrong," but to demonstrate facts and consequences. On this particular occasion, we knew that a man had gotten drunk and beaten his wife. The argument was noisy, a whole set of dishes thrown and broken, and everyone around here knew all about it. I said:

"You know exactly what happens when someone drinks; they say an alcoholic drinks up his children's lifeblood, and it's true. In a drunkard's house, there is never enough bread, there is never enough of anything, the wife is unhappy and so are the children. It is a real disaster."

I went to the board and I wrote — I had to give them three lines of writing a day, one in large handwriting, one medium, one small: that was the rule — "Alcohol kills." I had barely finished when I heard laughter behind my back. I turned around and said:

"What made you laugh, Rosa?"

She answered immediately: "Madame, *you're* making me laugh with that sentence."

I know of few classes where youngsters would have dared answer their teacher that way, but I had accustomed them to telling me what they thought whenever I spoke to them. I always told them: "Whether you agree or not, you must express yourselves," and it worked; it was an understanding between us established from the start: they were to take everything I did and said with a grain of salt. Without wanting to pat myself on the back, I can justly say that I instituted a dialogue between myself and the class long before it became fashionable, and that is why a youngster like Rosa dared say: "*You're* making me laugh with your sentence," without anyone being surprised.

"So," I said, "and why do I make you laugh?"

"Well, my father bought my mother a little keg of brandy, he thought when she drank it, she'd be sick to death of herself; well, Madame, the keg is empty and my mother's still around."

When a twelve-year-old child comes out with a response like that, it is hard to follow it up with a lesson on morals. My lovely sentence, straight out of the manual of ready-made ideas, did not carry much weight, and it was up to me to return to reality. That was all the more obvious since the story was true. The woman was still alive, and her husband went on supplying her with all the alcohol she needed; after the keg of brandy, he bought her a half barrel of wine, thinking that if she drank enough and soaked up all she could, she would surely stop. He had to face disappointment: his wife held out but she also had six children. They were the ones who paid for her lack of moderation, and one of the babies died of uremic poisoning.

There was another plague that I stood up to and fought: savings. At the time, official policy decreed that we teach children to save money. I remember voicing strong opposition in a meeting; I said I refused to teach my youngsters lessons on savings. I refused both in my own name and in the name of teachers in general, many of whom did in fact approve of "nest eggs." The basic principle was that as soon as a poor man put four cents together, he would run and invest them in a savings bank. They would deposit ten francs, then twenty, then thirty; at age ten, children were obliged to have a bankbook, and at school they were asked to deposit two sous per week in the mutual insurance company. To me, it was a crime to remain silent, not to tell them that with inflation, everything given to the government is eventually fit to throw into the garbage. I was adamant on this point and I would tell them:

"Don't ever put one cent in the bank, never buy bonds; take the little money you have and buy everything you need for your own well-being, buy the equipment you need, set yourself up, but never give one penny to the government."

It was the same with respect to war: how shameful to speak to children about the jingoistic France that is so fond of uniforms, that is never wrong. From the time I was a child, I abominated all the pages of our history books summoning us to remember only military victories and names of heroes. Obviously, I made every effort to remain within the framework of the permissible in class, but even so, I attempted to bring some life to the comic-strip images of history disseminated in our textbooks. When we reached the Wars of Religion, I spoke to them about tolerance; when we got to the Revolution, I told them that the sans-culottes° had been both pioneers of liberty and victims of universal suffrage; and as for the Napoleonic wars, I did my best to destroy the Little General's mythic image. I was implacable, saying:

"That man was a tyrant to all Europe; his motives are unimportant: nothing can justify the millions of deaths he brought about. That man was a criminal."

My words were sincere. When I was their age, I could not bear the tales of those battles, they sickened me. I remember my joy when Napolean finally began to beat a retreat. As a little girl, I sided with the Russian soldiers, I was for the Spanish peasants, and Waterloo: what a blessing! The tyrant was struck down.

These words may appear excessive or even naive, but I feel no remorse — on the contrary. Even today I wonder whether or not I got my ideas across to my youngsters. Nothing is less certain. When I hear them make nationalistic and chauvinistic remarks now that they are adults, I wonder if I was not too moderate in my own remarks.

For a schoolteacher, recitations are an extraordinary event. I have always loved them, and I believe that children are very sensitive to them, and that they often express themselves best through poems. I have already mentioned "The Death of the Jew" which gave me the chance to speak to them about racism. There is another poem I am particularly fond of since it was important to me never to forget that I had children of the soil sitting in front of me, little peasants, many of whom would remain in the village, and that it was my duty to show them the usefulness and nobility of the farmer. Even today, my nephew Auguste, who very nearly turned out illiterate, never fails to remind me of it when I go to see him. "That poem was so important to me," he says each time, "that I love to recite it. You want me to?" And I listen.

> A tale I will tell of Louis XII, dear friends,
> The father of his people whom we cherish without end,
> For goodness e'er retains its rights o'er heart of man.
> A noble lord, he heard, perhaps an excellency,
> To beat a poor farmer had shown the base temerity.
> Summons he the guilty man with no hint of his design,
> In his palace one day, compels the man to dine.
> Upon a secret order by the monarch passed,
> The noble lord is served a magnificent repast:
> All the very best that can imagined be
> Save only bread alone, and that by royal decree.
> The King comes by and asks: "Hast thou been well served?"
> "Yes, indeed, dear Sire, I have been superbly fed,
> And yet I have not dined, for life requires bread."
> "Go hence," says Louis XII, with countenance severe,
> "And learn the lesson well which thy sovereign holds dear:
> Since, my lord, for thee, the staff of life is bread,
> Learn to respect the farmer by whom thou art well fed."

A recitation like that was extraordinarily valuable for the pupils; it was an example that touched them directly and they were sensitive to the fact. Once they had done it, the lesson was obvious: the peasant grows the wheat, flour is made from the wheat, bread is made from the flour. They understood all that naturally, and above all they felt the solid bonds tying them to other people and other people to them.

I think there is nothing more beautiful than teaching school in the same village year after year when you are a child of the region. I knew everyone, the parents and the children; it was a unique bond tying me to them all. I knew the qualities and faults of each individual, and I saw the effects of my work, the changes slowly taking place within the families.

Thus it was that I shaped two generations in Val-des-Prés. It is often said: "No one is a prophet in his own country." I am not so sure. In any case, my pupils are between thirty and fifty years old today, and I have the impression that in spite of everything, they have retained something of what I taught them. I believe that had I not opened their minds, had I been reactionary, they would not have forgiven me — at least I think so. That day, not too long ago, when I asked them to band together to defend our valley from highway construction crews, they all answered present, just as they had in the days when they were all kids in smocks and high shoes with inkstains on their hands.

Chapter
30

Farewell
to
Jean Carles

Those were calm and happy years. The children were growing up, going to the lycée, and the older one was increasingly enthusiastic about skiing and ski competitions. We kept body and soul together with Les Arcades, we made our way "slowly but surely" as they say.

Then came the Algerian war. Carles's ideas and mine had not changed with the passing time; more than ever we were pacifists and dedicated antimilitarists. All during the years of the Indo-China war, we had spoken out against colonialism, and when our elder son reached draft age, we wished that he'd refuse to do his military service. We were prepared to make sacrifices to help him, but he loved his country too much, he loved his mountains too much, he wanted to be a ski instructor and prefered serving in the Alpine Chasseurs to becoming an expatriate.

Faithful to our ideal of liberty, neither Jean nor I ever interfered with our children's choices. At the risk of repeating myself, let me say that my husband always said that children should be allowed to live in freedom; and when the time for decisions came, we let them do as they wished. When the second wanted to leave school, my husband did not tell him that he was wrong and that one day he would be sorry. He had always said that a man did not need school to do what he wanted, on the contrary. And so he allowed the boy to choose.

When he got his brevet,° our son told me:

"Maman, don't think I'm going to vegetate at lycée desks: I don't like school."

"What do you want to do?"

251

"I want to be a pastry chef."

I immediately picked up the telephone and called a friend who was a pastry chef in Paris, asking her:

"Would you be willing to take on Michou as an apprentice?"

"Yes, of course."

"All right, then I'll put him on the night express and he'll be at your door tomorrow morning."

And that is what happened: my son left to do his apprenticeship just as he wished. He did wonders there and might even have stayed in Paris, except that he was like his brother: he could not do without snow and sun and so he came home. He too had skiing in his blood; he too did his basic training in an Alpine regiment. Unfortunately, it was at the time of the Algerian war and he went off to fight.

Carles was like a madman; he the anarchist, he the pacifist, could not bear for one of his sons to fight against Algerians with a gun. He would say:

"I do not want my children to kill anyone at all, especially not Algerians."

My husband had lived in North Africa for several years; he had made many friends among the Arabs and retained a special respect for them. There wasn't the slightest doubt in our minds that this was a dirty colonial war, a war in the interest of protecting the big colonials and their fat fortunes.

Jean said: "It is natural for the Algerians to rebel. No one here has any idea the way all those nouveaux riches treat them; to the colonials, Arabs are dirt, they exploit them, and they steal from them by pulling as much wealth as possible out of their soil. I am on their side, and I do not want my son to take part in this genocide."

But what could we do? Nothing, or so little. When we heard of some demonstration for peace or Algerian independence, we joined the ranks of the protesters. We would take old sheets and turn them into banners. Jean got out his paint pots and brushes to draw slogans for us. With Marie, we went down to Briançon; I was fifty-seven years old, but I was not slow to scream "Peace in Algeria" as we paraded through the streets with our streamers, playing hide and seek with the C.R.S.° One time, I was cut off from the group holding my sign and a kind fellow came over to say:

"Don't stay here, you'll get yourself beaten up by the cops."

"Well, what am I supposed to do? They're ruffians, and besides it's better for an old lady like me to be on the receiving end than a young person."

What looks I got from those Briançonnais! Especially the storekeepers behind their storefronts. They all knew me, and seeing me in the streets screaming and waving banners — well, that took their breath away. I realized then that there was still a great deal to be done to lift the wool from their eyes. I knew that the next day they would say among themselves that I had no common sense, whereas in reality, they were the people who had none. I had a number of serious quarrels on the subject. In those situations, I never minced words:

"But why did the French go there in the 1830s in the first place? How do you justify the conquest of a country living quietly and not asking anything from anybody? By what right have the French decreed that Algeria is part of France? It's a question of might makes right. Well, that's all over now; we've exploited them, pillaged them, and now they're kicking over the traces: they're going to throw us out like dirty cheats, and they'll be right."

Michou wrote to us from Algeria, saying that what he was seeing was far worse than we could imagine off in France. It was unbearable and he was in pain. One day he wrote:

A unit came back with two Algerian prisoners; the captain had them placed in the middle of the courtyard, surrounded them with four sheets of shiny metal, and left them directly in the sun without anything to eat or drink. Within twenty-four hours, one of them died of thirst and exhaustion and the other died the next day; the worst of it is that the whole time, the whole camp went right on living as if nothing was going on.

When I read letters like that, I trembled with fear and indignation. I'd tell my husband:

"Jean, do you realize what could happen if the censor or somebody picked up that letter? They'd take him off and shoot him as an example, and they'd shoot us along with him."

I wrote to my son to stay calm, adding: "You'll tell us whatever you like when you come home, but I beg you, so long as you are out there, do not write another word about those atrocities."

I admit that I was terribly frightened; it was the period when the F.L.N.° was operating in France and the D.S.T.° spared no one. Breaches against the security of the state were the only thing people talked about, and I did not want my son to pay for his sincerity.

A little later, we received a card announcing his selection for the army ski championship games, and saying that he would soon come to France to compete. Jean could not contain his joy at the idea of seeing his son again, and most important, he thought he'd find a way to keep him from going back to Algeria again. He would say to me:

"I'll never let him leave again; I'm likely to do anything, even break his leg with a shovel, but I can assure you, he will stay right here."

Alas, those were only dreams. The composition of the team was changed, our son did not come home, and Jean fell back into the apathy that was undermining his health.

He wasted away, a little more each day. I saw clearly that things were taking a bad turn, and when he got too tired he would say:

"Oh, it's nothing, just feeling knocked out all of a sudden; I'll stretch out for an hour or so and I'll be all right."

But the bouts of fatigue recurred with increasing frequency, and it grew harder and harder for Jean to recover his strength. He tried to rationalize the situation. "It's nothing," he'd repeat, "It'll go away, I'm worried about Michou," and I believed him. Even the doctor was taken in and didn't hesitate to reassure me when he listened to Jean's heart, examined him, and analyzed the results.

"You're very foolish to be alarmed, Madame Carles; your husband has the heart of a young man and lungs of steel. He's solid as a rock and he'll live to be a hundred."

Doctors do not work miracles, even with fine words. A week later, Jean left us forever. He died so suddenly and I expected it so little that I refused to believe it when it came. Just the night before he had been on his feet, insisting that I let him cook for a few guests. Marie and I could manage by ourselves, but we could not keep him away from his stoves.

Without blinking an eye, the doctor stated: "It's intestinal flu."

"But you told me a week ago that he had the heart of a twenty-year-old."

"One thing has nothing to do with the other," he replied. "It could not have been foreseen."

Later, much later, I told a young doctor friend of my son's:

"You know, I'm the one who emptied my husband's last bedpan. When someone is critically ill, there is always a change for the better they call 'the death-bed rally.' When I looked into the bedpan, I said:

"'You see, you tell me you're not urinating any more, but the bedpan is full.' The liquid was red-orange.

"He replied: 'But I didn't urinate, I moved my bowels.'

"Good lord, I thought to myself, if that's what his stool looks like, it's awful."

He was not worse than usual the day he died, but I simply could not leave his side; I stayed in his room, going around in circles, although I had a thousand things to do. It had bothered him.

"Come on now," he said, "you're being ridiculous. I slept well, I feel well, and I'm going to get up and help you with the rabbits."

When I finally made up my mind to leave the room, I stood paralysed just as I was about to cross the threshold, and I turned back to him, incapable of taking another step.

"What's the matter with you?" he said. "Go do your chores."

"Nothing. Nothing," I answered with a lump in my throat.

"You see I'm better, you know it perfectly well."

No, I didn't know anything of the kind. The proof came a few moments later while I was feeding grass to the rabbits. Marie came running, disaster painted on her face.

"My God, Marie, what's the matter?"

"Tonton° fainted."

By the time I raced to the telephone, called the doctor and reached his room, he looked at me and still had the strength to say: "Let me be," and it was all over: Jean Carles was dead.

His death left an immense void; for thirty years he had shone like a sun warming all who came near; through him, Les Arcades had become a seat of life and liberty, and he had served as guide to us all. Going through our papers, I came across a few pages in which our friend, Judge Rabinovitch, attempted to sketch a portrait of Jean Carles. Those few sentences are eloquent in their simplicity.

I like to visit Carles in Val-des-Prés; he welcomes me into his house, which is undoubtedly the most beautiful in the countryside around here. He offers me a glass of cassis, and then he talks to me about his life. Carles has traveled: Spain, Morocco, Greece, he went all around the Mediterranean with his four housepainter's brushes. He is a cultured man and a libertarian spirit; he has read not only anarchist literature but also journals like *The New Age in Literature,* the first set from Poulaille's time. He feels alone in Val-des-Prés, isolated, always treated like a stranger.

Carles is the pure anarchist who remains pure, and who will remain pure until the end; he knew the whole militant movement of prewar days; he was shaped by the working-class milieu to which he owes his perceptiveness and his critical mind. They told him: 'You have to read this and this and not just anything': they meant *Clarté, Monde,* and *Avant-Garde.* He had known anarchists in the days when some of them were advocating individual acts of violence; he could not get used to that idea: he was a workingman and he was nonviolent. 'You understand,' he would tell me, 'my father worked for the same company for fifty-two years, my grandfather, twenty-seven, that's my heredity.'

Carles was every inch a pacifist; he was against all wars, including violent social revolution; he often told me: 'War is the end of everything human,' and he advocated individual acts of refusal and opposition. He was hostile to all forms of corporate intellectualism: a fierce adversary of Fascists, he also denounced the Communists. Carles was for plain, unadorned human beings.

He told me: 'In my family, we're from the Ardèche: my father had honesty in his blood, he taught it to me, and as a result I did not get along as well as other boys my age. When my father died, my mother went to find a job in Paris. I was only a kid. I know what it's like to be hungry, I know poverty and men who will give you a cup of coffee if you let them rub your ass. And the night shelters? I slept there two or three times; in the evening, when you arrive, they give you soup and take your clothes to disinfect them, and the next day they give them back wrinkled. That's when you feel you've foundered for good. It's not the kids who are corrupt in Paris, it's the men.'

Speaking of Val-des-Prés, he told me: 'They're selfish boors. I've been living here for more than ten years, and I don't have a single friend, not one person I can talk to openly the way I do with you. To them, I'm a stranger and they make me feel it every day; they are underhanded rather than direct, and not one of my ideas or initiatives is appreciated. When I tell them I don't like money, it drives them crazy. Take flowers, for example. I say that they are beautiful, that we must raise them: the people here laugh at the notion, disregarding beauty simply because you can't *eat* flowers. . . . Oh, if I could write, it would make a devil of a book. Unfortunately, I begin to think when I walk out of the house; while I'm going along and I'm alone, a load of things bubble up inside me, and I think I ought to write them down immediately; but when I come back home, I don't remember any of it. I tell you, there is a novel in the life I've lived, if only I could write it.'

These few sentences by a true friend accurately reflect the feelings of all those who knew my husband and had the capacity to understand and appreciate him. As for me, what more could I add? Sometimes, I compare him not to a lone wolf, but to a stray dog intoxicated with liberty and refusing collar and master alike. Not once in his life did Carles capitulate to schemes and compromises with his principles. I saw him refuse pay for a job rather than accept a deal that seemed debasing in his eyes.

"I won't touch those few coins of yours, and let my gesture teach you to treat your workers better."

I have seen him refuse his rights and decorations as a veteran, refuse the pension he was entitled to, telling them:

"We're not former soldiers, just sold out; they never consulted me when they took away the seven best years of my life. Accepting your pension means accepting your mode of governing, and that I can never do."

Together we tore up his service record that day, with its inscription in red ink: "rebellious spirit, refused to crawl."

He was the one who taught me to read all the writers who spoke from the heart, from Louvain to Henry Miller by way of Louis Ferdinand Céline. He was the one who opened all the doors leading to humanism for me: Selma Lagerlöf, Neel Doof, Knut Hamsun,° Blaise Cendrars,° Panaït Istrati, Michel Del Castillo, Émile Arnaud, Henri Bérault, Ignazio Silone, Erich Maria Remarque and many others. You were sure to find the book of the month when you came to Les Arcades. Everyone knew and admired Jean for his love of books. My inspector could not get over it whenever he came to see me, he would say:

"Tell me, where did you come by such a cultivated man?"

He found it difficult to acknowledge that my husband might be simply a workingman and yet know so much. I would answer:

"My husband left school when he was eleven years old; he learned all the rest from books."

All of his friends were there with me to bury him. I had a simple inscription placed on his gravestone: "Jean Carles, Pacifist." One day, talking about his funeral, he had told me: "Above all, I do not want any flowers or wreaths; they're nonsense."

But I felt obliged to place that word: "Pacifist." It was the least I could do, and in so doing I believe that I have kept faith with his thought and with his life. An exemplary life.

Chapter
31 🖋

The Wolves
Are
Back

My life has become another life. The void left by Carles, the enormous hole in my heart has been filled in. A hundred details have made it possible.

Memories first of all: his indelible mark on people and things stood as living testimony to his existence. Carles went on living through all that he had done. Curiously, through our thirty years of married life, part of me had remained in the shadows. He shone, he was radiant, while I . . . how shall I explain it? I walked in his footsteps. My children told me so one day:

"You know, Maman, we never set much store by you, because you followed so closely in Papa's wake that he was the only one we saw."

That was true, but I never suffered from it and I have no regrets; on the contrary, my happiness lay precisely in our communion. It made me all the stronger and more decisive with Carles gone. I often thought back to the woman in René Allio's film, *The Shameless Old Lady*; we were different, of course, since I was far from emerging from the deepest shadows, but like her, I felt ready to take on the world. It was at that time that I truly learned the value of Friendship. I mean to speak of those indestructible friendships lasting fifty years and more, of my friend Justine from Puy-Saint-Vincent, of my friend Isabelle Guignon, a lacemaker from Amiens whom I met in 1918 when she was a refugee in Val-des-Prés and with whom I have corresponded for sixty years. There is yet another who breaks all the records. When she comes here for vacation, it is to look after the grieving widow. What a strange way for a nurse to spend her vacations!

"Your mother must get out," she told my children, "and I'll arrange it.

She'll come with me; we'll travel together and take the trips she couldn't take with your father."

That is how I got to know "La Bérarde" before it was plundered and sacked by promoters; I'd known it previously only through Pierre Scize's *People of the Summits*. I also got to know the Vallée Sauvage of the Fournel, the Dormiouze Waterfalls in the Fressinière Valley, Casset's mountain with its blue glacier and Lake Arcine, and Rif Belle: a peak in the wilderness reached by a narrow path. This simple, untouched nature is absolute beauty, offering solitude and purity. I remember those moments. What days those were! The little glass of anisette with spring water was so good; so were the melons chilled in the stream, the local ham, and the farm cheese, all washed down with a bottle of wine with a label reading: "Buou n'en che cantaras" — "Drink and you will sing."

Together we visited Bouchié, a village perched on the mountainside and abandoned now; fourteen men killed or missing in the war: all the women left after that catastrophe. And we visited Ratier, and the floor of the Vallée Verte, and Les Ayes, that chalet pinned on to the mountainside. My friend had found what was needed to fill my heart. It was then that I truly understood what Carles meant when he used to speak about separation and death. He would say:

"There will always be flowers . . . from the flowers, you must take nothing but the color and perfume; the sun will be there still, the river and the birds, there will also be salad to pick from the garden."

At a bend in the road, intoxicated with happiness, I could close my eyes now, and tell myself: "Goodbye, Jean. Our second life begins today."

"There will always be flowers!" Indeed, how could anyone imagine that the flowers in this valley might one day wither and disappear? How could anyone imagine that this totally unpolluted region might one day fall to ruin under the staggering blows of technocrats and the businessmen who think only of their profits? The idea alone is unbearable.

Nevertheless, alarming rumors began to circulate in the early seventies, rumors which gradually assumed the shape of reality. The government, it seems, was planning a superhighway — a major construction project in the national interest — linking Marseilles-Fos to Turin-Genoa by way of the Echelle Pass and the Clarée Valley.

Once I got over my initial indignation, I reacted violently when I heard about that monstrosity, telling everyone I met:

"We mustn't allow them to carry out a project like that; we must defend ourselves, and the sooner the better."

We had a meeting at Les Arcades, some ten of the commune's landowners and I, and we discussed what might be done. Everyone agreed on the principle of creating an association to defend the valley, but no one could bring himself to assume any responsibility, so we were about to leave the matter there, without establishing anything concrete. Finally, one of the peasants said:

"Well, if they ask me what we did, we're going to look pretty dumb when we answer: 'Nothing.' The very least we can do is set up an association with a president and officers, even if they're temporary."

There was an embarrassing silence. No one wanted to come forward. So I said:

"At my age, I wish I didn't have to, but rather than leave things up in the air, I am willing to be president of our association."

"Well, fine," they said, "so it's settled."

And that was how I was named president. We also elected a secretary, and decided to hold a meeting for the whole region in the town hall.

The mayor was not yet in on it; he was even against our initiative, and the first thing he did was visit the subprefect and tell him we'd held a meeting in decrepit, unsafe premises. Even so, we informed him of our intentions in a letter that went more or less like this:

In the course of a private meeting held in Val-des-Prés, representatives of the commune decided to form a Committee for the Prevention of a Superhighway in the Clarée Valley. A temporary executive board has been elected with Madame Émilie Carles as president. The next meeting will be open to the public and will be held some time in January 1974, in order to elect a permanent executive board whose job it will be to establish the by-laws of the Committee and to request recognition by the authorities in accordance with the Law of 1901.

In a second letter, we asked his permission to use the auditorium in the town hall for our public meeting. The date was set for January 12, 1974.

He was obliged to agree, and the meeting was an unprecedented success. Virtually all the people in the commune were present. From that time on the committee functioned actively. Throughout the year it never stopped working to win new support for the valley's cause. Informational meetings in Briançon, meetings with associations from other communes, leaflets, posters, letters to ministers, hearings at the subprefecture: we did everything within our power to sensitize and mobilize public opinion.

At the end of the year, during one final meeting at the casino in Briançon, we were forced to face facts: the Briançonnais were not interested in the future of their region. That evening, when I took the floor to address an audience of 150 people, I could not hide my disappointment and I gave them a warning:

"If we are to make our voices heard, large numbers of people must speak. If the general interest is defended by a mere handful, the movement is rushing headlong to defeat."

We had nothing but fine words. To achieve progress, we had to do something besides meetings and more meetings where speeches and discussions only wearied supporters in the end. I was aware that the situation was deteriorating and I stopped sleeping at night; hour after hour, I searched for an idea, for something that would pull the movement out of the impasse it had reached.

The idea came by chance, at a time when I was hardly thinking about it. I was in the bus for Ciotat, going off for a few days' rest on the Riviera, and at Gap we were blocked by a peasant demonstration: 150 tractors filing by in procession and totally cutting off the flow of traffic. Right away, there was an indignant outcry against the peasants; the passengers on the bus felt nothing but angry scorn for the demonstrators. With me, it was the opposite; I exulted and said to myself: Good lord, this is the first time I've ever seen peasants aroused. It's wonderful! I was so enthusiastic that people on the bus began to ask me questions. They did not understand why I was reacting so positively when all they saw was the inconvenience. They were saying:

"We're going to lose an hour, if not more; that's all they'll achieve. What's the point of all this monkey business?"

And I answered: "You don't know what you're talking about! You don't know what it means to be a peasant. Until now peasants have never had the white part of the leek. It's *not* a shame that they're waking up and demonstrating!"

I had been so carried away by the demonstration that when I returned to Val-des-Prés, I had to talk about it to the fellows on the committee. At our very first meeting, I told them:

"I saw 150 tractors parade in Gap, and in my whole life I've never seen anything so beautiful. Our peasants are finally waking up, and I don't have to teach *you* what a peasant's life is like. You've been pigeons your whole life long; my father got plucked just like you, and I tell you, if you were really men, we would demonstrate exactly the way they did it in Gap."

They took it as a joke at first, and that made me angry. I went on:

"You know what Jean Carles said?" I choked up just at the mention of my husband who would have agreed so intensely with what we were doing, but I got a grip on myself and, pounding the table with my fist, I shouted:

"He used to say we have the most beautiful countryside in the world, and *that*, that is something you do not know! And you do not love it! And you do not defend it because you have never left your stables, because you do not know that from everywhere there are streams flowing, that everything shines with light and purity. Of course, we won't be 150 strong like in Gap, but if all of us band together to parade through Briançon, to tell the sub-prefect that no one can take our valley away from us, then we will have taken a step forward."

I was so scathing and impassioned that night that I convinced them, and they all backed me up. All the men between twenty and forty in Val-des-Prés. All of them had been my pupils.

"So what must be done?" they asked me.

"Well, I'd like you to set a date for the demonstration and I'd like all of you to be there."

"Yes, Madame."

"Yes, Madame! It's not enough to say 'Yes, Madame.' Listen to me carefully. I don't want you to answer 'Yes, Madame,' and then tell me on the appointed day: 'Oh, *I* can't come, my hay is dry,' 'Oh, *I'm* up at two thousand meters and I'm not coming back down.' We'll be at the height of the season. I know you and I know the land; on that day, I don't want you to let me down; if you do, you're not men."

They couldn't get over my speaking to them like that, and I added:

"Look here, so I'll know what you're worth and whether I can rely on you, we are all going to the casino in Briançon next Saturday. People from Le Larzac° are bringing a film that will show you how peasants defend themselves."

"All right, Madame."

They said "Madame" the way they did in the days when I had them in class. On Saturday, when I reached the movie theater, I counted them. They were all there, and they came over to say hello since they were anxious for me to know they had come. They were interested in the film on Le Larzac, and they discussed it among themselves. From that day on, I knew I could rely on them. I said: "I have confidence in you now, and I know that you will come."

The demonstration was set for August 13 at 5:00 in the afternoon.

In the days before we descended on Briançon, I got things ready. Some young people and I made placards. I had torn up sheets and bought cans of paint, and together we painted our slogans: "Sheep not Trucks," "The Clarée Valley for the Peasants," "Leave the Mountain People in Peace." We also had a sign depicting a village caught in the claws of a power shovel, and leaflets for the Briançonnais.

We made all these preparations while our peasants were cutting and raking grass for the lambs. On the eve of the demonstration, a neighbor stopped by to see me.

"Madame Carles," he said, "we have to give up the demonstration because there'll be fifty of us at the very most, we'll look ridiculous and they'll make fun of us all over the Briançon countryside."

"Listen, Marcelin, do what you like; as for me, even if there is only one tractor, I will be on it and I'll take my signatures to the subprefecture. Even if I'm alone I will still go. I am not going back on my word."

Marcelin was not the only one who tried to make me change my mind. I had the privilege of phone calls from Briançon's crème de la crème. The police commissioner phoned and so did the subprefect, all wondering what was going to hit them, all singing the same tune:

"Madame Carles, this demonstration must stay within bounds, tourists are not to be upset. Beware of provocations and violence, Madame Carles, and inform us of your route, what you plan to do, how many tractors you will have, and how many people you will have at your demonstration."

"You're asking for too much," I told them. "Tractors? Well, you'll count them on the spot when you see them. *I* am not sure of anything; the same holds true for the demonstrations, you will see for yourselves. As far as violence is concerned, if anything happens, the fault will not be on our side."

We all planned to meet in Briançon on the appointed day. Obviously, I arrived early and stood waiting for my fellows to make an appearance. The minutes dragged by, each one seeming double or triple its actual length, and I said to myself: If only they come, if only the wind isn't knocked out of their sails.

Those were not idle thoughts, for I knew what it meant for them to come down from Granon in tractors on the thirteenth of August. They were all cutting "dog's tooth grass," some of them up as high as the Fort de l'Olive, at two thousand meters and more, and coming to Briançon meant a loss of hours on end.

When they arrived, I heaved a great sigh of relief and counted them: they were all there. We had thirteen tractors in the commune: thirteen were there and the men too, all those under forty. Some families numbered five people — well, all five were there. We were almost 300 strong at the outset, so it was a success already. I took my fellows and we went to see the subprefect.

We were a delegation of five — all they had authorized. The subprefect was seated behind his desk, looking rather aloof, uncomfortable. He listened to our grievances as he thumbed through the notebook full of signatures which I'd just handed him. When we finished, he said:

"Madame Carles, I do not understand you. There has never been any question of building an express highway in the region, only a high-speed road, and you're stirring up the whole countryside with tractors, demonstrators, and petitions: now tell me, what's the point? There is no scandal to bring to light."

I answered in the same tone:

"Look here, Monsieur Subprefect, we are not naïve altar boys, we are not going to wait until the surveyor's sticks are planted, because then it will be too late."

One of the landowners from Val-des-Prés took on from there:

"Madame Carles is right, and we all stand behind her because we want to keep our fields, our houses, and our valley the way they are. Naturally you call it a high-speed road, but you'll rebaptize it, and from one day to the next it'll turn into a superhighway."

The subprefect said nothing more. We left and went back to our fellows waiting on the tractors with their motors idling. Judge Rabinovitch spoke first, and I followed. Speaking for all of us, I said "we."

> We are the people who maintain the soil, we are the people who maintain life. What would become of our villages, if the earth were not tilled? It would mean the end of our fields of poppies and cornflowers. From time to time you come upon an amputee, and aren't you ashamed to have two arms when he does not? Well, they want to amputate our Clarée Valley and we must not let them have their way!

Once again my schoolteacher's trade had come to the fore. They listened to me like good children, the silence so complete you could hear a fly buzz between sentences.

Farther off, I saw the helmets of the C.R.S. shining in the distance — they too could hear me, and since most of them were children or grandchildren of peasants, I wished that they would understand me as well, and that they would retain something of what I said.

When I finished my speech, the fellows came up to see what we were going to do next. Many of them wanted to take the tractors down the Chausée.

"No," I said. "No one is going down that street. I gave my word that we'd stay away from the Chausée so we wouldn't interfere with traffic and alarm the tourists, and I don't want any brawls. It's been a magnificent demonstration up to now, and we have to end it magnificently too."

You always look foolish when you forbid something, and I sensed a wavering. I understood very well that they wanted to emphasize their point, but with the Chausée off limits, they didn't seem to know what to do next. Suddenly a young man came forward saying:

"But you didn't promise we wouldn't go along Avenue Lautaret, Madame."

I hadn't thought of that; it was a wonderful idea and I said:

"No indeed! Outside of the Chausée, I made no promises."

I didn't need to repeat it twice, all the tractors set off in the direction of Avenue Lautaret. We went all the way to the end, up to the traffic circle, and then we came back down toward the barracks, maintaining an even pace, with our signs, our leaflets, and our slogans.

I shall always remember that jaunt. There I was on the biggest tractor: there was only one seat for the driver, and I had been standing for the whole three hours of the procession. Three hours on a machine like that — you should try it, and don't forget that I was seventy-five years old.

We went up into the Old City, and when we reached the Gargouille,° my driver began to worry himself grey.

"God almighty, God almighty," he swore. "I told them not to go this way, there are shop windows, and crates of fruit sticking out over the sidewalk, and there'll be an awful fuss if we hit anything."

I just laughed, I was happy and I said: "Don't worry! We won't have any problems, let's just keep going," but he went on grumbling and called to his son who was ahead of us on another tractor:

"Hey, Pierre! Pierre!"

"Watcha want?"

"What about the cows?"

"The cows? Well, they won't get lost. We'll find 'em tomorrow if we don't tonight. We're doing good work here, it's more important than bringing cows in."

No one wanted to go home. The demonstration was splendid as it turned out: for once the Briançonnais saw peasants taking the bull by the horns, and they were astonished. A sizeable number of people joined with us and took up our slogans. The most wonderful part of it was the solidarity that emerged, with everyone feeling that we were truly together, united as if we were a single person. The young people were the most enthusiastic; they were becoming aware of their unity and their strength; they smiled from ear to ear, sensing that they were making their weight felt. It was a beautiful sight to behold! The subprefect, too, realized that our demonstration was not an inconsequential jaunt. He could see that all the people on the tractors were young men from Val-des-Prés; he heard them shout their resolve not to let themselves be had, he understood, perhaps, that all these men cared about their valley, cared about their land, and that they intended to remain in their region. Far from being ridiculous, our demonstration had been a complete success.

From that day on, I was the subprefect's bête-noire, a thorn in his side; and I was catalogued as a troublemaker to such a degree that the following winter, when Guy Lux did his television show "Interneige" — "In the Snow-belt" — from Briançon, I still made those gentlemen of the département quake in their shoes. Unfortunately, nothing happened because events had moved too swiftly and I did not have time to alert all of our supporters and plan a demonstration worthy of the name.

We were only a handful on the night of the broadcast, but when we reached the Champs de Mars — the military parade ground — a fellow came over and said peremptorily:

"So, Madame Carles, what are you going to come up with tonight?"

I looked at the fellow somewhat haughtily and replied:

"Me? Are you speaking to me? But I do not know you, sir. Who might you be?"

"Oh, so you don't know me! Well, I am the police commissioner of Gap, and *we* know *you*. They don't talk about anything else in the whole département since your exploits of last August. But don't bother getting any ideas today: if you have anything in mind, it won't be shown on Eurovision."

"Really!"

"Yes. If you make the slightest move, if you pull out any placards, if you shout, we will cut you off. Europe doesn't need to know we have any damn pains in the ass here in France."

"Look here," I said, "for what it's worth, I shall not be a damn pain in your ass today."

I was not going to tell him why we had decided to play it quiet that day. There were not enough of us, we saw that clearly, but *he* didn't have to know, and since he was afraid of the worst, it was just as well to let him think it. They hadn't stinted themselves on resources. We were about fifty strong, and there was practically one gorilla per person, not counting the C.R.S.° As soon as we budged, they followed us as if we were bandits ready for a holdup. I remember we all set off together from one end of the Champ de Mars to the other: right away, all the cops followed on our heels. It was so funny!

Eventually, I climbed the post-office steps and sent my people off home:

"That's enough for today," I told them. "We're not prepared, so we might as well part company without a fuss; we'll begin again soon, and on a larger scale."

We could not stop with a failure, especially since the fallout from our August march continued to reach us. I received expressions of support and signatures of sympathizers from all over France and even from Europe. It was no longer a matter of five thousand signatures, there were eight thousand by now! To give the movement new impetus, friends in the association got the idea of holding a press conference in Paris and they came to invite my participation. I was tired that day, weak from bronchitis and in a bad mood.

"It certainly is a good idea, but I am not going to Paris. Look at the condition I'm in. I'm too old for a press conference."

My friends insisted: "Madame Carles, we ask only one thing: come with us. We'll rent a hall, we'll decorate it, we'll take care of the invitations, the journalists, the paperwork. All we ask is for you to be there and speak."

"Well, in that case . . ."

That's how it all began; afterwards we laid out our plans to the people of Val-des-Prés; they agreed to the idea and we began preparations for our new operation.

We had to raise money. I thought of organizing a festival for the region. It wasn't a bad idea and the village mobilized immediately. We brought performers from Marseilles, set up games, lotteries, a dance, and a refreshment stand. It was for July, and though it began to rain on the appointed day, it was still a complete success. The local women had fashioned baskets of what we call "the wonders of Granon" around here; the men sliced ham and served wine by the glass. In spite of the rain, people stayed and danced until ten at night, and when we did our accounts, we found we had collected enough money to finance our press conference.

I arrived in Paris with all my followers. I would never have dreamed that I had so many, between my family, my friends, and a number of unwavering supporters, there were almost twenty-five of them. The conference was to be held on the boat owned by the Touring Club of France, anchored near the Alexander III Bridge. My friends had decorated it all over with posters and pictures of the valley, and there was even a buffet planned for the journalists and guests. Once again our demonstration was a complete success. Monsieur Richard presided over the meeting, presenting the various speakers: Judge Rabinovitch, Monsieur Vallier, and me. He said to the journalists:

"I am pleased to introduce Madame Carles to you: she is seventy-six years old, she is the person who founded this movement, she comes from Val-des-Prés, and she is the very soul of the battle. And now she is going to speak to you with the warmth and spontaneity that are her hallmark."

I had not prepared anything in advance, not a word, not an outline. I'll be hanged if I can remember now what I said that day; I don't remember a thing, but it seems that my words were ardent, that what I said came straight from the heart and all the journalists were won over by the old lady from the valley. When the meeting was done, they came over to ask me questions. Who was I? What was I doing to defend the valley? Why was I doing it? They all looked astounded. Why? Because of my age? Because of my spontaneity and my vehemence? In any case, they wrote articles in their newspapers and that was good publicity.

Since then, alas, nothing much has happened. We've gone back to our meetings and speeches. There's a dead calm on both sides, but in my opinion, it augurs nothing good. At the beginning of this year, 1976, I wrote to the President of the Republic for the third time. In my letter, I said:

> My name is Émilie Carles; I am a retired schoolteacher, seventy-six years old, and I have always lived in this valley, doubtless the most beautiful to be found in the Hautes Alpes. The threat hanging over us impelled me to write to you at Chamallières last August. Your reply gave us hope, but the months go by, and everything leads us to believe that our valley is going to disappear. We are but simple peasants and the attachment we feel for the land does not make us hostile to all progress; however, the contemplated projects will deprive us of our resources by despoiling our land. Thanks to its microclimate, the Clarée Valley is the last refuge for people with serious respiratory illnesses. Children come here to recover the health they lost in city smoke, and if the express highway was to be implanted here, within a few months, like you in the evening on the Place de la Concorde, we too would be asphyxiated!

On Saturday, January 24, a taped news telecast on Antenne 2° presented our Briançonnais, and in one of the spots, the Minister P. Dijoud, mayor of Briançon, discussed the town's projects. He brought up our problem, of course, and I saw myself passed off as a 'nice simple woman who talks without thinking.' That sort of insolence distresses me deeply, and everyone who wrote to me subsequently to express support will discover that I am not a woman to tolerate uncalled-for remarks. To be sure, my age is a factor and I am not brilliant like Monsieur Minister, but our claims shall not be silenced by a low blow of the sort: that would be too easy.

These fields, these meadows: over the centuries we have wrested them from the mountains. I can still see myself as a little girl helping my father and brothers construct and brace what we call 'clapiers' in the Alpine regions, that is, low walls laid up dry to hold off erosion of the land. What I want to protect from concrete is the labor of those men and those women. How could anyone believe that a major highway link between the cities of Fos and Turin would be restricted to two express lanes? Finished off with a single-track railroad? For reasons of safety and cost efficiency traffic would be routed almost straight through the center of the valley, whereas what we would propose is a road along the mountainside constructed so as to protect vehicles from the danger of falling rocks; this would have the advantage of preserving the site and placing limits on all improper extensions. Moreover, our peasants' common sense rebels when easier access to Briançon is used as an argument. Why would anyone think of making a detour of some ten kilometers to stay in a village without any attraction when nearby Grenoble offers the advantages of a city with everything people need already in place? And besides, is it not the nature of an express road to link distant points so that motorists can travel at high speed without being obliged to make stops far from the main centers? This valley is a tourists' paradise and it must not die; it is made for people who love cross-country skiing, both one-day outings and the *randonnée* kind that combines skiing and mountaineering. We do not have the renown of ski resorts that receive on a grand scale — we are simple people — but if you did us the honor of coming to our village, you would be won over, and you would not leave us helpless against concrete, asphalt, and pollution.

I could transmit the files of our association to you, the plans, the negative votes of the municipal council, the lists of names on petitions, or I could come to Paris. But would these documents be delivered to you, and would you receive an old woman? I will probably have to be satisfied with awaiting an anonymous reply before I apply to you once again.

I always got an answer; this time the letter talked vaguely about reviewing the plans in order to determine the solution best adapted to the situation. I wasn't fooled; it was only words. As time went on, I began to get used to that sort of response, whether it came from prefects, deputies, or cabinet ministers: they all had the art and craft of playing at words and promises, a game that made me think of cat and mouse.

It is hard to foresee today how our case will unfold. I get the impression that the peasants here in the village are growing tired. That is to be expected; they've cried wolf so long, they don't believe in it any longer. Recently, the mayor called them together to show them the land-use plan and the layout of the highway, telling them:

"You would be well advised to accept the layout as is, otherwise you run the risk of having decisions imposed on you without anyone asking your opinion."

There are sixteen farm families in Val-des-Prés at the present time. In the beginning they were all members of the association; some have already left, not many, two or three, but if the mayor keeps on talking in that vein, it may very well spread like an oil slick. The old people, the skeptics, try to undermine the young, saying: "She can do whatever she likes, Old Lady Carles; if they want to build their highway, it'll get built." The young people answer back: "With asses like you around, it surely will get built."

Membership is not enough. They've lost their enthusiasm and they're coming to meetings less and less. Even so, I tell them: "You have to pay attention to timing; there comes a moment when time works against us, and that's where we are now. Take care, don't doze off!"

Still worse are the underhanded "black and whites": those who are both for the highway and registered members of the association. I know a few of them and they're the most dangerous. It all adds up to a situation that is far from propitious, and to the fact that we're far from the enthusiasm of August 13, 1975.

What would have to happen is for the commune's people to realize that this highway is not meant for them. Those who think it is are mistaken: the highway is and will be for people travelling long distances. Perhaps it will be good for the tourist industry, but what kind of tourist industry will that be? The kind that will drive people to go through the valley at 140 kilometers an hour. Aside from that, no one here will benefit from it. I try to explain, I tell them:

"When will *you* use that highway? To go to Briançon or Névache? Maybe, providing there's a feeder road from Val-des-Prés. But nothing is less likely. What then? To go from one end of the village to the other, to go to Plampinet or La Vachette, what road will you take? Still the same one, the old road, while the tourists will drive by overhead leaving you their exhaust. Unless they build a new road there too, wider and faster. That change will be added to the rest, to the express road and to the railroad they're planning. Our valley won't be anything but an immense concrete corridor, noisy, smelly, and polluted. It will be the route for the trucks carrying fluorine; at least two or three thousand per week are projected at the outset: that notorious fluorine that deposits its dust everywhere, burning and destroying vegetation, grass, and lungs. The Clarée will turn into another Maurienne Valley, a dead valley where the foliage has been destroyed and the sheep compelled to go elsewhere."

That's what they must get through their heads: this highway and everything that goes with it is not conceived with the good of the village and its peasants in mind. Should that monstrosity become reality, Val-des-Prés would be Val-des-Prés no more. In a few months the valley would lose its whole character, and those who came here to recover lost health, to breathe pure air, to camp or go canoeing: they too would go elsewhere.

To that slow but inevitable ecological pollution would be added the more rapid human pollution, for if it takes twenty-five years and more to bring trees low and to kill grass, this second pollution would proceed far more swiftly. In a few years, Val-des-Prés would become a ridiculous and hellish place of no further interest to those who were once drawn here by their love for nature.

This is what the peasants must come to realize, it is around these themes that they must mobilize and fight. Today more than ever.

Obviously, it all comes down to a question of power. It is difficult to speak of the highway without calling to mind the upcoming elections. Although, whatever the results may be, I am afraid there won't be much change. It is a harsh thing to say, but you'd have to be crazy to believe otherwise. Around me, in the papers, on television, the only thing I see and hear are men solely concerned with success and power. What sickens me the most is the blablabla, the eternal blablabla rising up from all sides: from the center, from the right, and from the left. What these men want is to win votes, get elected, and trumpet everywhere that they are the strongest and the best. They are far from sharing the true interest and deep wishes of the people who work and produce. In my opinion, the big guys, the ones they call the big politicians, do nothing but repeat the same words, Liberty, Equality, Fraternity; the worst thing is that with many people it works: they're such practiced demagogues that many believe them and follow them. I, however, am like Gilles Vignault in his song, when he says: "Liberty, you scarcely hear me, Equality, you don't at all, Fraternity — well, let's not bring that up anymore."

With people repeating those words ever since 1789, we should certainly find out what they really mean someday. But we don't. They make promises, they get themselves elected, and then they forget, or else they use lack of funds as an excuse. I think those professional politicians ought to be set to work in a mine a thousand meters down, if only for a day; maybe then they would understand what it means to be a worker, what it means to be a miner spending one third of his life underground; maybe then they would understand that a four-hour day is sufficient for an underground worker! But they don't, the men who run the show, the money men, do not know what it is to sweat. I'd like to see them work on the assembly line, go down into the sewers, collect garbage, dig up the earth, plow or reap. I'd like them to know what a worker's or peasant's day means. Once they have felt it in their flesh and in their minds, perhaps they would be the first to shout: "That's enough!" And perhaps they would favor reducing the length of the working day.

But it's the same with that as with the highway, only force and compulsion will make them do it, ever. Neither bosses nor politicians will work that change. Nor elections. Change can only come about through those who work and struggle. "We must unite and fight," I tell them; what is true for the highway is also true for the rest and I tell them:

"Stop taking your wishes for reality, stop playing the nouveau riche game! Just because you've known poverty and want, and because today you've got enough change in your pocket to put butter on your spinach, there's no reason to believe everything's all right. That's not a sound outlook on life. Who do you think you are? You're people on salary, working people like the others, and it's time you gave up your quarreling and left your absurd principles behind. Always you've been taught that workers dislike peasants and you've been taught to despise workers in return; well, *I* don't see any difference between you: you are all proletarians, and I believe that if you stood together the bosses and the bankers might forget their alms and bend the knee, I believe they would open their money chests and share without putting up an argument." Jean Carles used to tell me:

"A strike with all the workers twiddling their thumbs for one week would put the capitalists up against the wall. Everything would shut down, nothing would get done, because it is the workers and the peasants who produce the world's riches and make the world go round."

Alas, triple alas! Men have not yet reached that level. Governments stuff their heads with twaddle and in the end all they dream of is imitating the rich. I knew a woman, a simple schoolteacher like me, who sweated blood and tears to raise her children, and one day she told me:

"To think that I work like a slave and I can't even buy myself a diamond ring!"

When I hear that, proletarians whose ideal is owning a diamond, all I have left are my tears to weep. What is the point of a diamond ring in a human life?

While you wait for people to realize what's what, you have to vote. We have a Socialist mayor in Val-des-Prés at the moment. It's new, but it's not very clear, just as it's not clear what game the Socialists are playing in general. Besides, that's not the problem; the real problem lies in the union of the left, and in a region like ours, the next question is whether people will agree to vote for the Communists. I remember what happened here over fifty years, from 1928 to today. There was one Communist vote at first, Jean Carles's, then two, then three; when women got the vote, that made four and five votes; and finally, with the young people added, there was a record number of thirteen. Thirteen Communist votes in Val-des-Prés: it was a miracle.

I say a miracle, for in a region like ours, people have always voted capitalist because they take themselves for capitalists. With a house, a bit of land, a tractor, a binder, and a little nest egg for an excuse, they think they've gotten rich and they vote for the Right. For those people, there is no difference between the Common Program° and Communism, and not just any Communism, the old, ridiculous Communism in the shape of a bloodthirsty bear with a knife between his teeth. What other idea could they have? They never read newspapers, and when Marchais° speaks on television, they rush to change channels.

If at least everything were clear on the Left! But with the elections only a few months off, they're fighting each other. Socialists and Communists are hurling accusations, tearing each other apart and making extravagant promises. They too have come out for the army, the strike-force, nuclear power; when the time comes, they too will be for the endangered Fatherland and, why not, for the sacred union of Saber and Aspergillum: Army and Church.

Under these circumstances, who can know how to vote and for whom? Whoever does know is very lucky; to my mind, voting is simply a little better than doing nothing. In the final analysis, the French have no choice but to vote for the lesser evil, according to the dictates of their hearts. Where is progress in all that? Where is the opening up? Where is man and the dignity of man? And what is the Communist game? After five years of the Common Program, they've suddenly become purists. Their conscience is clear because they're attacking capitalism: what a great discovery to repeat in 1977 that capitalists are the source of all evil! I call that a self-evident truth. On top of that, the Communist Party has proposed a new goal: one million members! Why make those million cards? To print the number on posters? To shout it out in speeches? To take power, you need determination and sound ideas, not a million members. Let the Communists take power, let them throw themselves into the arena, let them grapple with economic problems inch by inch, let them apply their social principles, and let them topple the capitalists otherwise than on paper. If they do, if they really do, they won't just have a million cards, they'll have millions upon millions of convinced followers.

It's not really complicated! In the long run, if workers are to gain a comfortable life, a few people have to take the bull by the horns, they have to throw everything the hell out, start out from scratch and, above all, mount a serious attack on capital assets, abolish wealth, and excessive fortunes. But no one dares, for in France, great or small, Capital is sacred.

When I think about the money and luxury at the disposal of some few, while the others sweat and slave, while whole peoples struggle against hunger in the Third World, I am ashamed for the human species. Never would I dare lead a life I might denounce as harmful to other people. One day a "good friend" told me:

"*You* can't be a Communist because you have houses and land, because you're a schoolteacher, and your husband runs a hotel."

"Oh, you don't think so!" I answered. "Well, let me tell you, the day I saw youngsters in my class wearing a wooden shoe with a hole on one foot, and on the other a leather shoe worn down at the heel. If I held back from giving them a pair of shoes, it was out of tact and not to lapse into charity; but on that day I understood that I could never sleep in peace until those youngsters had the same advantages as my children. My life will be fulfilled when all the children in the world are fed and clothed like my own. For that, I am ready to give everything I have. What do I need extra possessions for? I would be much happier if I knew that no human being was suffering. Not a single one."

Chapter
32

November 11, 1977

The first snows have just fallen; the whole country-
side has been transformed in a matter of hours, with the warm colors of
autumn giving way to the white layer of snow on which the trees' black
silhouettes are projected. After autumn, winter is here. It reminds me that
this book — writing it at least — has gone on for the space of the four seasons.
I began to arrange this bouquet of wild herbs at the end of May; November
has come, and I think that it is done.

For years and years I'd been thinking of writing this book one day; we
were already talking about it in Jean Carles's time. We would tell each other:
"We have to write a book, we'll get to it one day, we still have time to mull it
over," and time went by without anything getting done. Well, here it is, done.
As I wrote, I put in all my heart and all my sincerity; may these pages
communicate my love of people and nature, and my revolt against injustice.

Since May, life has gone on. Fatigue, illness, the hospital, and now
convalescence have followed one upon the other like the ineluctable elements
of a game of chance. Instead of moving toward recovery, I might just as
easily have died. But death wouldn't have me, not yet.

It's not that I am afraid of death. Jean Carles used to say on the
subject:

"It is the logical culmination of life; every man knows that he must die
one day, and there is no shame, no fear in expecting and accepting death
when it turns up."

I am like him, and I do not fear what is beyond death. When I tell
myself that death should not take anyone by surprise, I am thinking of

believers and nonbelievers alike. Believers must be happy to die because they will be returning to eternal Paradise; as for unbelievers like me, what can they fear from a hereafter they do not believe in? I tell myself: If there really is something afterwards, what do I risk? I can't be punished for anything; I've never done evil: on the contrary, my whole life long I have striven to do good.

I believe it is splendid to leave life with the thought that you have done the maximum possible to defend the ideas you believe just and human, and to help those who need to be helped without discrimination. For me, that is a wonderful feeling. The day I found out that I could still be useful by bequeathing my body to medicine, I did not hesitate, I made a gift of my body and my eyes since it seems that my corneas can give a blind person sight. It is the last good deed I can do.

What I fear most are suffering and physical or intellectual decay. I have no reason to complain; everything around me combines to make my old age a gilded old age. I live at home, in my village, and my children live nearby. What more could I ask? It's wonderful to take walks around my house, play a game of *belote*° with old friends when you like, to be in the region where you were born, with its customs. I am so attached to this village I could never have lived anywhere else. When I go off on a trip to the Midi or anywhere else, I find that I yearn to come back. Val-des-Prés is my cradle: nothing can replace it. I have everything here: my joys, my pain, my memories.

To be sure, living alone is hard sometimes; even with my children to look after me, I feel it. I have to get up, have to make my breakfast, and when you're alone, there are days when you would just as soon let yourself go. On days like that, I think of those who do not have what I have, of old people without enough to provide for their most basic needs. It is sickening, unacceptable, but alas, there are still far too many in that bind. I am lucky enough to have a comfortable retirement, and I would like every man and every woman to enjoy the same rights, so that after forty or fifty years of work each one is assured of enough for a decent life, and none is a burden on anyone or forced to ask the state for charity.

Just a few days ago, I happened to turn on the television one morning. It was November 11 and I came upon the ceremony in which war veterans were being decorated by the President of the Republic. Waiting for their medals were a few ghostlike old men, survivors of '14-'18, and watching as they lent themselves to that sham I could not hold back my tears of rage. Right before my eyes was the display of a time I thought was dead and gone. Behind the veterans of Verdun came younger faces, all of them heroes of '45, Algeria, and other places, moved and proud to be decorated with the Legion of Honor. To me, those little red ribbons invented by Napoleon symbolize only the shedding of innocent blood. Instead of exalting and rewarding patriotism, playing the "Marseillaise" — "that stupid song," as François Closet calls it — we would do better to sing the memory of the gallant Louis Lecoin. With his fifty-two-day hunger strike and daily letters to his former classmate, Charles de Gaulle, that greatest of all pacifists achieved the protection of law for conscientious objectors. Gallant Louis! I salute you just as I did the day I saw you in Brussels. We had gone there to see Claude Autant-Lara's film, *Thou Shalt Not Kill*, because, in France, Land of Liberty, it was prohibited.

Through you, Lecoin, we have taken a giant step in the direction of peace, and we thank you, but many things remain to be done, and that I expect from women. They are the ones who bring children into the world. I saw a young ewe lower her head and charge dogs one day because she thought her baby lamb was threatened: within a few seconds those dogs had seized her and bled her to death. Where is the woman capable of doing as much? We let our children do their military service, which is as much as to say we let them rig themselves up like bandits, because underneath the uniform precious few human feelings are left. We let them go off to Korea, Indochina, Africa, or other places, even within France where they're sent around on absurd maneuvers, stupidly risking their lives.

Women, you who have had a child, who carry one in your womb, or who want a child, never give a second glance to a man in uniform, to anyone who bears arms, to a munitions manufacturer or an arms merchant — not because they do not deserve love, but first let them earn it by recycling themselves. If the military budget were used for all the hospital services, leaving the young men at home, and using the career army for humanitarian works — and there's no want of them — soldiers would be less stiff and more human. In 1789, France summoned Europe to revolution; why should she not give peace to the world now by casting the seeds of a general disarmament? Our example would be followed swiftly, I am sure, because it means saving humanity from a cruel and monstrous end toward which we are advancing day by day.

Who benefits from progress? Why must we have eight-hour days? With a work day of four to five hours, unemployment would be eliminated and everyone could have a job. Let us learn to live very simply: one table, four chairs, a bed: that's all we need, let us learn to make use of our leisure time, get as close to nature as possible. Let us learn to read, because reading means strengthening our minds through the minds of others, steeping our hearts with feelings that please, and struggling with an author according to whether our ideas and feelings agree with his or diverge. Learn to live by knowing how to live and let live. Never take anything in life but flowers, and from flowers, only the perfume; drop the religion that has the largest number of followers: I am talking about the religion of money. A Belgian writer has said: "Power of goodness and gentleness, it is you who should rule the earth. Alas, that currency is altogether too ideal to circulate on our planet. . . ." That is not true; fortunately, there are people for whom it is real: I know couples and families where it is the only currency in circulation, and it is beautiful, it is splendid, and we must all reach toward it for so long as we shall live.

I know perfectly well I'll be called a utopian. It's true! And I say: Why not? We must have utopias so that one day they may become realities. Less than a century ago, social security, unemployment benefits, and paid vacations were utopias; today we have them and everyone takes it for granted. The same is true for everything: what for the moment seems unattainable will be tomorrow's reality. With less selfishness, less indifference, we are bound to achieve greater justice, greater equality among people. But we must fall to work immediately, expecting nothing from our elite bureaucrats, the "Enarques."°

And so at the end of our lives, perhaps, we will not find ourselves alone and sad like the retired captain Jean and I met, and who told us:

"Oh, you have every reason to be proud of your lives, you've accomplished something through the fine roles you've played, you've done useful things. Not me. I'll go off leaving nothing good behind. You cannot imagine how weighed down I am by the emptiness and futility of my profession." Brave captain, who had come to understand that the army was a thing of naught.

There it is!

To finish, because you have to finish, what more is there to say?

No to violence, no to injustice.

Yes to pacifism and to all that is Human.

Too bad if that sounds like a slogan: for me it is a slogan of love. I have believed in it, I believe in it still and always, until the last breath of my life.

Afterword

"The Clarée Valley is safe! They've just named it a protected natural site. So you don't need to get those petitions signed."

My guide in Briançon spoke exultantly when I called from Paris on August 1, 1990, to say goodbye and thanks before flying back to New York. The fight launched by Émilie Carles sixteen years earlier had been won at last. The wolves will not be back.

Like many of Carles's readers, through her words my husband and I had fallen in love with a region we did not know, and had become concerned over the fate of the valley. Like other readers, we had gone to see it for ourselves. There are three two-lane roads into the Briançonnais: one comes west from Italy, one north through Gap from the Riviera. We took the third, southeast through Grenoble. Crossing the Lautaret Pass through the Alps at approximately seven thousand feet, we were surrounded by peaks, mountain behind mountain behind mountain, to infinity, it seemed. A few miles north-east of Briançon, touted as the highest city in Europe, we entered the lovely Clarée valley, a narrow area, strewn with many-colored wildflowers over which butterflies danced, bordered on each side by the sharply rising Alps, and cut by the clear, cold waters of the river, a rapid mountain stream rarely more than fifteen feet wide. Even today this area is largely untouched. Carles was right. Her valley is one of earth's beautiful places. A superhighway would have destroyed it utterly.

The valley's single road is barely two cars wide, except in towns, where vehicles moving in opposite directions patiently take turns going through. The tiny villages — Val-des-Prés, Plampinet, Névache — show a degree of prosperity now, largely due to vacationers who have come to the region in search of clean air and exercise.

In Val-des-Prés, we met with members of the Collective for the Defense of the Clarée, signed their petition and took copies with us to circulate among our French and American friends. The group, working out of the mayor's office, is quartered in a small building with the words "Communal Oven" still visible where long ago they had been cut into the stone over the broad, low, semi-circular doorway. And so we found ourselves in the place described by Carles, where generations of villagers had baked their yearly supply of bread. We saw Les Arcades close by, freshly painted. Now owned by the commune, it is leased to the local branch of the Union des Centres de Plein Air (Union of Fresh Air Centers), an organization offering low-cost out-of-doors vacations to young adults, thus realizing another of Carles's hopes for her region.

We learned that Georges Carles is a successful hotelkeeper in nearby Serre Chevalier, that Michou's only son Christophe is learning the business working for his uncle, who has no children of his own. Judge Rabinovitch, now dead, served the judiciary in Briançon; he had shared Jean Carles's ideas and was concerned with environmental issues. His wife still lives there; his daughter, now in Paris, translates into French such authors as John Dos Passos, Joyce Carol Oates, and Jerzy Kosinski.

In Val-des-Prés we also visited the cemetery by the church, and we stood silent at the tiny family plot within sight and sound of the river. On this simplest of gravesites, small, white enameled hearts, hung on a black filigree metal cross, designate Joseph Jean Allais and Catherine Orsat — we hadn't known her married name until then — above a marker so blackened by time or the elements as to be virtually unreadable. Was it for Nini? Right in front lay a neat white stone marker, engraved in gold with the words "Jean CARLES / 1889–1962 / Pacifiste." Émilie is not present; true to her humanistic values beyond the grave, she had bequeathed her body to science.

"Just as well she's not there," someone observed. For although Émilie Carles inspired followers to fight her good fight to the end and save the valley, she and her book, we discovered, have not been universally admired. No doubt it is too soon. "She didn't have to wash all that dirty linen in public, didn't have to put in all those names," you will hear. And you wonder what they're talking about, since Carles mentions practically no family names but her own. The problem may well be that people recognize themselves and each other. Paradoxically, as people protest at having their secrets made public, they vehemently deny that Carles told the truth. Older villagers and conservative, middle-class Briançonnais alike are embarrassed that the outside world may judge them as backward and brutish. Some were ambivalent about the idea of a superhighway, wary of the tourist invasion it threatened, but attracted by the money it promised.

The high point of our visit to the valley was surely the afternoon we spent with Marie Ritz, Carles's niece ("little Marie" of the book), at her freshly painted small house in Plampinet near Névache. We went to thank her for supplying descriptions of local herbs and definitions of old patois words; for it was to her that librarian Catherine Fromm had turned when I wrote for help. She is a tiny, energetic peasant woman in her mid-sixties, eyes sparkling with intelligence and humor. Now retired, she spends her time gardening, and gathering herbs along the Clarée as her aunt used to do. Her house and tool shed are perfumed by the herb bouquets hung to dry for cosmetic and medicinal use. The garden is lush with vegetables and flowers, in accordance with Carles's view that human beings have esthetic as well as utilitarian needs. At the garden's edge stand plastic containers of varied sizes, and even an old bathtub, filled with water warming in the sun to be used for watering the plants when it reaches the proper temperature: this is the secret of her success as a gardener, explains Marie, who treats both people and plants with tenderness and understanding.

We sat on the modest stone terrace facing the garden. Nearby stood the wooden armchair where her mortally ill Mémé (Aunt Émilie) had sat taking the sun when she came from the hospital to stay with Marie after her operation. She chose to die in the Vivier, though, the house she and Jean Carles were building for their old age, but still unfinished when he died in 1962.

Together we looked at the photographs in her copy of Carles's book. "Was the family always so unsmiling?" I asked.

"Yes. People weren't happy in those days. They never relaxed, worked all the time. Mémé was the same till she met Jean Carles. He changed her. Took her out of it, taught her how to smile and laugh."

Of both Jean and Grandfather Allais, Marie said: "They were everything to me," for they had given her the affection denied by her father. Grandfather would take her on his knee, talk to her in patois, never using the familiar form, calling her "Paoro cocoa" — poor little thing — as he once had called his own little Émilie. She describes Jean as goodness incarnate, accepting everthing and everybody as they were, finding no task too menial or domestic, even ironing the clothes Émilie washed. Marie is eternally grateful to her aunt and uncle for refusing to abandon her to the welfare system despite their limited means. As for local criticism of her aunt, she has this to say: "People didn't like her because she told the truth." And she looks you straight in the eye as she speaks these words.

Just a few months ago she had the joy of watching the final telecast of Bernard Pivot's immensely popular literary talk show "Apostrophe." Pivot showed snippets of his own favorite interviews with authors over the fifteen years of the program's life, among them Jane Fonda, Vladimir Nabokov, and Émilie Carles. Summing up such a person as Carles is difficult, even for one so eloquent as Pivot. But he found the right epithet, I think: "C'était une sacrée bonne femme — She was one hell of a woman!"

Glossary

ACADEMY: The educational district in France.

ALPINE CHASSEURS: The French army's designation for its ski troops.

"ANT": When Jean calls Émilie "the ant," they both know he is referring to La Fontaine's seventeenth-century fable, "The Grasshopper and the Ant." While the ant spends the summer gathering food for the winter, the improvident grasshopper sings (that is, enjoys life), and has nothing set aside when the barren months arrive.

ANTENNE 2: A television channel in France noted for its news broadcasts.

BELOTE: A card game similar to pinochle.

BÉRAULT, HENRI: A misspelling of the name Béraud. Journalist and writer (1885–1958). His death sentence (1944) for collaboration with the Nazis was commuted to imprisonment at hard labor until 1950.

BOCHES: The French colloquial and pejorative designation for German soldiers in the First World War.

BREVET: Certificates called brevets used to be awarded upon the completion of primary studies, and then on completion of secondary studies.

BREVET SUPÉRIEUR: Certificate which used to be awarded for study at the secondary level. Rigorous oral and written examinations had to be completed over a period of three years in math (including algebra, geometry, and trigonometry) psychology, history, geography, literature, a modern European language, the natural and physical sciences, music, drawing, sewing (women), and mechanical drawing (men). To earn it not only with distinction but also with the congratulations of the examiners shows truly exceptional achievement.

Bugne: A type of fritter peculiar to Provence.

Le Canard Enchaîné: Highly popular weekly paper, extremely well-informed on government affairs, which makes its revelations in the comic mode. (Referred to by its French name in current U.S. publications.)

Céline: Louis Ferdinand Destouches (1894–1961). His *Journey to the End of the Night* was written in 1932. *Trifles for a Massacre (Bagatelles pour un Massacre)*, published in 1937 and never translated into English, is a set of virulently anti-war and anti-Semitic essays. A Nazi sympathizer, Céline fled to Berlin in 1944 and then to Denmark before returning to France in 1951.

Cendrars, Blaise (1887–1961): Swiss-born French novelist and poet, an early associate of the poet Apollinaire and of the Cubists. An insatiable traveler who worked at many different trades, even joining the Foreign Legion and losing an arm in the First World War, he wrote tales of adventure which take on a special dimension through his visionary language.

'Certificat d'études' or certificate: The certificate for primary studies was often what in Great Britain is called a "school leaving certificate," indicating the end of formal schooling. The *certificat d'études supérieures*, or a certificate earned at the university level, was awarded on completion of the *licence* (see below). Certificates at both levels were awarded upon successful completion of an exam.

Chalabréi: Along with chonzio, drouille, and langue bogne, a plant found in the mountainous Briançonnais region; whether or not it may be found in other areas with a similar geography I have not been able to determine. Chalabréi, like drouille, is used both as animal feed and as an herb for human food.

Chonzio: See *chalabréi* above.

Clairette: A slightly bubbly white wine.

Common Program: In 1972, French Socialists under the leadership of François Mitterrand and the Communists under Georges Marchais developed a "union of the left" with a shared program and candidates in an effort to win the legislative elections of 1973. While they had a measure of success, they did not elect enough deputies to the National Assembly to topple the government of Georges Pompidou.

COMMUNE: The smallest administrative subdivision in France, it has no corresponding unit in the U.S. system. It is governed by a mayor, deputy mayor, and a municipal council.

C R S · Compagnies Républicaines de Sécurité — the uniformed, elite national police in France, organized on military lines but responsible to the Ministry of the Interior. They are called on for emergency situations much like the state police in the U.S., or the Royal Canadian Mounted Police.

DAUDET, ALPHONSE (1840–1897): Best known for his charming stories set in Provence, such as the *Letters from My Windmill* (1866).

"THE DEATH OF THE JEW": Actually "The Peddler's Death" ["La Mort du colporteur"] from the *Jocelyn* (1834), an unfinished epic by the romantic poet Alphonse de Lamartine (1790–1869). His peddler is also a Jew. The text offered by Carles begins with the original poem's third line, omits lines 9–10, and changes punctuation. However, the fundamental anti-racist message remains intact. It should be noted that such poems have traditionally been part of civics lessons in the primary grades.

DÉPARTEMENT: The centralized French Republic is subdivided into administrative départements which have nothing like the independence of a "state" in the American federal system.

THE DEVIL'S POOL [*LA MARE AU DIABLE*]: George Sand's novel of country life, written in 1846.

DROUILLE: See *chalabréi* above.

D.S.T.: Direction de la Surveillance du Territoire or Internal Surveillance Agency — a national security force that operates in plainclothes, similar to the U.S. Federal Bureau of Investigation.

ENARQUES: Graduates of the Ecole Nationale d'Administration, and thereby set on the path to the upper levels of national government administration. Admission is through competitive examination.

F.F.I.: Forces Françaises de l'Intérieur, or French Forces of the Interior — the Resistance Army at the end of the Second World War.

F.L.N.: Front National de Libération, or National Liberation Front — the Algerian independence guerilla army.

GARGOUILLE: Literally, culvert or drain. The steep, lively main market street of the Old City of Briançon is named the Grande Gargouille because of the open channel of fresh water running down the middle, for use in case of fire. No more than fifteen feet wide, it must have made a dramatic site for the procession of tractors from Val-des-Prés.

THE GENERAL AND THE MARSHAL: General Charles de Gaulle and Marshal Henri Philippe Pétain.

THE GENERATION OF 1870: 1870 marks the Franco-Prussian War, a crushing military defeat and national humiliation that was one of the causes of the First World War.

HAMSUN, KNUT (1859–1952): A Nobel laureate born in Norway to a peasant family named Pederson. After two years in America, he returned home and published his best known novel *Hunger* (1894), which made him instantly famous.

THE HUMAN HOMELAND [*LA PATRIE HUMAINE*]: Pacifist weekly, founded in 1931.

HUMANITÉ: The Communist daily paper (referred to by its French name in current U.S. publications). It was founded as a socialist publication by Jean Jaurès, first Socialist Party head in France. One segment of the group split off to become the French Communist Party and took the paper along.

The index: Index Librorum Prohibitorum — a list of books that Roman Catholics may not read without permission of the Church or unless the books have been expurgated.

ISTRATI, PANAÏT (1884–1935): Romanian-born author who wrote in French and led an adventurous life in the Balkans, the Middle East, and Italy which is reflected in his books. His most popular novel was *Kyra Kyralina*, 1924.

JIM, THE REBEL PEASANT [*JACQUOU LE CROQUANT*]: Eugène LeRoy's 1899 novel of a peasant uprising in the Périgord region of France.

LA FOUCHARDIÈRE, GEORGES DE: Journalist and writer; a cofounder of *L'Oeuvre* in 1916. He wrote "Hors d'oeuvre," a regular humor column on topics of current interest.

LANGUE BOGNE: See *chalabréi* above.

LE LARZAC: A high plateau south of the Massif Central devoted to raising sheep. In the early 1970s, the peasants of the region demonstrated against the establishment of a military base in the region.

LIBERTY, EQUALITY, AND FRATERNITY: "The Declaration of the Rights of Man and the Citizen," written by Lafayette and modeled on the American

Declaration of Independence, consecrates these values which became the watchwords of the French Revolution and of all French Republics ever since. Carles often uses these words ironically.

LICENCE: A university degree beyond the French baccalaureate and roughly similar to the U.S. master's degree.

LYCÉE: French secondary school whose curriculum includes the material of roughly the first year of a U.S. college.

MAQUIS: The French underground resistance during the Second World War.

MARCHAIS, GEORGES (1920–): Head of the French Communist Party since 1972; he has always taken a hard-line approach.

MATERNELLE: Nursery or preschools included in the French national educational system.

MONSIEUR LE PRÉSIDENT: Form of address to a presiding military or civil judge.

NEW AGE IN LITERATURE [*NOUVEL ÂGE LITTÉRAIRE*]: This could be either the *Nouvelles littéraires, artistiques et scientifiques*, a weekly founded in 1921, or *Le Nouvel âge*, another cultural weekly published by a writers' cooperative starting in 1931.

NOTARY: Whereas the American notary public functions only as an official witness, the French notary exercises a number of the functions of a U.S. lawyer, mainly in the domains of real estate, contracts, and wills. To become a notary, one must pass an extremely rigorous competitive examination.

ON THE OUTSIDE [*EN-DEHORS*]: Published monthly starting in 1922, it advocated individualism, ethical freedom, sex education, and free love.

"PARIS IS WORTH A MASS": Statement attributed to the Protestant leader Henri de Navarre who converted to Catholicism on ascending to the throne in 1589 as the first Bourbon king, in order to restore peace and order to the largely Catholic nation torn by decades of the Wars of Religion.

POILUS: The French colloquial designation for soldiers in the First World War, corresponding to the American "doughboy."

THE POPULAR FRONT: The name given by analogy with the Spanish Republic's *Frente popular* to the coalition of the parties of the left, under the leadership of Léon Blum. It came to power in June 1936 as a result of the world-wide economic crisis, the political developments in Europe, and the rise of the French right. After instituting major social reforms such as paid vacations for all salaried people, the forty-hour week, and higher wages Blum's government fell in 1938, having permanently changed the conditions of workers' lives.

PREFECT: Known as Commissioner of the Republic (Commissaire de la République) since the March 1982 law creating administrative decentralization in France. This functionary is the administrative head of a département (see above).

ROSTAND, EDMOND (1868–1918): Neo-romantic poet and playwright, best known for *Cyrano de Bergerac* (1897).

THE ROUSTAN LAW: Since, according to the French Civil Code, it was illegal for a married couple to live apart, this law, passed in 1921, required a given percentage of vacant posts to be set aside for government functionaries separated from their spouses by the place of their employment. In 1925, the law was amended to make special provision for married teachers. Note that in the centralized French education system, public school teachers at all levels are civil servants.

SANS-CULOTTES: This term originally applied to the volunteers of the revolutionary army early in the Revolution of 1789. They tended to come from the poorer classes at first, but eventually included the ultra democrats or so-called "rabid" revolutionaries (*"les Enragés"*). They characteristically wore long trousers, the *pantalon* (rather than the kneebreeches or *culottes* associated with the Old Regime), a short coat called the *carmagnole*, the red phrygian bonnet signifying liberty, and, often, wooden shoes or *sabots*. Their influence ended when Robespierre fell in 1794.

SEED BIN: The *maille au grain* (a regional expression) was a wooden chest used for storing grain and hams.

SUBPREFECT: Known as Deputy Commissioner of the Republic (Commissaire adjoint de la République) since 1982, this functionary is responsible for the day-to-day operations of his/her *arrondissement*, a major subdivision of a département (see above). This person is responsible to the Commissioner of the Republic (formerly the prefect, see above) of the département where he/she serves.

THURSDAY: The French school week comprises four complete days and two mornings. The latter are Saturday and Wednesday. However, until the educational reforms of the late sixties, the free weekday afternoon was invariably Thursday.

"TONTON": Affectionate word for uncle.

Town hall and the church: In the eyes of French law, marriage is a civil affair; the wedding must take place and the requisite papers signed at the town hall. If they choose, the bride and groom may have a religious ceremony as well.

Tu: see *vous*.

Vieille France: Scion of an old, upper-class family, living by an obsolete system of values and code of behavior.

Vous: The formal second person pronoun. The Guillestre uncle is afraid Émilie will grow up using the familiar form "tu" exclusively, and therefore not know how to address people in "polite society."